M<small>AJOR</small> T<small>AYLOR</small>

MAJOR TAYLOR

THE EXTRAORDINARY CAREER OF A
CHAMPION BICYCLE RACER

ANDREW RITCHIE

The Johns Hopkins University Press
Baltimore and London

Copyright © Andrew Ritchie, 1988
All rights reserved
Printed in the United States of America on acid-free paper

Originally published in a hardcover edition by Bicycle Books, San Francisco, 1988
Johns Hopkins Paperbacks edition, 1996
05 04 03 02 01 00 99 98 97 96   5 4 3 2 1

The Johns Hopkins University Press
2715 North Charles Street
Baltimore, Maryland 21218-4319
The Johns Hopkins Press Ltd., London

Library of Congress Cataloging-in-Publication Data will be found at the end of this book.

ISBN 0-8018-5303-6 (pbk.)

FRONTISPIECE: Paris 1901. At the prime of his athletic career, Major Taylor posed with promoter, manager, and journalist Victor Breyer.

DEDICATION

TO THE HUNDREDS of anonymous newspaper and magazine reporters and photographers, whose careful and colorful accounts at the turn of the century made it possible to tell the story of Major Taylor's life.

TO MRS. SYDNEY TAYLOR BROWN, Major Taylor's daughter, who has waited a long time for this book.

AND TO MAJOR TAYLOR himself, a heroic man, whose life and great sporting achievements should not be forgotten.

CONTENTS

ACKNOWLEDGMENTS

My special thanks to the following people who helped me in many different ways during the research and writing of this book.

SYDNEY TAYLOR BROWN for encouraging and helping me from the beginning of the project and for sharing with me her thoughts and feelings about her father's life; most crucially for giving me access to Major Taylor's scrapbooks and papers.

CHRISTINA NAU and ROB VAN DER PLAS, my publishers, for believing in the importance of the book and working with me to overcome its many difficulties. And ESTELLE JELINEK, my indispensable editor.

ROLLO TURNER for support, advice and penetrating late night discussion in Pittsburgh.

JUDY KEENE for her diligent research into Major Taylor's early life in Indianapolis.

ROLAND SAUVAGET, JACQUES SERAY, SERGE LAGET and BERNARD DÉON for patient help locating information and photographs in Paris. MICHAEL DAVIS for friendship in Paris.

JIM FITZPATRICK, who generously lent me a typescript of his as yet unpublished book, *Major Taylor Down Under, A Black American in White Australia, 1902—1904* and permitted me to include some of the information from it in Chapter 10. Hopefully, his book will soon be published, adding yet more detail to the story of Major Taylor's two summers racing in Austrlia.

DANIEL DOLE, HOWARD SUTHERLAND and MARVIN COLLINS for support in Berkeley. KEITH KINGBAY and BLAKE DAVIS in Chicago; WAYNE KIRK in Somerville; FRED WILLKIE and PETER NYE for insight and advice.

MALCOLM E. BARKER, for help and assistance at many different stages of the project.

LELAND MEADER, of the Schwinn Bicycle Company, for allowing me access to the Schwinn archives.

LIBRARIANS who tolerated my compulsive searching in the Bibliothèque Nationale, Paris; Chicago Public Library; Boston Public Library; Worcester, Massachusetts, Public Library; Library of Congress, Washington, DC.

MANY OTHER PEOPLE who helped me and with whom I had correspondence about Major Taylor.

1
PROLOGUE

IT IS DIFFICULT for us today, to reach back in our imagination to recreate the thrill and excitement of bicycle track racing between 1890 and 1910. Yet it was, nearly a hundred years ago, a hugely popular and surprisingly modern sport. In fact, among spectator sports in the United States during those two decades, it was certainly as popular as, if not more popular than, baseball, boxing or horse racing.

About a thousand professional bicycle racers competed fiercely for lucrative prizes, and a few big champions walked away with the coveted honors. Huge crowds attended race meetings, hungry for the speed and drama of sprint racing wherever there was a good track and an enterprising promoter.

Bicycle racing appealed to people from all social strata. Fashionable women in colorful dresses and huge hats and men in smart suits and bowler hats rubbed shoulders with working men in sweaty clothes and knit caps. The races took place in an atmosphere of festivity and gaiety. Military bands played waltzes and marches. Vendors hawked sodas and popcorn and photographs of the stars. Bicycle and tire manufacturers advertized their products with huge posters.

Competition was fast and intense, often rough and dangerous. The riders watched each other carefully, jockeying for position before they accelerated with a fierce jump. As they lunged and wrenched themselves over the finishing line, a vast cheer went up from the crowd. Then came the bouquets and the lap of honor, the applause and adulation, interviews with the press, the awarding of medals and prizes. The racing continued into the long summer evenings, and the crowds spilled out of the track into the gathering darkness to take the street-cars home.

In a world without cars, motorcycles or airplanes, racing cyclists were the fastest humans on earth. Champions had an air of bravado and panache about them. They were heroic and glamorous figures. If they were successful, they made a lot of money.

Riders tended to come from what was often referred to as the 'un-educated class,' that is, the working class. They were mostly down-

USA, 1878—1932

to-earth, no-nonsense men accustomed to hard physical labor. For them, bicycle racing was a way out of the drudgery of a job in a factory or on a farm. It was a highly unstable existence, but the top racers enjoyed substantial fame. They were interviewed, quoted, discussed and admired. Their form was analyzed, their chances evaluated. They were stars in the modern sense.

At the top of the sport, a certain polish and suavity reigned, the style of the well-paid champion. A fine suit was a must, as well as a good hat and a decent room at a well-known hotel when he was out on the circuit. After all, the rider had a responsibility to his employer and it was vital that he make a good impression off the track as well as on it. There was no other sport in the 1890s to rival bicycle racing for drama and excitement.

INTO THIS supercharged sport a small, wiry and extremely fast black teenager emerged – Marshall W., nicknamed 'Major', Taylor . In a world where black people were expected to know their place and not to challenge the dominance of whites, the success of this plucky, determined youngster against white competitors came as a disturbing shock and his astonishing speed as a revelation.

Taylor first appeared as an amateur in races around Indianapolis and Chicago and later in Massachusetts, Connecticut and New York. Soon recognized as the 'colored sprint champion of America,' he turned professional when he was just eighteen years old and astonished everyone who saw him with his prodigiously talented performances.

In just a few years, he climbed right to the top of his sport. He became world champion in 1899 and American sprint champion in 1899 and 1900. He broke a series of world records and in 1901 received rapturous acclaim during a triumphant tour of Europe – the most important international tour of European countries ever undertaken by a black American athlete. Against the best bicycle racers in the world, he enjoyed a position of unequalled supremacy.

The story of Major Taylor's racing career is the story of his battle to establish the right to participate in professional bicycle racing in America. It is a dramatic social saga of those difficult, segregated times. He won that battle, but not without a struggle of epic proportions, one that ranks him as the earliest, most extraordinary, pioneering black athlete in the history of American sports.

USA, 1878—1932

He was almost certainly the first black athlete to be a member of an integrated professional team, the first to have a commercial sponsor, the first to establish world records. He was the second black world champion in any sport, preceded only by George Dixon, the bantamweight boxer. He was the first black athlete to compete regularly in open, integrated competition for an annual American championship. In all of these achievements, he set an example of accomplishment and pride to black Americans. He was also a representative of black America abroad at a time when many people in Europe had never seen a black person.

IF ALL THESE claims are true, why is Major Taylor's name barely mentioned in the histories of black participation in American sports? Why has he received so little recognition? Why is his career only familiar to a few people interested in the history of bicycle racing and to those who know something about his later life in his hometown of Worcester, Massachusetts? Why has it taken so long for this forgotten black hero to be rewarded with public acclaim?

It is not difficult to explain why Taylor's name sank into obscurity in the United States. First, bicycle racing as a professional sport declined drastically in popularity in this country as the twentieth century progressed, and by the end of World War II, it had almost disappeared. A dead sport does not remember its own past, and the entire dramatic story of bicycle racing at the turn of the century receded almost into oblivion.

Second, the same racism that was instrumental in trying to suppress Taylor's accomplishments while he was competing continued to suppress the memory of his achievements after his retirement from racing in 1910, at the age of thirty-two. When he died in 1932, it was a long time since the peak of his career. Jessie Owens and Joe Louis were about to begin their pioneering exploits, and only Jack Johnson had played out his sensational, rabble-rousing career. Taylor's turn-of-the-century achievements stood alone, in unique isolation from the general currents of the time. With bicycle racing no longer a popular sport, his meteoric sprinting was easily forgotten.

Yet Major Taylor has not been forgotten in France, where bicycle racing has an uninterrupted history as the national sport. In France today, there are people who still talk about his 1901 races as if it was

USA, 1878—1932

just yesterday. A prophet without honor in his own country, Taylor is still revered and idolized in France.

WHEN MAJOR TAYLOR died penniless in 1932, in Chicago, at the height of the Depression, he was buried in a pauper's grave. There was no fanfare of eulogies for him. Even when he was reburied in 1948 and his achievements praised at a Chicago memorial ceremony, it was still not the right moment to elevate him to his true stature as one of the preeminent black American sports pioneers. His name remained in obscurity.

When writing his autobiography, looking back over the distant beginnings of his bicycle racing career as a young boy in Indianapolis, Taylor himself had called it 'a freak of fate' that started him on his long and difficult journey to fame and glory.

Perhaps it was a 'freak of fate,' in a sense, to have been born at the right time and in the right place, to have had the opportunities that Taylor had, chances rare enough for a black youngster in America at that time. But if there was some luck in the possibilites he was offered, there was nothing but determination in the way he embraced his opportunities.

Marshall Taylor, even as a very young boy, was never slow to seize the chances that came his way. Only a very determined child, a disciplined, enthusiastic, willful child, could have come so far, so fast, and made such rapid progress as a teenager.

The story of Taylor's emergence from humble, rural beginnings in black America into the spotlight of international stardom as a champion bicycle racer, and his rapturous reception by huge crowds at races in America, Europe and Australia, is the story of a young man propelled, not by an accident of birth or fate, but by his own ambition and drive, by a fierce determination to overcome obstacles, and by the astonishing development of his own marvelous athletic ability.

USA, 1878—1932

2

EARLY GUIDANCE
AND INSPIRATION

MARSHALL WALTER TAYLOR, the son of Gilbert Taylor and
Saphronia Kelter, was born on the outskirts of Indianapolis on
November 26, 1878. He was one of eight children, five girls and three
boys, raised in humble, rural poverty not far from the noise and bustle
of a rapidly expanding industrial city. The oldest of these children
may have been born in Louisville, Kentucky, where Gilbert and
Saphronia were married. From imprecise information in his autobiography, Marshall appears to have been one of the youngest among
the eight children, certainly born after the family had arrived in Indiana.

Both Gilbert Taylor and Saphronia Kelter were born into freedom
in Kentucky of parents who had been slaves and who moved over
the state line into Indiana, a free state, either before or during the Civil
War.[1] * Indianapolis was not very far from the southern state of Kentucky, but far enough to give the family a measure of security from
those who might question their right to freedom. In fact, Indianapolis
lay on one of the routes of the 'underground railroad' from the South
into Canada. The couple's move north into Indiana was part of the
vast upheaval among blacks caused by the Civil War. Their initial arrival in Indianapolis may have been as refugees from the conflict.[2]

Gilbert Taylor fought for the North in a black regiment during the
Civil War. Later, in the 1860s or 1870s, after leaving the army, he bought
a small farm, from which he eked out a living to support his increasing family responsibilities.[3]

In about 1887, when Marshall was about eight years old, his father,
an experienced horseman, turned to the city for employment and became coachman to the Southards, a wealthy white family in Indianapolis. He took the job either to supplement his farming income

---

* Notes are numbered per chapter and may be found starting on p. 267.

or as an alternative to it. He probably worked at one of the splendid, ornate, Victorian houses the wealthy were building all over the country on exclusive, tree-lined, suburban streets.

For the young Marshall, his father's new job was a decisive event. There, in the stables of the big house, he got his first opportunity to expand and enlarge his experience beyond the obscurity and anonymity of the farm.

Later he would call it a 'freak of fate,' which started him on what was destined to be his racing career.

"Occasionally my father would take me to work with him when the horses needed exercising," Taylor recalled in his autobiography,

> ... and in time I became acquainted with the rich young son Daniel Southard, who was just my age.
>
> We soon became the best of friends, so much so in fact, that I was eventually employed as his playmate and companion. My clothing was furnished and we were kept dressed just alike all the time. Dan had a wonderful playroom stacked with every kind of toy imaginable, but his workshop was to me the one best room in the whole house, and when there I was the happiest boy in the world.
>
> The rest of Dan's playmates were of wealthy families too, and I was not in the neighborhood long before I learned to ride a bicycle just as they did. All the boys owned bicycles, excepting myself, but Dan saw to it that I had one too. I soon became a big favorite among them, perhaps because of my ability to hold up my end in all the different games we played, such as baseball, tennis, football, rollerskating, running and cycling, trick riding, and all the rest.

Young Marshall's easy interaction in the social life and sports at the Southard house underlines the fact that, even at an early age, he had a remarkable and atypical relationship with the white world. He was already lucky enough to have access to expensive toys and bicycles and to compete and express himself athletically. Living at the Southards', he was now separated from his own family surroundings, but was not, as the black coachman's son, restricted to playing in the stable yard. On the contrary, he was welcomed into the life of the family, his role was to be 'companion' to Dan Southard, apparently an only child considered in need of company his own age.

INDIANAPOLIS, 1878—1893

"It was an arrangement where he *lived* in the house and was treated like their son," Sydney Taylor Brown, Taylor's only child, who is now in her eighties, recalls.

> He wasn't living around the stables. ... He was reared like their child, and the Southard boy had a tutor, he didn't go to public school. *He* sat *there*, and my *Daddy* sat *here*, and the tutor taught them....He lived there, he slept there, he went to school and he ate there. He was the *companion* to this boy. ... A white man back in those days who hated the Negro group often had one Negro that he was fond of, or one Negro family that he would die for, but as far as the whole race was concerned, *that* was a different matter.

This period of living and learning in the Southard house lasted for several years, from the time he was about eight to twelve or thirteen. The experience, of course, had a profound impact on Taylor's development. The values and self-confidence he must have garnered from his own parents were now, in his formative years, supplemented and enlarged by his experience in this new world, so utterly different from the poor, rural home of his family. He was introduced to a class, a race, and a world of wealth and privilege. The Southard's house opened his eyes to other possibilities, expanded his horizons enormously, and gave him great expectations.

There, at the Southards', besides learning to read and write from a private tutor, he learned to talk, think and relate to others in ways different from those he would have learned at home or at a simple rural school. Gradually, he was weaned away from the farm and its values. He grew accustomed to the comforts of the white world, nice clothes, linen table napkins, material possessions. And he learned to relax around white people, to talk to them confidently and assertively. In Indianapolis at that time, the Southards must have been a very unusual family. Apparently, the young Marshall was not considered 'uppity' there.

It was not surprising, therefore, that when he visited his parents' humble home, he saw it in a different, perhaps negative, perspective. "There were occasions when he would go home," says his daughter:

> He didn't go, say, every weekend, but he kept in contact with his family when he lived at the Southards'. But he alienated himself. The word 'alienate' is perhaps a little strong – but he was the one sibling in that group the other children didn't care for, because he was different from them. You see, *they* were farm kids. *He* had all these manners, white

Indianapolis, 1878—1893

damask napkins and fine clothes and the speech. He liked to eat well, he was *different* from the rest of them. So when he came home, he never was popular with his brothers and sisters.

At a very early age, then, Marshall Taylor, the black farm boy who had graduated to the status of companion to the son of a wealthy white family, had his feet planted in two different worlds, but belonged totally in neither. He gained confidence in dealing with the white world, while learning to respect and defer to it. At the same time he was distancing himself from the farm, his family, and his roots.

The relationship with the Southard family – with its echoes of the paternalistic slave patterns of the past – and the separation of the young boy from his parental home might have had disastrous consequences for him, teaching him a lesson of inferiority and subservience. But it had exactly the opposite effect, creating in him instead a feeling of confidence and self-assurance and allowing him to think of himself as an equal to his friend, Dan Southard. Most remarkably, there is, in the description of the two boys "kept dressed alike all the time," a compelling image of racial equality. Marshall was encouraged to see himself and think of himself as being identical to, and equal with, his white companion. He was, in fact, adopted by the white family.

It is not improbable to suggest that, even as a child, Taylor had special qualities that made others notice him and single him out. Why would the Southards have taken the son of their black coachman into their family as a companion to their own son, if they had not seen in him qualities they liked? It would not have been done solely on the basis of compatibility of age or simply because he was available. Something in him attracted adults, his politeness and intelligence perhaps, his ability to concentrate, and his capacity to learn. That he was a pleasant, cooperative child, and not a troublesome one, is obvious.

Taylor's progress through childhood and youth suggests a continual curiosity to learn and absorb experience, to make the most of the chances that came his way. At the Southards' there was equality of a sort. He learned to measure himself against his white playmates and understood he was their physical equal. But this integrated, privileged life could only exist in the cloistered security of the Southard household. The world outside was not so generous.

INDIANAPOLIS, 1878—1893

That he was black and that there were limitations on what he could do, where he could go, and what he could expect to achieve, were lessons Marshall could not accept so easily. When the white children went to the Indianapolis branch of the YMCA to exercise and play, he was excluded from the gymnasium because of his color. As he recalled later:

> It was there that I was first introduced to that dreadful monster prejudice, which became my bitterest foe from that very same day, and one which I have never as yet been able to defeat. Owing to my color, I was not allowed to join the Y.M.C.A., and in consequence was not permitted to go on the gymnasium floor with my companions. The boys protested to their parents about it, but they, even with their powerful influence, were unable to do anything about it. Consequently I could only watch the other boys from the gallery go through their calisthenics, and how my poor little heart would ache to think that I was denied an opportunity to exercise and develop my muscles in the same manner as they, and for really no reason that I was responsible for.

HAVING BEEN taught this first bitter lesson about his social status, Marshall was soon thrust out into the real world from the artificial comfort and security of the Southard family when they decided to move to Chicago. "Because my mother could not bear the idea of parting with me," he wrote, I was dropped from the happy life of a 'millionaire kid' to that of a common errand boy, all within a few weeks."

With his most prized possession, the bicycle the Southards gave him when they left Indianapolis, Marshall began to earn his first few dollars doing what so many other children do, getting up early in the morning to deliver newspapers. It was a job that strengthened and developed his cycling ability, where speed and stamina certainly helped.

Living at home on the farm on the outskirts of Indianapolis and delivering newspapers to make a small contribution to the income of his struggling parents, Marshall found that his bicycle also gave him independence and freedom. Though he probably learned to ride on a high-wheel bicycle, the machine he was riding at this time was probably one of the earliest 'safety' bicycles, which had been introduced around 1890, with solid rubber tires, probably a heavy but still smooth-running machine. It was certainly quite unusual at the time, for a young black farm boy to have a bicycle, since the expense of buying one would have been beyond the means of his parents.

Marshall learned to do tricks on the bicycle and soon became adept at it. "The same perseverance that later played such a prominent part in my successful career on the bicycle track evidenced itself while I was a barefoot boy. After long hours of practicing, I became a pretty fair trick rider," he wrote. Exhibitions of trick riding were quite common at the fairs and bicycle races of the time, and he was inspired to imitate them.

One day, when he was about thirteen, probably early in 1892, Marshall went to the shop of Hay and Willits in Indianapolis to have his bicycle repaired. "After the repair had been made," he remembered later,

> I made a fancy mount on my bicycle in the middle of the store and immediately drew the attention of Mr. Hay. He asked me who taught me that trick, and when I replied "myself," he smiled doubtfully. I told Mr. Hay that that was one of my easiest tricks and that I had a number of others that I would like to show him if he was interested. He was, and he ordered the store cleared to a certain extent and I did a number of my homemade tricks for him and his guests of the occasion that made them fairly gasp. In fact, the exhibition was so good that Mr. Hay, his mind ever alert for good advertising for his store, invited me to repeat them in the street in front of his place of business. In a short time there was so much congestion on the spot that the police were called to open it for traffic.

> Going into the store later on Mr. Hay's invitation, he asked me how I would like to go to work for the firm. I told him I was peddling a paper route and earning $5.00 a week at it and that, of course, I would expect a little more for my services if my mother would allow me to work for him. My eyes nearly popped out of my head when he said, "I will give you that $35.00 bicycle and $6.00 a week if you will come to work for me." I told him I would consult my mother and let him know shortly. I went to work for him in the course of a few days.

Once again, just as with the Southards, Marshall had impressed an adult with his confidence and ability and opened a door for himself. At Hay and Willits, a young bicycle store ready to expand into the boom years of the mid-1890s, he had put his foot on the bottom rung of the ladder in the professional bicycle world.[4] Having any kind of job at all in the city at the age of thirteen was quite an achievement for a farm boy. His main duties in the store were the typical chores of the shop boy, to dust and sweep, arrange the shelves and open the door for the customers. But there was a respite from the drudgery each day, when Marshall had the chance to show off his skill as a trick cyclist and to do the publicity work for which Tom Hay had employed him. "Every afternoon, at four," he wrote, "I was booked to give an exhibition of trick and fancy riding in my nice new uniform out in the street in front of the store."

The 'nice new uniform,' a soldier's uniform with bright buttons and braidings, worn with a little military cap, was a publicity gimmick designed by Hay and Willits to attract attention to the snappy young trick rider and to entice new customers into the store. It was also responsible for Marshall Taylor acquiring the nickname which was to become his permanent name for the rest of his life.

There are many subsequent, contradictory accounts of how Marshall became 'Major' Taylor to everyone but his wife, Daisy. One explanation is that at school, "he was always at the head of a group of children playing soldiers and he was the Major and he held a large baton in his hand." Another explanation, given in a French newspaper, was that he was called 'Major' at school "because of the incredible thrashings he used to hand out to the other pupils who made fun of him because of his color." Even Taylor himself confused the issue at times, seemingly unwilling to explain the simple truth. "The title 'Major' has no military significance, as many suppose," explained an Australian newspaper in 1904. "Asked recently where he got his rank, Major Taylor replied, 'Well, I got it from my parents when they christened me. My Christian name is Major.'"[6]

The truth seems to be simply that the young boy, dressed in his military uniform, whose appearance was eagerly awaited each afternoon on the sidewalk outside Hay and Willits, became the 'Major' – and the humor and appropriateness of the name stuck.

Later, the name had an undeniable impact in contributing to his public and professional identity and mystique. It evoked an image of dominance, of authority and command, which strengthened and defined his professional presence. Even as a boy, it gave him pride and a positive identity. He was a performer. He wore a uniform and had a new name. It was something different and made him feel important.

INDIANAPOLIS, 1878—1893

IT WAS WHILE Taylor was working at Hay and Willits that he won his first race, an event he still remembered very vividly thirty years later when he was writing his autobiography.

A gold medal for an upcoming 10-mile road race promoted by his employers was put on display in the shop window, and Taylor spent more time fondling this medal than doing his job dusting the shelves. "It seemed to me that would probably be the only chance that I would have to be near such a valuable prize," he recollected. "I recall clearly being so bold one day as to pin the medal on the lapel of my coat and strut with it for five minutes in front of the mirror." His eventual entry into the race was, as he remembered it,

> ... an accident pure and simple. I had gone out to witness the event, which attracted the cream of the amateur riders of Indiana, and had taken a vantage point near the start, when Mr. Hay spotted me. ... Mr. Hay insisted that I take my place on the starting line. I rebelled, but he fairly dragged me and my bicycle across the road, saying, "Come on here, young man, you have got to start in this race." I was badly scared at the thought, as one may well imagine, since I had never seen a bicycle race before.
>
> Although the band was playing a lively tune and the crowd was cheering wildly, I was crying. When Mr. Hay saw that he started to lift me from my wheel, but stopped and whispered in my ear, "I know you can't go the full distance, but just ride up the road a little way, it will please the crowd, and you can come back as soon as you get tired."
>
> Crack! went the pistol, and with tears in my eyes I was off with a fifteen-minute handicap on the scratchman.* There were hundreds of cyclists stretched along the route, and it seemed to be a friendly sort of cheer and one that encouraged me and inspired me to keep on going even after I had begun to feel very tired. Those words telling me that I could turn back after a short distance inspired me on when it seemed like fatigue was about to overtake me. They made me all the more determined to show my employer that I could go the distance. ...
>
> After I had ridden some distance, I noticed a group of riders coming to meet me. As they drew closer, I noticed Mr. Hay among them. He had the gold medal that was hung up for the first prize and dangled it in front of my eyes as we rode along. As he did so, he informed me that I was a mile ahead of the field and had half the distance left to go. The

---

*   See the Glossary on p. 285 for explanations of bicycle racing terms.

thought flashed through my mind that I had a chance to own that medal. ... The sight of it seemed to give me a fresh start, and I felt as though I had only just begun the race. The thought of that gold medal becoming my property spurred me on to my greatest efforts. The act on Mr. Hay's part was the psychological turning point of the race for me. From then on I rode like mad and wobbled across the tape more dead than alive in first place about six seconds ahead of the scratchman. ...

Once across the finishing line, I collapsed and fell in a heap in the roadway. Kind hands revived me shortly and I recall clearly that the first thing I saw on regaining consciousness was that big gold medal pinned on my chest. I had been through a nerve-wracking, heart-breaking race, my legs pained me terribly, but I felt amply repaid for my efforts as I scanned that medal. My first thought was to take it home to show it to my mother. ... My mother laughed and cried in turn as I related the incident of my first race. And one may well imagine my enthusiasm as I told her about the race, as I was but thirteen years old at the time.

SOMETIME IN 1892 or 1893, Taylor left Hay and Willits and began to work at Harry Hearsey's bicycle store, an older and more established store, also on North Pennsylvania Street, the 'Bicycle Row' of Indianapolis.[7] At Hearsey's, Taylor was promoted to teaching bicycle riding, and had a much more responsible and personal relationship with customers.

Hearsey, who was about thirty at the time that Taylor first went to work for him, was a pioneer in the bicycle industry in Indianapolis. A cyclist himself, trained as a mechanic in the bicycle factories of New England in the 1880s, he had opened a store in Indianapolis in 1886, where he sold and repaired the old high-wheel bicycles. Since he was English himself, he had been curious about the pioneering developments in bicycle technology going on in Coventry, England, in the mid-1880s, when John Kemp Starley was refining his ideas for the first Rover safety bicycles, and he had imported the very first example of the new safety bicycle ever seen in the city.[8]

Thus, as the safety bicycle grew in popularity and American manufacturers began to produce their own designs – the first examples of the bicycle as it still is today – "Hearsey was in a position to become the central figure around whom the bicycle activities of Indianapolis revolved. His shop was headquarters for all the famous racing men ... and he was a leading spirit in the great meets which were as much events in the 1890s as automobile races have been since."[9]

Taylor was employed in Hearsey's store principally to give bicycle lessons, a common practice at the time, when many people who bought a bicycle had never ridden one before. HEARSEY'S PRIVATE RIDING SCHOOL – LESSONS FREE TO OUR CUSTOMERS, a newspaper advertisement for the shop announced, adding laconically: "Kindly bear in mind that our spacious Riding School, in which our customers may practice free of charge, is provided with padded walls. This is a comforting thought."

Out of the enthusiasm for the bicycle grew a new sport, and many of the cyclists who went to Hay and Willits' store organized themselves into the Zig-Zag Cycling Club, which moved to a home of its own in rented quarters as it grew to a membership of about 200 in the early 1890s.[10] Tom Hay, Bert Willits, and Harry Hearsey were the leading lights of the club, organizing runs and races, promoting advertising gimmicks and launching themselves into a hectic round of social events, dinners, and dances in the winter months.

Taylor was involved in all these activities, but not eligible for full participation, since his color excluded him from the white club's formal social activities. His daily environment was the bicycle shop, among the white customers and employees. At the shop, there were social limits to be observed, a position of servility had to be adopted by necessity. He was participating in and entering into the life of the store, but there was always the danger of stepping out of line. At night he went back to the farm, back to another world, racing his bicycle through dark, deserted streets. There was always riding and racing as a way of expressing himself, of proving himself. That was something nobody could take away from him.

AMONG THE CROWD of people in the bicycle world of Indianapolis who frequented Hearsey's bicycle shop when Taylor was working there was a tall, good-looking, humorous man called Louis Munger. He was nicknamed 'Birdie' by all his friends for reasons unknown, possibly something to do with his prominent nose, or with his position on his bicycle, or his jovial disposition.

Louis de Franklin Munger, born in Detroit in 1863, arrived in Indianapolis in the early 1890s from Chicago, where he had been living for a number of years. He was busily occupied in setting up a small factory to manufacture the light and carefully designed racing bicycles more and more sought after by racing cyclists of the early 1890s. Perhaps he came to Indianapolis to learn some of the skills he needed from Harry Hearsey, or he may have wanted to take advantage of the already bustling bicycle trade in the city.

Munger was a star in bicycle racing. He was not one of the biggest, certainly not as big as the champion Arthur Zimmerman, but he was a well-known record breaker and sometime holder of the 1-mile world record on the track on the old high-wheel bicycle. He was a big enough star to become a hero in the eyes of the youngsters at Hearsey's, Taylor being one of his admirers. At the age of thirty, he was past his prime, but he had not completely retired from racing.

Munger was a good example of the bicycle fanatic of the time. He lived, talked, ate, and slept bicycles. He raced them, he rode them for pleasure, he earned his living making and selling them, he expressed himself creatively by experimenting with them and designing them, and his social life revolved around them. He moved in a bewitching, compulsive world of technological advance and economic opportunity.

Munger's greatest racing exploits had been in the heroic days of the high-wheel bicycle in the 1880s. He had been one of the best racers who had followed the circuit around Chicago, at Peoria and Springfield, Illinois (the mecca of bicycle racing in that decade), and up and down the East Coast. Officially amateurs, these men competed for splendid prizes, gold cups and medals, horses and wagons, and of course, new bicycles. They often accepted, nevertheless, the sponsorship of bicycle manufacturers, and sometimes turned their prizes into cash by selling them. They were devoted full-time athletes, often more professional than truly amateur.[11]

In Indianapolis, Birdie Munger soon started his own business, the Munger Cycle Manufacturing Company. An advertisement in December 1893 encouraged his potential customers with large exclamation marks: THE MUNGER! WAIT FOR IT! IT IS A STUNNER![12] Needing a servant or valet for his new quarters, Munger did not have to look any further than Hearsey's, where Taylor, the energetic and mature black teenager, was giving lessons in the riding school. Munger also knew about Taylor from having seen him competing in the boys' races in Peoria, Chicago and Indianapolis. Taylor, impetuous and likable, was

always badgering Munger for advice and information. He followed
him to the track, begging to ride his bicycle. He went riding with him
on Sundays or hung around Munger's workshop, always inquisitive,
asking questions. It may be that *he* chose Munger as his new boss as
much as Munger chose *him.*

Munger had grown to like Taylor. He recognized in him the same
qualities that others had seen. He was serious and determined, quick
to learn and trustworthy. And he was also useful. Soon Taylor was
working for Munger rather than for Harry Hearsey and was installed
in Munger's house as his "cook, chambermaid and general man of all
work." His morning and evening rides to and from his parents' farm
came to an end, and the intensity of his bicycle world was now complete.

"Mr. Munger's bachelor quarters in Indianapolis became famous
among the bicycle racers and bicycle salesmen throughout the
country," Taylor wrote in his autobiography. "Many of them made
their home with Mr. Munger while in the city on business. When I
was not tied up with tasks in the factory, I served as a helper around
the house."

Once again, the drudgery of working for a white man, which might
have been a burdensome, thankless task, creating resentment, had a
dramatic silver lining. For at the house he met important people and
expanded his horizons even more. "In this capacity, I came to know
all of the leading bicycle racers of the country," he wrote, "but what
is more I won the admiration of Mr. Munger and he became one of
my staunchest supporters and advisors."

A later description, from a Boston newspaper, tells the story of
Taylor's ascent to stardom after he became the American sprint champion at the end of 1900. It gives an interesting glimpse of his initia-
tion into bicycle racing in those early days in Indianapolis.

> The Major's entry into the bicycle game is as unique as the position
> which he holds today. ... Many years ago, when some of the profes-
> sionals, including Birdie Munger, ... were quartered at Indianapolis, the
> Major, then quite a kid, was hanging around the quarters where the
> cyclists put up. He was stuck on bicycle riding. Being a bright kid, the
> cyclists, just for fun, used to make him try to ride their wheels. At first
> it was tough work for the Major, but he succeeded ... in being able to
> push it to the front of the others so often that today he can give the

laugh to those fellows whose shoes he polished a few years ago, and who would now be glad to accept orders from him.

When hanging around with those fellows, he used to run errands, do a little cooking and general chore work, all the time doing a little dickering with the bicycle. He used to essay a little trick riding, particularly when the present safety came into vogue, and he used to make lots of fun for the racers who were in training. Because he was able to afford them some amusement, the riders looked on him with favor and allowed him many little considerations. He used to go on centuries with them, and developed into a strong rider.[13]

ONE OF TAYLOR'S meetings with famous bicycle racers of the day remained firmly imprinted in his memory. That was the extraordinary thrill of being close to the greatest champion of them all, the famous Arthur Augustus Zimmerman, the most famous bicycle racer in America, and probably in the world, when Taylor, a fourteen-year-old lad, met him in the summer of 1893.

Zimmerman, who had an extraordinarily triumphant season in 1893, his last season as an amateur, was invited to race in Indianapolis on August 24. Nearly every important champion had been invited to the meet, organized by the Zig-Zag Cycling Club, with Tom Hay, Bert Willits, and Harry Hearsey as the main promoters of the occasion.

"The citizens of Indianapolis will have an opportunity on Thursday next to witness a day's sport far superior to anything of the kind ever seen in the world," gushed the *Indianapolis Sentinel* the day before the big race. "It is the first time in the history of cycling that all of the champions of the various nations were ever assembled at one meet. Bicycle races are far more interesting than horse races; they are run off with great promptness. No score, no jockeying; every race for blood."[14] In truth, "the champions of various nations" amounted to one white South African rider, but Zimmerman and Willie Windle were there. *They* were the star attractions.

As the visiting 'cracks' arrived in the city for the event, a committee from the Zig-Zag Club met them at the trains and escorted them to their quarters. They came from Cleveland, Chicago and other cities. Munger sent Taylor to the railroad station to meet his old friend Arthur Zimmerman. For Taylor, it was the chance of a lifetime.

"It had been arranged that Zimmerman would be the guest of Mr. Munger, and I was delegated to conduct him to the Munger home," Taylor remembered:

> I recognized my hero from pictures of him that had been printed in the newspapers. While hundreds surged about the train to welcome Mr. Zimmerman to Indianapolis, where he was a prime favorite, and a brass band rent the air, while a welcoming committee stood by, I worked my way to the great cyclist's side. Quickly I gave him my message and Zimmerman smiled as he grasped my hand and asked my name. He insisted that I ride in the carriage with him to Mr. Munger's house and he talked with me continuously en route.

Taylor told Zimmerman about his exploits, the gold medal he had won in his exciting first race and about the boys' races he had been winning since then. When they arrived at the house, "Mr. Zimmerman asked his host about me. Mr. Munger confirmed all that I had told Mr. Zimmerman about my races and a lot besides. 'I am going to make a champion out of that boy some day,' said Mr. Munger. And at Mr. Zimmerman's request I sat down to the dinner table with them – a great honor indeed."

"I have told Major Taylor that if he refrains from using liquor and cigarettes, and continues to live a clean life, I will make him the fastest bicycle rider in the world," Munger told Zimmerman at dinner. Zimmerman reminded Taylor that he still had a long way to go, but added, "Mr. Munger is an excellent advisor and if he tells me that you have the makings of a champion in you, I feel sure you will scale the heights some day."

The day before the race, the competitors all went to the track to familiarize themselves with it and to work out. In the afternoon, "all the stars were shining at the Fair Grounds," reported the *Sentinel.* "They pronounced the track one of the finest they ever rode over and Zimmerman expressed himself as able to make some very fast time, far below the record now."

In the evening, "the riders of the city and all the visitors took part in a magnificent lantern parade," organized by the Zig-Zaggers,

> ... in which they vied with each other in the brilliancy of their decorations. There were lanterns and bunting and bright colored decorating paper in abundance, and the streets over which they passed looked as though peopled with harlequins from some other sphere for the time being.

INDIANAPOLIS, 1878—1893

The streets were lined with people and the street cars stood still while the boys passed. The streets were for the time given over to them and all were willing to concede them room without any discussion of the question of the rights of vehicles or pedestrians.

It was the largest parade of the kind ever given in the city and was a fitting opening to the races today. The whole parade was the subject of much favorable comment.[15]

The next morning, while the bustle of final preparations for the races was going on, Taylor, with the sparkle of the lantern parade still in his eyes, met another big champion, an even more established rider than Zimmerman: Willie Windle, the sprint champion of America from 1889 to 1892, whose dominant position as a sprinter in the late 1880s had been challenged by Zimmerman's ascendancy. "While on my way out to the race track on an errand," Taylor wrote later, "I found myself sitting alongside one of the other big champions of the day, Willie Windle, of Millbury, Massachusetts. That gold medal of mine arrested his attention and Mr. Windle inquired as to its history. I was the proudest boy in the world as it became noised about that I had shaken the hand of the two outstanding bicycle greats of the bicycle circles of the country – Zimmerman and Windle."

The Indianapolis Military Band welcomed the crowd and the riders to the State Fair Grounds on the afternoon of August 24. Dan J. Canary, "the world's famous trick and fancy rider," held the crowd spellbound "with his natural, bewitching grace and beauty and his extraordinary cleverness," a performance which Taylor watched with an attentive and critical eye. The day was perfect, "with the exception of a wind which came in sharp gusts, blowing from the west." But as the afternoon wore on, "the wind died away to a perfect calm and the riders had it all their own way."

Zimmerman won the big race of the meet, the 1-mile open, the prize being a gold, diamond-encrusted cup worth $1,000 presented by the Zig-Zag Club. Windle could only manage fourth place. Munger, who also competed in the race, could not get into the prizes. Zimmerman not only won, he also set a new world record of 2 minutes, $12^4/5$ seconds for the mile, beating the old record of George Taylor, who was second in the race, by $2^3/5$ seconds

Zimmerman shot by the grandstand like a stone from a catapult. … He received an ovation which would have caused most any man to have swelled visibly, but he paid no attention to it, and ambled along to his dressing room like some green, country boy who never seems to know where to put his hands. The secret of his apparent indifference is his extreme bashfulness. He never knows what to say or what to do, so very wisely does nothing. When he is called upon to make a speech or respond to an address of presentation, he blushes and stammers and gets as nervous as a school girl, and yet he can go out on the track and whip the world riding.[17]

T HE IMAGE of athletic greatness that the fourteen-year-old Taylor witnessed that afternoon was a striking one. The famous cyclist, Zimmerman, had won an important race and set a new world record, yet he was so shy that he hardly knew what to do with himself as he bashfully accepted the applause of the crowd.

And it was not just the excitement of meeting the two famous champions, Zimmerman and Windle, in Indianapolis, which touched Taylor deeply. He was also impressed by their attitude towards him, which was not one of condescension or hostility, but of friendly interest. "I was especially impressed with the friendliness of the two of them," he wrote, "especially towards me, a colored boy. In my youthful mind the thought flashed that men can be champions and still be broad-minded, in strange contrast with the would-be champions that I had met in and about Indianapolis. There was no race prejudice in the make-ups of Zimmerman and Windle, they were too big for that. And that expression has been fresh in my mind ever since that day."

Without role models from his own race, the fourteen-year-old Taylor had nevertheless found heroes to worship. They were white heroes, but they were kind to him, and they listened and understood his infatuation with the bicycle. And Munger, acting more or less in the role of his father now, encouraged him, advised him, and pushed him forward. Small wonder, then, that in such an environment Taylor made rapid progress. He had the chance to develop and improve and, just as he had with every other opportunity that had presented itself to him, he embraced it with vigor and determination.

INDIANAPOLIS, 1878—1893

3
BICYCLE BOOM
AND JIM CROW

TAYLOR'S JOBS at the bicycle shops in Indianapolis and the beginning of his bicycle racing career occurred just at the moment when
the bicycle was entering American life in a serious way, when it was
becoming common and accepted and a useful tool of everyday life.

In the 1880s, a small group of devotees had ridden and raced the
old high-wheel bicycle, or 'ordinary' (so called because the first of the
new safety bicycles, low and very peculiar-looking at first, were
thought extraordinary). They had ridden it in and around the cities as
a sporting and utility vehicle. But this difficult to manage and
dangerous bicycle, with its solid rubber tires and the rider perched
dangerously high up off the ground, had never gained wide
popularity. It was a young man's fancy – dashing, risky, and romantic – opening up new vistas for those with courage and energy, but
far too adventurous for most people.

The extraordinary records made on dirt roads and specially built
tracks by the earliest bicycle racing pioneers, including Zimmerman
and Munger, showed the potential of the high-wheel bicycle as an alternative to the horse, but it could not replace the horse for most
people. It was a daunting prospect to ride the grandiose and tricky
high-wheel over the unsurfaced rocks, mud, and sand of the roads of
the 1880s. Only the very athletic and committed set out on long rides,
and long-distance records were hailed in the newspapers as great
achievements.

It was the development of the safety bicycle, first designed and
commercially produced by John Kemp Starley in Coventry, England,
in the mid-1880s, and the invention and introduction of the pneumatic
tire by John Boyd Dunlop in Ireland a little later, that revolutionized
the bicycle industry.[1] The combination of these two improvements
led to a huge and sudden increase in the demand for bicycles in
Europe and America because they were now accessible to the mas-

USA, 1889—1895

ses. With increased demand came further refinements in technology and design and increased production quickly created a whole new industry, which employed thousands of skilled machinists and assemblers and flooded the market with bicycles.

Between about 1889 and 1895, the bicycle business in America boomed. Sizable fortunes were made quite rapidly in the production, distribution, and retail sale of bicycles and their components. New York City, Chicago, and New England were the major business centers of the industry, but every large city had its 'bicycle row,' where retailers competed for the sale of nationally advertised brands, such as the Victor, the Rambler, the Crescent, and the Columbia.

The customers for these finely made mass-produced bicycles, which sold for between $50 and $100 each, were initially the more affluent middle class. One hundred dollars was a substantial amount of money at a time when the average worker's wage might be only a few dollars a week. But as cheaper models and second-hand bicycles became available, bicycling soon became much more democratic, more freely available to all. It increased people's mobility, saved time, bypassed the high cost of keeping a horse, and became an important recreational activity. And it was the means by which a new sport was developed and introduced to the public on a much larger scale than before. Spectators reacted to the speed and excitement of bicycle racing on the road and track with intense enthusiasm, and new stars of the sport were created, of whom Zimmerman was the earliest.

The bicycle of the 1890s was the link between the horse and the automobile in personal transportation. For a twenty-year period, between 1890 and about 1910, it was the most common means of making short journeys. The automobile did not come into general use until well after 1910, and even then it was still a rich man's toy.

By 1894 and 1895, the energetic economic vigor around the bicycle had become a social avalanche.[2] Newspapers constantly discussed the bicycle and its social implications and significance. It was recognized as extremely healthy for the national economy, an excellent example of entrepreneurial capitalism at work, bold, expansive, inventive, enriching. It was also hailed for encouraging exercise and creating good health, as the benign developer of sound bodies and sound minds, as an economic leveler, and as a means of expanding people's horizons.

USA, 1889—1895

Social clubs centered around cycling sprang into existence at all levels of society. The upper-crust clubs and the appearance of the socialites of the smart set on their brand-new bicycles in the parks and boulevards of New York City, Chicago, Boston, and Washington gave a new and short-lived impetus of respectability to the bicycle boom. The affluent soon tired of their new toy and went back to their horses and automobiles, but factory clubs, institutional clubs, neighborhood clubs, Czech clubs, public library clubs and even black clubs united their members around a common interest and gave the mostly young men and women who were their members the chance to organize runs and rallies, races and parades, and the excuse to celebrate at several rowdy dinners throughout the year.

The background, then, to Taylor's employment, first by Hay and Willits and then by Hearsey, and to his finding a niche with Munger in Indianapolis, is a rapidly developing bicycle craze, which would get bigger and bigger through the middle of the 1890s and become a boom by 1895. One cycling magazine called Indianapolis "a beehive of cycling industry" and claimed that "no city excels Indianapolis in the magnitude of its bicycle industry."

Taylor grew up into this feverishly expanding commercial bicycle world and served his apprenticeship in it. His employment in these stores was unusual at a time of restricted possibilities for black people. As a young boy, he saw an economic opportunity and leaped right into it. The unique thing about his leap was that he was a black boy leaping into a white world and treading a path that no black boy had ever trodden before.

EQUIPPED WITH one of Munger's ultralight racing bicycles, Taylor was soon training seriously on the road and at the track, developing his racing skills and especially his sprinting, at which he excelled. The quick transition he had made from being Munger's houseboy to being his protégé was outlined in a newspaper article at the end of 1897, describing how he had climbed those first few rungs of the ladder of success.

> Taylor was but a lad when he came to Munger. 'Birdie' placed him in his bachelor quarters ... and Major Taylor was an important factor in those quarters, as cook, chambermaid and general man of all work. Munger was a racing man and the Major soon gained the enthusiasm of the race track. He cared for the wheels of Munger and soon grew to

be a lover of a fine wheel, such as Munger made. Taylor finally had a 14-pound wheel all of his own, and from that time on he was a poor man for the quarters. He spent his time at the race track. Munger stormed and stormed, but it did no good.

One day, he decided to go out to the track to see for himself what Major was doing. That day the colored boy electrified his master with an un-paced mile in 2 minutes 9 seconds. The World's Record was but 2.07 at the time. Munger placed the lad in road races and he came out of them all right. He placed him in track races, and his place was always in the front ranks.[4]

On Sunday June 30, 1895, Taylor won a seventy-five-mile road race from Indianapolis to Matthews, a town across the plains to the north-east of the city. The man who promoted the race was George Catter-son, who was described as "an active and pushing young man, of fine physique and an ardent lover of athletic sports, taking especially great interest in bicycling and frequently making century runs."[5] Catterson had invested in real estate and the construction of a railroad in the Matthews area and wanted publicity for his enterprises. He was also interested in giving Taylor a chance to prove himself because word had spread about his being barred from the tracks in Indianapolis be-cause of his color.

Bicycle racing was definitely the thing of the moment, and Catterson's sense of timing was shrewd. "The bicycle craze in In-dianapolis seems to grow rather than diminish in its intensity," the *In-dianapolis Sentinel* reported. "The many pretty roads about the city and the pleasant rides that may be had are conducive to the increased sale of wheels. In all directions from the city there are pretty roads and good roads to travel. ... Indianapolis lies in a plateau broken by few hills and the riders do not have the unpleasant work up and down hills." [6]

Under the headline, BICYCLING AS A SPORT, IT IS OUTSTRIPPING FOOT-BALL, TENNIS, CRICKET, AND BASEBALL, another article asserted that, "the frequent reports of the doings of the sport in the daily press, the use of the cycle as an adjunct to business, the discussions in the medical press as to the value of cycling as a cure for common ailments ... and its present growing popularity among the aristocracy, all testify to the fact that its place as a sport and a pastime is beginning to gain a recog-nition that has never been achieved by any other open-air amuse-ment."[7]

USA, 1889—1895

EARLY ON SUNDAY morning, at the start of the race to Matthews, a large crowd of people almost blocked Massachusetts Avenue in Indianapolis. Taylor's participation was kept secret and he was entered in the scratch position, that is, starting last, behind the other twenty or so competitors. "I trailed along in the rear for several miles," Taylor recollected,

> ... and was resting up in good shape before they were aware that I was in the race. They made things disagreeable for me by calling me vile names, and trying to put me down, and they even threatened to do me bodily harm if I did not turn back. I decided that if my time had come I might just as well die trying to keep ahead of the bunch of riders, so I jumped through the first opening and went out front, never to be overtaken. ...

> When I took the lead, we had covered about half the distance and were on a weird stretch of road that was thinly inhabited, with weeping willows on one side and a cemetery opposite. The thought ran through my mind that this would make an ideal spot for my competitors to carry out their dire threats. Spurred on by such thoughts I opened up the distance between my wheel and the balance of the field to make doubly sure that none of them caught up to me and got a chance to do me bodily injury.

The rain had begun to fall in torrents almost immediately, and the dusty clay turned into a thick mud. "The condition of the roads was such as to make it impossible to make any kind of time," a reporter commented. "For a number of miles the wheelmen say that the road was like a trough of water. At some places the clay so clung to the tires as to make it almost impossible for them to run through the forks." Two of the riders almost got to Muncie, at about the three-quarter-distance mark, but were both "so overcome from exhaustion that they could not go another step. They shook hands and agreed to quit."[8]

At Muncie, where the six riders still left in the race were dripping with water and covered from head to foot in mud, some of Major Taylor's friends had agreed to meet him, to pace him into Matthews, and had taken the streetcar out there to wait for him. But, because of the awful conditions, "they had given him up and were at dinner when Taylor pedalled into the place. They hurried out, however, and took him over the ground at a good clip."

The 'little black wonder' left all his friends behind. Pressing on through the torrential rain, "he finally rode into Matthews alone,

USA, 1889—1895

covered with mud and his clothes weighing more than did his trusty thirteen-pound Munger," the *Sentinel* reported.[9]

Catterson was waiting in Matthews when Taylor arrived at 3:35 P.M. In fact, he was the only cyclist to finish the race . The *Indianapolis Sentinel* headlined the event as A WONDERFUL ROAD RACE, and praised the "little colored boy," who had "proved himself a wonder." The first prize was a house lot worth $300 in the center of Matthews. Taylor tucked the deed in his pocket and rushed home to present it to his mother. "I had not previously told her of my plans to enter the race because I felt that she would worry about me until I returned home," he wrote later; "Of course she was elated over my success, but she made me promise that I would never ride such a long race again. I was only 16 years old at the time."

BY 1895, when the determined young Taylor won this hard race from Indianapolis to Matthews, the presence of black people in the sporting and social world of cycling had become a serious issue for the white riders. As the bicycle boomed and clubs and races were increasingly organized, it was inevitable that racial prejudice would be directed at those black riders who wanted to participate.

Since its founding in Boston in 1880, the League of American Wheelmen , or LAW, had protected and furthered the interests of the growing number of bicyclists, or 'wheelmen,' in America. It fought to establish the legal rights of cyclists on the roads, persuaded railroads to carry bicycles as baggage, and published and distributed a newsletter and thousands of maps and guidebooks. It grew rapidly, providing an organizational and social focus for bicycle-related activities. Soon its many concerns included the promotion and control of bicycle racing in the United States and a campaign that lobbied successfully for better roads.

As the high-wheel bicycle became outmoded by the safety bicycle in the early 1890s, and as bicycling became more accessible to many different kinds of people, the LAW grew in size and influence. It was a large, politically active organization, with state divisions, a central committee, and an annual convention, at which national policy matters were debated and voted on. In just one year, from 1896 to 1897, the number of members jumped from 40,000 to nearly 75,000.

As the bicycle democratized society, black people also began to ride for recreation in considerable numbers, especially the relatively better-off blacks in northern cities. When they sought to join the LAW, it became a hotly debated issue whether or not to admit them as members. The question was, of course, whether blacks should be accepted as the equal of whites in the League, with all the privileges that such membership gave, the entry to social events, dinners, dances and rallies.

Many people, especially Southerners, were emphatic that blacks should be excluded. At the 1892 annual convention, a group of delegates, led by Colonel Watts of Louisville, Kentucky, tried to introduce a motion banning 'the Negro' from membership. But the assembly refused to consider the question. An editor of *Bicycling World* summarized the mood of racial integration and tolerance that dominated the northern and eastern delegations:

> When a negro sends in his name and two dollars, and asks admission to the League, I claim that by that act he exhibits symptoms of patriotism and intelligence which puts the burden of proof on the pale faced dyspeptic who would keep him out. ... We want every member and every dollar and every vote that is to be had. A black *gentleman* is infinitely superior to a white *hoodlum*. Let us size up the applicant by his behavior, not by his color. ... For Heaven's sake, let's draw the line only at respectability. If the colored man wants to come in, let us take him, not only willingly, but gladly. And after we have taken in the man, his money, and his vote, let us behave ourselves well enough so that he won't be ashamed of us.[11]

In 1893, at the LAW convention in Philadelphia, members of the antiblack southern faction tried again to get their voices heard, this time more forcefully than before, and managed to gain considerable support for their proposal to introduce the word "white" into the membership rules. They did not gain the two-thirds vote necessary for their motion to pass and become LAW policy, but the issue had become an emotional one, threatening to disrupt the relationship between northern and southern delegates.

"It was quite evident at the Philadelphia convention that the Southern delegates came all primed to make a strong fight against admitting the negro to the League," wrote columnist Roland Hennessy, in the Indianapolis *Wheelmen's Gazette*, in March 1893, voicing his approval of the LAW's rejection of the southerners' racist proposal.

> I think that the action of the Assembly on the color question voices the sentiments of every fair-minded L.A.W. man. If you, or I, or some other

man, doesn't like the negro, that is no reason why he should be treated as if he had no rights or privileges. The Southerner has a natural antipathy to the colored man, and in view of the conditions of the colored man in the South, they cannot be blamed for not wishing to mix with them socially. That's for them to settle. If they don't want negroes, they have their remedy. Let their local divisions settle the difficulty. Here in the North where prejudice is not so pronounced, or at least, where it is better concealed, we can handle the matter to our own satisfaction. Thus the North and the South are enabled to settle the color question to suit themselves, while the L.A.W. as a national body does not take any responsibility in the matter.[12]

A month later, the Associated Cycling Clubs of Chicago, affiliated to the LAW, proved that the northern attitude toward the 'colored brother' was not always liberal either, when it barred black riders from participating in the famous Pullman Road Race, one of the most prestigious road races on the annual calendar. The contradiction was glaring. Hennessy, writing again in the *Wheelmen's Gazette*, reacted to the Chicago incident:

If we allow the colored man to come into our house, surely we should not turn our backs on him as soon as he enters. It does seem strange for a body of sportsmen to hold forth the hand of good fellowship one day and pull it back with great vehemence the next. ... We of the North have been very denounceatory of the South and its treatment of the colored rider, and yet on occasion have we not been just as inconsiderate and far more hypocritical? Have we not praised him with our tongues and turned our eyes away from him when he has presented himself for participation in our affairs? In other words, have we not treated him unjustly according to the rules we have wished to lay down for others?[13]

Colonel Watts, who saw himself as fighting a crusade on behalf of southern opinion, was a very determined man. The 1894 LAW convention was held again in Louisville, Watt's hometown, and he lobbied and prepared carefully for the occasion. He and his supporters had "worked like beavers during the past year," and had succeeded in introducing a 'color line' in their own local Kentucky constitution.[14]

When the delegates from all over the United States assembled at the convention in Louisville, 'Negro exclusion' was the burning issue. Watts made an energetic speech to the whole assembly, explaining his reasons for wanting to insert the word 'white' into the constitu-

USA, 1889—1895

tion, so that it read, "Any amateur (white) wheelman of good character, 18 years of age or over, shall … be eligible to membership in this league." The failure in 1893 to bar Negroes from membership, he said, had resulted in the resignation of members and also in a loss of potential southern members. The League would get 5,000 new members in the South if his motion was carried, he argued. He made no reference to his personal feelings against black people, but presented his arguments merely as a matter of expediency, namely, the necessity for the growth of the League in the South.

Then Watts took the extraordinary step of reading a letter sent to him by Frederick Scott, president of the Union Cycle Club, of Louisville, the largest black cycling club in the South, which he claimed supported him in his efforts to keep the league all white. "Dear Sir," the letter said,

> … the undersigned club, composed of twenty-five members, is fully acquainted with the amendment offered by you whereby a color line is proposed to be established in the constitution of the League of American Wheelmen. And being so acquainted are of the belief that it is offered for the good of the organization, in that its membership will be largely increased in the southern states.
>
> And as this club of twenty-five gentlemen desires to see carried out the great objects of the League, of which highway improvement is one, and believes that the adoption of that amendment will materially increase the membership in the southern states, we take this method of assuring you that you have our best wishes for ultimate success. If we can be of any service to you, command us. Fraternally, The Union Club.[15]

With Scott and other members of the club present – they had been publicly offered a case of whiskey by Watts – there was no further discussion. The consensus was that the issue had been discussed at great length already and that the battle lines were clearly drawn. The constitutional amendment to bar blacks from membership was put to a secret vote and was carried by 127 votes to 54, the Massachusetts delegation voting unanimously, as a block, against it.

The reaction to this decision was immediate and strong, with widespread debate and comment in the national and cycling press. Members threatened to resign, and some from the traditionally liberal states of Massachusetts and New York did so. The *New York Tribune* said that "wheelmen generally must look with disfavor upon the outcome of the convention of the League of American Wheelmen at Louisville. ... Fair-minded men will condemn the exclusion of colored men."[16]

In Boston, reported *Bearings*, the outraged black LAW members, many of whom belonged to the Riverside Cycling Club, held a protest meeting with "a few of their leaders in the legal fraternity and their Representative in the House, and they expressed their great indignation at the L.A.W., and endorsed the action of the Massachusetts delegation in casting a solid vote for the colored man."[17] They also wondered whether the letter of support from Scott and the Union Cycle Club of Louisville was authentic, since they could not understand why a black club would have taken such an action against itself. They suggested that Colonel Watts himself had written the letter and bribed Scott into signing it.

The Riverside Cycle Club sent a letter to the Union Cycle Club asking for an explanation of their action. "Believing you gentlemen incapable of forgetting yourselves so far as to stand in your own light," it said, "and knowing that among our white oppressors there is no limit to low, mean and inhuman acts, we are in doubt as to whether or not said actions be true. As a brother cycle club, we feel justified in seeking for an explanation."[18]

The *Bearings'* correspondent in Louisville called on Scott to question him about the whole affair, and "found him a pleasant and intelligent man and very willing to talk about the matter." Scott said that Watts came to him and explained that the failure to carry the amendment would mean the withdrawal of the southern members from the LAW and that no Negro could be admitted in the South anyway. "Mr. Scott is one of the few who do not care to force themselves where they are not wanted," explained the reporter, "and persuaded his club to the same opinion. For having the courage to express his opinions, he has been strongly condemned by negroes all over the country and is receiving many letters asking about his support of the amendment."[19]

Black cyclists in Boston were supported in their protests by Robert Teamoh, a newspaperman and the only black member of the Massachusetts House of Representatives at the time, a man described by *Bearings* as "a young colored politician with more push and nerve than brilliance, and more of the quality which sometimes places him in social gatherings where he might better be conspicuous by his absence."[20] Teamoh talked in heated terms to the *Boston Journal* and introduced a resolution of censure into the Massachusetts House in March, which hit hard at the LAW:

> Whereas the National League of American Wheelmen ... voted to exclude colored persons from membership in said organization, which exclusion affects the members of the organization resident in Massachusetts; resolved, that the General Court deprecates the action of the organization above referred to, and regards the enforcement of discrimination of this character as a revival of baseless and obsolete prejudice."[21]

The resolution was lost in committee, for there was really no legal recourse against the LAW. But the black cyclists of Boston continued during the next few years to put pressure on the LAW for the removal of the white-only ruling. Membership in the League declined drastically, by about 10,000 members during 1894 and 1895, a fact which completely undercut the twisted logic of Colonel Watts' reasoning.

The sharpest edge of comment on the Louisville convention appeared in the *Referee*, a weekly cycling trade journal with a large circulation, where a columnist called 'Phoebus' said that he did not understand at all why the press was making such "a mighty hulabaloo" about the whole affair and that he thoroughly approved of Watts' campaign:

> Personally, I am heart and soul with Mr. Watts in his manly and impersonal crusade against an evil which would sooner or later have ruined the L.A.W. in the great southland. ... Were these enthusiastic lovers of the blacks to question those who know, they would learn that the negro has little interest in anything beyond his daily needs, his personal vanity and a cake walk or barbers' hall now and then.

> The darkey is essentially a creature of today. His interest (unless it be in the advent of a circus next month) is taken up entirely with the matters just at hand. He is a lazy, happy-go-lucky animal wherever he is, but much more so on his native heath than in our northern clime. ... In the south, where he is better understood, the people who do not want him in the league or any other white man's organization put up with his indolence, his lack-brain carelessness and his thievish and other uncomfortable proclivities, and when he is hungry feed him and let him go the even tenor of his care-free ways. The negro, outside of a few lemon-hued and saddle-colored specimens with enough white blood

to make them cheeky, have no wish to belong to the L.A.W., and mighty few of them have the necessary $2 to spare. ...

I have no desire to deprecate ... the race. But it really wearies me to read labored essays from Tom, Dick, and Harry, whose only acquaintance with the black man is in the matter of "A shine, boss?" or as a waiter in a second-class restaurant, ... who feel that we ought to champion the much-abused Sambo, even though they know they themselves would not eat, sleep, marry, or tolerate as a companion the creature with the flat nose and black skin.

The League does not need him. Why should it admit one with whom not one of its members would dance at a public or private ball? ... Let us be calm and think it over. Our white brothers of the south feel safer and better and our black brothers don't care a tinker's damn. Therefore let us remember that the L.A.W. officials have done a wise act and say no more about it.[22]

The details of this struggle within one small area of society – the organized bicycling world – exemplify the world in which Taylor was growing up. Black Americans were not only limited and segregated, but discrimination was actually increasing as it was becoming codified and legalized.

What is most clearly expressed in these maneuverings and political battles within the League of American Wheelmen over this three-year period is the harsh and bitter feeling that many whites had towards blacks. "So long as blacks were slaves, so long as they posed no threat to the political and economic supremacy of whites, people were content to live with them on terms of relative intimacy. But when the slave became a citizen, when he got a ballot in his hand and pencil and paper, there were demands for laws and arrangements that would humiliate him and keep him in his place."[23]

While in some ways prospects for black people seemed to be improving – in educational opportunities, for example, and in ownership of property – "in other respects their status, North and South, actually deteriorated. Southern opinion was becoming more extreme than ever, and Northerners were becoming increasingly indifferent and even hostile towards Negroes."[24]

During the 1880s and 1890s, many of the rights won by blacks during Reconstruction were attacked and reversed by 'Jim Crow' laws. Blacks were denied the vote in many areas of the South by the introduction of educational or other requirements designed to exclude

USA, 1889—1895

them. Segregation in trains, streetcars, restaurants, in fact, in any public place where the two races were likely to meet, became more and more general across the South and increased in the North.

This new legal codification of white supremacy was an attempt by the white power structure in the South to turn back the clock and prevent blacks from challenging white control. The rising discrimination went unchecked by the failure of the Supreme Court to rule in favor of the civil rights of blacks in a series of test cases, culminating in the notorious case of *Plessy v. Ferguson* in 1896, which held that "separate but equal" facilities did not violate the 14th Amendment of the Constitution.

Where the new segregation laws did not succeed in keeping the black man in his place, white Southerners took the law increasingly into their own hands. More lynchings took place in the 1890s than in any other decade. Between 1890 and 1900, 1,217 lynchings by hanging, burning, shooting, and beating were recorded, the vast majority of them of blacks. Between January and October 1900, newspapers reported 114 lynchings, all but two of them in the South. "It is evident that the white people of the South have no further use for the Negro," wrote an Arkansas minister, E. M. Argyle to the *Christian Recorder* in 1892. "He is being treated worse now than at any other time since the surrender."[25]

This combination of factors helped to create a decade frequently described as the darkest period in race relations in U.S. history. It was within such a social context that the League of American Wheelmen's debate about black membership was being conducted and a black teenager named Marshall Taylor was working in the bicycle shops of Indianapolis and beginning to compete in races against white cyclists.

While the racist message of the 1894 LAW ruling was loud and clear, its practical interpretation was not that easy and caused disputes between the national committee and the state divisions. Massachusetts made its disapproval very clear and continued to support black cyclists. But what would happen, for instance, to those blacks who were already members of the LAW? The reply was that they would be allowed to remain in the LAW as long as they paid their annual dues regularly. Then, what about racing? Could a black rider enter a race now that he was barred from membership? Yes, ruled the Racing Board. A black rider was still eligible to enter a race held under LAW rules, even though he was not a member of the LAW.

The number of blacks affected by the LAW ruling was comparatively small, but the 'Negro exclusion' was significant as a sign of the times. It set a standard that was ambiguous in its practical interpretation, and it was up to individuals to interpret it. As Taylor's career developed and he quickly became prominent, his presence became a test of the beliefs and attitudes of the white officials and riders with whom he came into contact. Because he was the only black bicycle racer who became successful, his presence was provocative and controversial from the very beginning. It was a litmus test of racial attitudes.

Taylor may not have read carefully the newspapers and bicycling magazines that undoubtedly lay around in Hearsey's bicycle shop and Munger's house, with their accounts of lynchings in the South and the banning of blacks from membership in the LAW. But he was certainly aware that there were two classes of people in his world, black and white.

He had been pretty lucky, in general, in his experiences in the white world. It had given him many more opportunities than most young blacks could hope for. And the LAW ruling banning black membership, ironically, at this point in his young career, had the effect of stimulating the growth of black cycling clubs and black races, and it was there that Taylor decided to serve his racing apprenticeship for the next year or so.

USA, 1889—1895

4

PRECOCIOUS TEENAGER, COLORED CHAMPION OF AMERICA

MAJOR TAYLOR grew in confidence and experience throughout the summer of 1895. The victory at Matthews encouraged him and created a lot of publicity. He was more aware now of the hostility likely to be directed at him if he insisted on entering the same races as white riders. The 'colored wheelmen,' in fact, were talking actively of forming their own national cycling organization, the Afro-American Cycling Union or Afro-American Cyclists, as an alternative to the LAW, and they finally agreed on a name, the Colored Wheelmen's Association. With the encouragement of Birdie Munger, Taylor decided to explore what he could achieve within the black bicycle racing world – his own racial community.

He became a member of the See-Saw Cycling Club, a black club organized in response to the exclusively white Zig-Zag Cycling Club in Indianapolis. Like the Zig-Zag Club, the black club decided to hold a 10-mile road race on July 4. In the aftermath of the racial tension created by the Matthews race, it seemed like a safe decision and became an annual event in Indianapolis for several years. According to Taylor, "It was announced in advance of the event that the rider who won would represent the club in a big 10-mile road race in Chicago, all expenses being paid for by the club, including a trainer." Taylor won the coveted trip to Chicago, easily beating the local black opposition.

> About a thousand men and women, most of them armed with revolvers and firecrackers, stood in the broiling sun in Meridian Street and waited forty minutes for the finish. There were large and small colored riders among the thirty-three starters. One rider wore a suit of pink underwear, half a dozen or more wore bathing suits, and others were at-

tired in riding uniforms so 'loud' that they could be 'heard' long before
the wearer could be seen. When the riders left a tent in the grove to
begin the race, one might have thought, from the bright colors displayed, that a tribe of Indians were going to a pow-wow.[1]

Taylor, though, always an earnest competitor, had no time for such
fun and games. Chicago, that summer of 1895, was in the midst of a
road racing fever as the cycling craze continued unabated. On Saturday afternoons throughout the racing season, dozens of cycling clubs
staged races on the flat roads radiating like the spokes of a wheel
from the center of the city, and huge crowds turned out to watch
them.[2] It was these crowds, and the inconvenience they caused to
traffic, that eventually brought about a ban on road racing in many
areas and the transferring of bicycle racing from the public roads into
the more convenient arena of the race track.

One of these events was the 10-mile road race of the Douglass Cycling Club, at which Taylor had won the right to represent the See-
Saw Cycling Club. The Douglass was an all-black club, and the race
was open only to black riders, who came from all over the country.
It was, in fact, a black championship event, and, as such, it was an
important occasion for the sixteen-year-old Taylor, who remembered
clearly the psychological impact that his strongest opponent, Henry
Stewart, the 'St. Louis Flyer' had on him that day. His rival was older
and much more experienced, actually twenty-nine years old. "Stewart
was a man of powerful physique, having well-developed legs and
muscular arms and shoulders," Taylor wrote.

> He ridiculed me and requested the secretary of the event to give me
> the limit handicap, as he said he felt I looked as though I needed it.
> His sarcastic remarks proved to be his undoing, however, as they stirred
> me up as I had never been stirred before. Instantly, all my fighting spirit
> rushed back to me, and I jumped into my racing togs determined to
> beat Stewart at any cost.

> When the starter sent us away, Stewart promptly jumped into the front
> and started to sprint from the very outset. ... He set a heart-breaking
> pace in an effort to shake me off in the first half-mile, but finding me
> right up even with him, he decided that he had better settle down and
> let me do a share of the pace-making. However, I had an advantage
> over him as his big frame served as a fine wind-shield for me, while I
> was so small that he did not get a similar advantage while riding at my
> rear wheel.

USA, 1895—1896

At about the halfway point, a puncture put an end to Stewart's chances and Taylor romped home to set a new 10-mile road record for a black rider of 27 minutes 52 seconds.[3] The puncture meant, of course, that in spite of Taylor's record, the result was inconclusive, and the two leading black cyclists met again at the fairgrounds in Rushville, Indiana, about 30 miles southeast of Indianapolis, at a Labor Day race meet and carnival organized once again by the See-Saw Cycling Club. This time they raced over 5 miles on a track.

The 'St. Louis Flyer' made the same tactical mistake at Rushville he had made in the previous race, choosing to do too much of the hard work at the front, with a very fast sprinter tucked in behind him. Taylor was now the one who was playing a psychological game. And he was also showing his tactical superiority. He enjoyed the benefit of the protection that a large man like Stewart provided. He sat in his slipstream and then, just at the right moment, 'the black wonder' shot out from behind him and beat him with a flourish, passing him, said the *Indianapolis Sentinel*, "as though he was standing still." But the citizens of Rushville, with a majority of 300 Republicans, refused the See-Saw Cycling Club "a hall wherein it could while away the hours dancing while awaiting their train," and so there was no merriment in Rushville that evening, when the races were over.[4]

Within a week or so, Taylor had journeyed to Lexington, Kentucky, where he wound up his "very colorful racing season by winning three races at the Fair in that city under the auspices of the colored citizens."[5] It was not bad work for a lad still a couple of months away from his seventeenth birthday.

M AJOR TAYLOR became more conspicuous as he continued to race and win through 1895. Already known in Indianapolis as the young lad who had attracted the attention of crowds with his trick-riding outside the Hay and Willits bicycle store and who coached the smart white cyclists of the fashionable set in the riding school at Hearsey's, Taylor now had a growing reputation as a racing cyclist. His name had been in the newspapers on several occasions. He was known as a black rider who was so fast that he could not only beat the black champion Stewart, but was also a threat to some of the best white riders, whenever he got an opportunity to race against them.

Birdie Munger, who had decided to employ Taylor because he was intelligent and responsible and because he had experience in the bicycle business, found himself becoming more and more paternal towards him. He advised and encouraged him in his bicycle racing activities, and he built him his own superlight racing bicycle, the best that was available.

Munger trusted Taylor's judgment about racing matters enough that he made him his coaching assistant. The Indianapolis high schools and colleges featured bicycle racing in their athletic programs, and Munger lent racing bicycles to some of the young athletes. "I was assigned to instruct them on the track," wrote Taylor:

> Before I started to instruct the youths, Mr. Munger would inform them that he would permit every one of them who led me over the tape to use the racing wheels in the meet. The young athletes realized they had little or no chance of beating me, and some of them tried to bribe me to let them nose me out. After their training preparations Mr. Munger would ask me to name the athletes who were in my opinion the best riders. They got the use of the wheels.

Taylor was thus not only in a teaching and advisory capacity, but he was also able to put in some useful training against his white peers, which, he said, "helped mightily in rounding me into championship form."

Soon, however, Munger was being criticized for becoming too closely involved with the talented teenager. People in Indianapolis and in his company began to talk. Possibly the criticism even came from people like Tom Hay and Harry Hearsey, who had themselves been helpful to the young man and who felt that Munger was pushing him too hard. Munger's response to this criticism, reported by Taylor, shows what high expectations he already had of his protégé:

> One day, a member of the firm asked Mr. Munger why he bothered with that little darkey, meaning myself. He answered that I was an unusual boy and that he felt sure I had in me the makings of a champion bicycle rider. "I am going to make him the fastest bicycle rider in the world," said Mr. Munger. "He has fine habits, is quick to learn, is as game a youngster as I have ever seen, and can be relied upon to do whatever he is told. He has excellent judgment and has a remarkably cool head. Although he is only sixteen, he can beat any boy in the city right now."

Munger's ambitious claims could only increase the tensions surrounding the encouragement he was giving the black boy. The relationship

USA, 1895—1896

was considered not merely a personal matter but a public issue as well. Some felt that Munger had overstepped the imprecise demarcation between having a black servant and a black pupil or protégé. While it was acceptable to educate and make use of a reliable and trusted servant, many thought it unacceptable to encourage Taylor to go his own way, especially when that way included challenging and beating white bicycle racers, older and much more experienced than he. Munger was perceived as perpetrating social disruption, discouraging Taylor from "knowing his place in the world," giving him an appetite for independent thought and action, for creating his own future.

According to Taylor's autobiography, their close relationship and Munger's refusal to heed the quiet warnings from his colleagues were the principal reasons behind Munger's decision to relocate his business to the East Coast, taking his valet and budding young world champion with him.

"There was a dark lining to my silver cloud," wrote Taylor. "Members of the firm objected strenuously to Mr. Munger's befriending me simply because of my color, and I was inadvertently the cause of Mr. Munger's severing relations with the firm and his decision to establish a bicycle factory in Worcester, Massachusetts. At Mr. Munger's proposal I came with him and have since made my home in that city."

Taylor exaggerated the cause of Munger's severing relations with the firm. Munger's hopes and expectations for him were certainly a factor in his decision to move east, but he had other reasons for deciding to leave Indianapolis. He was an ambitious businessman, whose bicycles were much sought after. He saw brighter prospects on the horizon on the East Coast, and had received offers and invitations from there. The bicycle boom brought with it the prospect of a substantial expansion of his business, and that was what attracted Munger to the East Coast. Thus, Munger's hopes and expectations for Taylor's future career coincided with his own professional ambitions, and the decision to leave Indianapolis suited them both.

What is certain is that Munger was an extremely good judge of athletic ability and potential. He had been around bicycle racers for more than ten years, and he recognized an exceptional rider when he saw one. He was not taking Taylor to the East Coast as his houseboy or servant, with some vague hope that he might succeed as a racer. On the contrary, he was convinced that Taylor had a prodigious talent,

USA, 1895—1896

which he had nurtured and seen develop over a number of years, and he was sure that the boy would succeed.

Munger also had a very clear view of the racial climate in Indianapolis and was aware of the activities of the racist faction of the Louisville LAW division, led by Colonel Watts, not far south of Indianapolis. He had no illusions about the seriousness of the racial opposition that Taylor would continue to encounter in the future if he stayed in Indiana. Massachusetts, Munger knew, was much more liberal. He was familiar with the efforts of the Massachusetts LAW members to protest against the league's exclusionist policy, and he knew that Taylor's prospects would be brighter there.

It was certainly an interesting couple, united by affection and a love of bicycles and bicycle racing, who waved goodbye to family and friends as their train pulled out of Indianapolis in that autumn of 1895. A thirty-year-old businessman, looking for expansion and new business opportunities, accompanied by a sixteen-year-old boy leaving home for the first time. Though Taylor had not led a cloistered existence and had already lived apart from his family for several years, this was his first big separation from his roots.

In other people's eyes, Taylor was merely Munger's 'boy.' But at the same time that Munger was Taylor's boss and employer, his advisor and protector, he was also his friend, his father-figure and his athletic coach.

"Before our train pulled out of Indianapolis," wrote Taylor later, "Mr. Munger informed his friends that some day I would return to that city as champion bicycle rider of America," and Munger's prophecy was realized. Taylor did return, not just as champion of America, but as world champion, sooner perhaps than either could have dared to anticipate on that day in 1895.

WHEN MUNGER AND TAYLOR arrived in the fall of 1895, Worcester, Massechussets, was a smaller city than Indianapolis, but bustling and energetic all the same. With about 100,000 people, it was heavily populated by Irish, Swedish, and Armenian immigrants. Its black population of less than 1,000 had much deeper roots in freedom in the North than the blacks of Indianapolis, who were mostly descended from slave families.

Worcester was similar to Indianapolis in that it was a hard-working and prosperous commercial and manufacturing city. It was linked with the bigger commercial centers of New York, Boston, and Pittsburgh by excellent railroads and an extensive streetcar system connected it to Boston and to the other manufacturing towns of New England – Springfield, Fitchburg, and Waltham in Massachusetts, and Hartford and New Haven in Connecticut.

All these manufacturing towns, with their tradition of metal working in small machine shops and a skilled labor force used to working with machine tools, were an ideal ground for the growth and development of the bicycle industry. Boston, Springfield, and Waltham had been the home of high-wheel bicycle makers since the early 1880s. The technology of bicycle manufacture was a craft that had grown out of the traditional metal-working skills and was a field that offered the possibility of personal advancement, not only to managers and entrepreneurs like Munger, but also to the ordinary working man.

> Worcester has developed from a country town to a great manufacturing city in less than ninety years. Within that time the steam-engine, the railroad, telegraph and commercial use of electricity have enormously increased the productive power of labor. The improvement in the condition of the laboring classes is no less marked; contrary to the opinion once held, the introduction of labor-saving machinery has advanced instead of lowering wages; has reduced, instead of extending, the hours of labor. ... Many of our mechanics own their own homes, and are naturally deeply interested in the welfare of the city. Avenues for advancement are always open to the capable and industrious. From their ranks will come the leading businessmen of the next generation, upon whom the continuance of prosperity will depend.[6]

These were exciting times in the bicycle world. The bicycle had quite suddenly become astonishingly popular in the mid-1890s, and the makers were having to expand their production enormously to keep up with public demand. "There is fierce rivalry among the bicycle dealers," reported a news item in October 1895, "and they disagree on many points regarding machines, but on one all are harmonious, and that is that this has been the most phenomenal season the bicycle trade has ever known." Most of the manufacturers the reporter talked to said that it was difficult to come up with an exact figure for the total number of bicycles produced in the United States during 1895. "It's all guess work," said a manager for the Western Wheel Works. "A person can hit a direct estimate about as well as he could guess the democratic or republican majority at a coming election." But they

USA, 1895—1896

agreed, nevertheless, that somewhere between 200 and 250 makers would probably have sold about half a million bicycles by the end of 1895. The average price of a bicycle was about $75, with total sales worth more than $30 million.[7]

During such an expansion, technical skill and organizational experience were eagerly sought after, and Munger had both. The creation and capitalization of new companies catering to the huge public demand for new bicycles was a major financial activity on the New York Stock Exchange, and it was not a business for the slow or timid. Expert financial management had to be accompanied by efficient production in the factories and on the shop floor, and Munger's work would be on a much bigger scale than the small factory he had run in Indianapolis.

The new company was called the Worcester Cycle Manufacturing Company, and with an impressive amount of capital to work with, Munger and his partners proceeded to buy buildings and install machinery. In New York, Worcester Cycle had offices first at 55 Franklin Street and, then, by the end of 1896, at 45 Wall Street, an address that indicates just how important a sound financial base was in the bicycle business.

In Worcester, the company bought a building formerly occupied by the New England Steel Works on about seven acres, where they began making a high-quality bicycle called the 'Boyd,' after the president of the company, Charles Boyd, with whom Munger was in partnership. "The Boyd wheel," said the *Bearings* reporter who visited the new company, "bids fair to be a strong competitor of most of the old established makes, and Mr. Boyd expressed himself as having unbounded confidence in the success of the machine."[8]

In Middletown, Connecticut, 65 miles to the southeast of Worcester, they bought another factory. "These magnificent works were ... completely fitted with the most modern machinery suitable for high-grade bicycle building. It is in this factory that L. D. Munger is superintending the manufacture of the Birdie Special bicycle, and to judge from the facilities with which he is surrounded and the ample means at his command, aided of course by his well-known ability as a bicycle builder, it is not unreasonable to suppose that the Birdie Special in 1896 will be the *ne plus ultra* bicycle."[9]

USA, 1895—1896

THIS THEN WAS the background to Taylor's new life on the East Coast. In fact, it was not so much a new life as a continuation of the old one in a different location. Taylor was still Munger's 'boy,' but much more now his employee and assistant than his valet or servant. Munger had married early in 1895 and had less need of help around the house. Though Taylor may have been staying at the YMCA in Worcester or with his friend, Ben Walker there, he and Munger were still constantly together.

Taylor spent time with Munger in the factories in Worcester and in Middletown, where he worked as a machinist in the factory. Increasingly, Munger entrusted him with delivering samples or important messages between the two factories, traveling by train and streetcar. They went together to important bicycle trade shows held in Chicago and New York, where the company's products were on display and to which they transported large wooden crates containing all the specially made display models. Taylor always had money in his pocket, and he kept meticulous notes of his expenses in a tiny notebook to make a good accounting to his employer.

Taylor's knowledge and experience of the bicycle trade were extensive by then, for he had served a good apprenticeship under his three employers. He was much better qualified than most young men of sixteen or seventeen to earn his living in the bicycle world, but both he and Munger knew that his future lay in racing, not in making or selling bicycles, and Munger had no intention of relenting in his determination to make a champion out of his protégé.

Later in his life, Taylor remembered his cordial welcome in Worcester:

> I was in Worcester only a very short time before I realized that there was no such race prejudice existing among the bicycle riders there as I had experienced in Indianapolis. When I realized I would have a fair chance to compete against them in races, I took on a new lease of life. … I shall always be grateful to Worcester as I am firmly convinced that I would have dropped riding, owing to the disagreeable incidents that befell my lot while riding in and around Indianapolis, were it not for the cordial manner in which the people received me.

His reputation had preceded him to Worcester, and anyone connected with the cycling game had already heard of the 'Negro champion' of America. "It did not take me very long to get acquainted in Worcester,"

USA, 1895—1896

Taylor wrote, "especially when its riders discovered that I owned a fine, light, racing wheel on which I could ride with the best of them."

In spite of Worcester's small black population, there were enough black cyclists there that in June 1895, before Taylor arrived, a black cycling club had been organized. COLORED CYCLE CLUB COMING, announced the *Worcester Telegram* to its readers in a characteristic headline: LATEST FAD AMONG THE DUSKY DENIZENS OF WORCESTERTOWN – ONE HUNDRED TWINKLING WHEELS FORM IN BRIGHT ARRAY – MAIDS OF EBON HUE WILL LIKELY JOIN IT, TOO. [10] A meeting was held at the house of one of the members, and "it was unanimously voted that a colored bicycle club be formed at once," the article reported.

> There are nearly a hundred wheels owned by the colored residents of Worcester, and several of the riders enjoy the distinction of having crossed the line ahead of their white brethren on several occasions. There are also several excellent riders among the young colored ladies of the city. The young men who are especially interested in the formation of the club are aware of the fact that an excellent example has been set them by the Riverside Bicycle Club of Boston, which is composed entirely of colored members, and which stands second to no organization of its kind in that city.

A number of names were suggested for the new club, but in the end, the name chosen was the Albion Cycling Club. Taylor paid his $5 dues and became a member as soon as he arrived in Worcester. It was through the Albion Club that he met Benjamin Walker, who also raced but not with the same seriousness as Taylor. They soon became good friends and eventually lived together at 13 Parker Street, when Taylor was not traveling on the racing circuit.

At the end of October 1895, when the leaves had already fallen and a memorable racing season for Taylor was drawing to a close, the Albion Cycling Club held its first race, a 10-mile road race. Munger acted as referee, starter, and timer, and Taylor, Munger's "protégé and mascot," won the event from scratch from a field of 16 riders, starting last and overtaking all but two of the other competitors. The wind was cold and blustery, and his time of 29 minutes 15 seconds was not good enough to break the course record held by a white rider.

"Everybody was anxious to get a glimpse of the chap from whom his friends expected such great things," observed a reporter from the *Worcester Spy.* "Taylor is not well known here, but he has a reputation of being a very fast man and his work Saturday, in the face of the strong head-wind, demonstrated this fact." The reporter went on to give his readers some details about the winner's recent racing career, describing him as "an unassuming, modest sort of chap, who has not been in the city very long. In all, he has won 20 firsts and has got a place in every race in which he started. It is not very generally known that he is the champion colored rider of the United States, and at present time holds the colored championship at the quarter, the half, the mile, two miles and five miles."[11]

Taylor's happiness at finding himself welcomed and recognized in Worcester and able to race so easily was heightened when he discovered that he would be allowed to join the YMCA and use its gymnasium. Munger went with him to see Edward Wilder, the athletic director, and Taylor was "pleased beyond expression" to learn that there would be no racial barrier to his training there through the winter. The memory of his exclusion from the Indianapolis YMCA was still a painful one for him.

Wilder noticed that Taylor's legs, not surprisingly, were well muscled for a seventeen-year-old, but that his chest, shoulders, and arms were badly in need of development, and he outlined a program of winter training for him. "Following his instructions to the letter," Taylor recollected, "I succeeded in building the upper part of my body into excellent physical form, but not until I had put in two or three winters' work in a gymnasium. I used light dumb-bells, Indian clubs and a Whitely exerciser in my room regularly, even while traveling, and became adept at deep breathing, through long and patient practice."

But it was not all discipline and hard work for the young man. A New Year's Eve dinner was organized by the Middletown factory of the Worcester Cycle Company where "a large number of the gentlemen were in evening dress, and the costumes of some of the ladies were very handsome ... and the festivities continued until about 3 o'clock, when Wells Brothers' orchestra concluded the program with the waltz 'When We Meet Again.'" Taylor delighted and amazed the guests with a display of trick riding on the Munger wheel. A reporter described some of the difficult feats he performed, riding "up a plank eighteen inches wide to the height of six feet, across a platform and down a flight of stairs consisting of fourteen steps, which, considering the amount of room at his disposal for the start and finish, was a most extraordinary undertaking. Taylor is, without a doubt, unequaled in this section of the country, as a trick rider."[12]

THE RETURN OF SPRING meant only one thing to Taylor, the opportunity to get out on the road once again and really get down to training. The 1896 season would be an important one, and he planned to enter as many races as possible. With the more liberal racial attitude of the organizers of races in Massachusetts, Connecticut, New York, and New Jersey, he would be able to measure himself against the best of the amateur bicycle racers in the country. The cycling craze was continuing unabated, in Worcester just as in Indianapolis and Chicago. "The Wheelmen live in race fever," said the *Worcester Telegram* in June of that year.[13] There had never before been so many opportunities to break into bicycle racing.

The first big event of the season was the Telegram Trophy Race, sponsored by the *Worcester Telegram*, the winner of which would be presented with an enormous gold and silver cup, elaborately decorated with figures of racing cyclists on their bicycles. The race was held on Saturday, May 9, and a vast crowd of people, 50,000 strong, said the paper, "the biggest crowd ever got together by day light in Worcester," came out to see the 30 contestants, lining the course from start to finish, climbing the trees to get a better view, bringing the normal business of the town to a standstill.[14]

It was quite a spectacle. Two cyclists who arrived breathlessly from New York told a reporter that it was rare to see so many people together in one place, even in New York. For two or three hours before the race, "the fields in the vicinity of the start were covered with thousands of happy, interested and good-natured people, and from a little distance it looked as though a great army had bivouacked there for a rest and was being visited in camp by several thousand pretty girls."

The occasion was given additional spice by the presence of many Bloomer girls, who were the object of much discussion in the press. "The lady bicycle riders were up to a thing or two in the racing line," wrote the *Telegram* reporter, "and it is suspected that many of them have the genuine sporting element in their blood. ... There was one little girl there in bloomers, and her stockings fitted her like the skin of a sausage. Before the race she started out to ride the course, and her progress was marked by a chorus of male 'ahs' and one of female 'ohs' for the entire distance of 10 miles. And that little girl rode fast when she need not have hurried a bit."[15]

The race itself, when it finally got under way in the crush of people, was a hectic tussle through dusty city streets. James Casey, of the Vernon Bicycle Club of Worcester, was the winner, with Taylor, who led the Albion Club contingent, in sixth place. When it was over, the children, who all along the course had "climbed the trees thicker than birds, dropped down from their perches and came back to town in droves."

The most remarkable thing about the race was something that the *Worcester Telegram* reporters, in their long and colorful coverage of the event, did not even bother to remark upon, because to them it was not unusual. The Albion Club's black members competed on equal terms with the white cyclists, and the Albions participated in official duties too, the starting and timing of the riders and the marshalling of the course. It was an integrated competition, and there is not a single mention of any protest or hostility over the presence there of Taylor or his teammates, Bert Williams and Bert Hazard. That was the difference between Worcester and Indianapolis.

The following weekend, the Albion Cycling Club had its second 10-mile road race, and Taylor came in first, winning the same cup as the year before, but this time it became his to keep. Then he went on to New Jersey, where he finished sixth in the famous Irvington—Millburn 25-mile road race, "the classic Derby of the East," held on the outskirts of Newark on a course "which is noted for its terrific hills, which dishearten the brave and most nervy of the road racing contingent."[16]

In this race, Taylor had a "beautiful duel" with Monte Scott, who he called "the best road race rider in the country," until about half a mile from the finishing line. Here a bucket of ice cold water was thrown in his face, and "before I recovered from the shock Scott had crossed the line a winner." Taylor made light of the incident, maintaining that it was an accident, that "many of the riders arranged for such a stunt, and some trainer evidently miscalculated when he showered the ice water on me." But in view of later opposition to his participating in races, it seems highly likely that it was an intentional 'accident' calculated to prevent him from winning.

At Lyndhurst, New Jersey, Taylor was once again the fastest rider over a ten mile course. He won prizes at track meets in Meriden and New Haven, Connecticut, where he received "a wonderful ovation

USA, 1895—1896

and a gold watch which I promptly presented to my friend Mr. Munger in appreciation for some of the many kindnesses he had extended to me." And he went to Jamaica, Long Island, where he won his first 25-mile road race from a field of 60 starters.

For Munger, who, as one newspaper put it, "has unlimited faith in his colored prodigy," Taylor's continued successes were a constant reminder of his promise. So intimately were their lives now linked that the young champion clearly had no problems with money or with equipment. Although he was still officially an amateur, the resources of the Worcester Cycle Manufacturing Company were solidly behind him. He was, in fact, already a thinly disguised professional. He kept the prizes he was winning – watches, dinner sets, and cups – or gave them to Munger, or sent them home to his mother in Indianapolis.

Taylor, even though he had not yet celebrated his eighteenth birthday, was the acknowledged champion of the black riders on the East Coast.

IN AUGUST 1896, Taylor and Munger returned temporarily to Indianapolis because they had received news of some interesting developments there and Munger had some business affairs to look after. There had been a lot of talk during the previous year about building a new bicycle racing track in the city, to attract the big-name bicycle racers. With the collapse of the all-white Zig-Zag Cycling Club, which had proved a little too rowdy for its own good, there was an organizational gap in cycling circles. Throughout 1895 and 1896, a movement had been under way to establish a new club, with the specific purpose of undertaking the building of a new track. The *Indianapolis Sentinel*'s cycling columnist complained that,

> Indianapolis has 10,000 wheelmen among all classes, but it is a hard matter to interest them in securing good roads, let alone giving a dollar or two a month for the support of a club.
>
> Indianapolis ought to have a cycling club of which the city could be proud.[17]

The same reporter was overjoyed when the plan to build a track was finally announced. "Indianapolis is now an important manufacturing center of wheels," he wrote, "and with a one-third-mile track built, there is no reason why the eyes of the wheelmen of the country should not be turned in this direction."[18]

USA, 1895—1896

George Catterson, who had promoted the road race to Matthews, became the president of the new club, which was to be called the Capital City Cycling Club. With his experience of dealing in real estate, he soon had the negotiations for the track under way. In mid-July 1896 it was begun, and by mid-August it was ready for its grand opening. Several leading professional riders were engaged, and afternoon and evening races were planned for August 18. Walter Sanger, a burly 200-pound sprinter from Milwaukee, who had just become a professional, was there, and so was Ray MacDonald, just returned from a European tour. The first meet was a great success and Sanger established a track record of 2 minutes $19^2/5$ seconds for the mile.

For Catterson and the new club, what better way to publicize and promote the new track than to engage Major Taylor, the most outstanding local rider, just back from the East. Catterson had been friendly towards Taylor in the past and again gave him a chance to show off his abilities. Catterson and Munger understood the risk as well as the appeal and attraction of lining up Taylor against Sanger and Mac-Donald, but the temptation to pitch him into this top-flight competition on his own home ground was irresistible. Munger especially was anxious to measure Taylor against some of the top professionals, and he saw the opportunity here. As an amateur, Taylor could not race against professionals in open competition, even if they were prepared to compete with a black rider, but he could be sent against their time records, and that was what they encouraged him to do.

Taylor did not just chip a fraction off Sanger's three-week-old mile record; he assassinated it, taking $8^1/5$ seconds from the white rider's time. He was paced by some of his friends on tandems, who, Taylor wrote, "were spurred on in their efforts by the thought that they were fighting for a principle, as well as for my personal success." The newspaperman, in one of the colorful vignettes that give almost as much life to the print journalism of the period as a photograph, said that Taylor,

> ... all the way around the track, was yelling to his pacemakers to "Go on! Put on more steam!" The boys on the big machines were doing their best. But right behind them, with scarcely six inches separating wheels, came Taylor, bending low over the handlebars, and riding for dear life. On the last lap he swung clear of the pacemakers and made a sprint for the tape, going the last lap in much faster time than any of the other four. He crossed the tape like he had been shot out of a gun, and when

USA, 1895—1896

it was announced that the colored boy had beaten Sanger's time by $8^1/5$ seconds, the crowd gave an enthusiastic cheer.[19]

It was a new track record!

After a short rest, Taylor came out again and took his place on the starting line, breathing deeply, ready to spring into action. This time, he took two-fifths of a second from MacDonald's $^1/5$-mile unpaced world record, set that spring in Paris. Taylor's record was unofficial and could not be submitted for recognition, but Munger and several other experienced timekeepers had held their watches on him, and there could be no doubt about the accuracy of the time. Taylor was showing phenomenal promise for a seventeen-year-old. This was his first world record, even though unofficial.

Munger and Taylor's friends were thrilled at the improvement they saw in his riding since he had been east. But the reaction to Taylor's presence on the Capital City track and to his being paced by white riders was not all friendly. He and his friends, wrote Taylor, "incurred the enmity of a group of narrow-minded people. As I passed through them to my dressing room, I heard several threatening remarks aimed at me. They were not only angry at me for having broken two records, but also at the track manager for having allowed me to race on the track, even though I had no white men opposing me." The threats against him were a reminder that Indianapolis was not the same kind of place as Worcester.

In challenging and beating Sanger and MacDonald, Taylor offended white sensibilities. He had stepped out of his appropriate place in society. And those white people like Birdie Munger, George Catterson, and the white pacemakers, people with 'dangerous ideas,' were also the object of criticism. 'Negroes' were supposed to be shown where their place was, not encouraged to have mistaken notions about their own importance. Even though he had beaten only the times of the white riders, not raced with them, Taylor's rides were seen as a provocation, an attempt to stir up trouble. He was banned thereafter from that particular track in Indianapolis.

Taylor, with his advisor Munger, was relieved to be on the train once again, heading back to Worcester, after this bitter reminder of the fierce, racist opposition he would certainly continue to encounter if he tried to pursue his racing career in Indianapolis.

5
RISING STAR

THE BREAKING of Walter Sanger's and Ray MacDonald's records in Indianapolis was a turning point in Major Taylor's career. If he could beat two of the top professionals, Sanger, with five years' experience in top-class racing, and MacDonald, just returned from success in Europe, Munger felt Taylor was now ready for professional bicycle racing.

Back on the East Coast, having turned eighteen in November, Taylor paid the fee to the League of American Wheelmen to register as a professional. Apparently there were no problems with the Racing Board in New York. Though he could not become a member of the League, the Racing Board had no objection to registering him as a professional rider. All professionals were obliged to be registered. It was a good thing for the health of the sport, they reasoned in New York, to have a talented new rider in the professional ranks. New York was not in sympathy with the racist legislation voted into the LAW constitution in Louisville in 1894. Certainly Munger's friends among the officials in New York were extremely useful in giving Taylor the opportunity to register.

Munger encouraged Taylor to turn professional because they were both aware of the money he could earn and the championships he could win. Cash prizes were good, with $200 for a win common, and it was possible to earn several hundred dollars in a successful day's work. In many respects it was a straightforward business proposition. Taylor was certainly well qualified, he had served an excellent apprenticeship, and his list of wins over the past year and a half was impressive.

A young black man's horizons were extremely limited in 1896. What other avenue could offer Taylor as many possibilities? He had already tasted something of the drudgery of the retail bicycle business and the toil of the shop floor as a machinist. The lure of big money and bright lights was strong; the bicycle racer was a hero, the man of the hour.

USA, 1896—1897

In an article entitled CYCLE RACING AS AN OCCUPATION: SOME POINTS FOR WOULD-BE ZIMMERMANS, the successful cycle racer's lot was viewed as an ideal one. "He is a hero in the eyes of the people. He is admired and courted and flattered wherever he goes. He is lauded and talked about wherever wheelmen congregate. He is one of the idols of society." But, the writer warned, young riders should not make the mistake of letting themselves "be dazzled and dream fantastic dreams of a life they really know nothing of." He reminded the "would-be Zimmermans" that to succeed they had to be outstandingly good:

> If the young racing man is really possessed of phenomenal speed and has in him the making of a great racer, he will be speedily snatched up by some one of the managers who are constantly on the lookout for good men. Phenomenons, however, are not the rule, but the exception. For every phenomenal rider who plunges headlong into the business and makes a swift and brilliant success there are ten mediocre aspirants who are permanently sidetracked in the ranks of the also-rans.[1]

That was the danger, of course: there was only room at the top for a few, the very best riders.

Munger could have advised Taylor to break himself gently into his career as a professional, to pick and choose his first professional races carefully. But instead he pushed him into the thick of things, entering him for his first engagement in one of the toughest, most controversial of all bicycle races, the spectacular six-day race at Madison Square Garden in New York held in December. Munger sent him with Robert Ellingham, who was working for the Worcester Cycle Manufacturing Company in Middletown, to Brooklyn, where Taylor became a member of the South Brooklyn Wheelmen and began his training for the long, hard race on the roads that ran out of Brooklyn onto Long Island. He needed to build up as much stamina as possible for the six-day race, and he put in some long days' work on the roads in cold winter weather to prepare himself for the ordeal ahead.

It was a risky choice for a debut from an athletic point of view, but Munger knew that whatever happened to Taylor at Madison Square Garden, the publicity would be intense. It would be a baptism of fire, that was certain. But it was unlikely that the liberal New York crowd would be unfriendly towards the black competitor.

The six-day race was one of the most agonizing endurance tests yet devised by bicycle racing promoters. Begun in Britain in the days of the high-wheeled bicycle and growing out of the late-Victorian passion for feats of endurance, it gave cyclists the chance to test the extreme limits of their physical powers. It also gave spectators the chance to witness their sufferings, like a horde of noisy voyeurs.

The six-day race was that, quite literally. The cyclists rode as continuously as possible for six days and six nights, individually, not in pairs or teams, covering as many miles as they could on the dangerous, steeply-banked indoor track. The winner was the rider who covered the greatest distance. Taylor had never before raced more than 75 miles, and he had never raced on a small indoor track. It was a sudden plunge into the most commercial, show business-like, aspect of bicycle racing: professional sport at its most intense and competitive, at its most wild and romantic – and at its most insane. If Taylor could last there, Munger reasoned, he could last anywhere.

With the six-day race scheduled to begin at just past midnight on Sunday night, a curtain-raiser in the form of a series of short races, was held on the Saturday night before, to get things warmed up. Madison Square Garden was packed with 5,000 people. Electric lights suspended from the ceiling illuminated the bright yellow pine track brilliantly. The best seats in the house were clustered around the edges of the track so the privileged could get a close-up view of the action. The cheaper seats were lost up in the darkness of the roof, and the whole place was filled with noise and cigarette smoke. "Enthusiasm ran rife, and the people cheered and howled frantically at every opportunity, even including the spills." And there were plenty of crashes. The riders could not get used to the uneven banking of the newly erected track and "tumbled about like tenpins in every heat, and the falls became so numerous that keeping count of them was out of the question."[2] A couple of the riders went right off the edge of the unfenced banking of the track right into the crowd, but no one, fortunately, was seriously injured.

Charles Murphy, later to gain fame as 'Mile-a-Minute' Murphy for his daredevil ride behind a train, created a sensation when he first appeared on the track dressed in a racing suit patterned on the American flag. "It was excessively patriotic. The shirt was made of the blue field and stars of the national colors, and the trunks were made of stripes. A big gold eagle ornamented the front of the shirt."[3]

USA, 1896—1897

As the races got under way, the pace was fast and furious. Taylor did not take very long to make an impact. "The jewel of the evening's entertainment," wrote the reporter from the *Referee*, "flashed in the bicycle world in the form of a veritable black diamond, the ebony mascot of the South Brooklyn Wheelmen, 'Major' Taylor, who chose the half-mile handicap for his professional debut." In the first heat, "this black meteor jumped at once from the thirty-five yard mark" and easily beat the field. He was "at once enthroned as a popular idol, the band playing 'Way Down South in Dixie' as a coronation anthem."

In the final of the half-mile handicap, Taylor beat Eddie Bald, the reigning American sprint champion, an outstandingly strong rider who had been the topmost professional sprinter for several years. Starting with a substantial handicap advantage, Taylor managed to stay away from Bald to win the race, and the spectators went wild

> The crowd howled itself hoarse over the victory of the colored man. But his victory in the heat was nothing compared to the final, which was the last event on the card for the evening. After his great performance in the heat the crowd was expecting big things from the dusky wheelman, and it was not disappointed.
>
> With the crack of the pistol, the rider jumped forward. Round and round the track whirled the colored rider, pedaling away like a steam engine. ... In the meantime Eddie Bald, who started from scratch, was straining every nerve to catch the runaway African. ... But to every one it looked as if the darkey held his own. It is a ten-lap track and with five laps to the half- mile the Major sat up after going four laps, thinking the race was over. He rode half way round again before he discovered his mistake, and in the meantime Bald was coming up rapidly. The crowd was shrieking to Taylor to go on and the latter suddenly realized that he had another lap to go. He ducked his head and away he went again, and beat Bald over the line by twenty yards. The South Brooklyn contingent went wild over their 'dark secret,' as they called him, and he was easily the hero of the evening.[5]

It was an astonishing display of virtuosity for this tyro to beat one of the best known, most highly paid riders of the moment. Taylor won $100 for this race, his first cash prize.

When the six-day race began the next day, attendance was good again. "One of those throngs marvelously mixed of every stratum from almost the dead hard slums to absolutely the exclusive upper crust that only a great sporting event can gather in Madison Square Garden" was on hand at the start, shouting and screaming and filling the air with thick smoke from hundreds of cigarettes and cigars.[6] They listened impatiently to a concert of sacred music as Sunday evening drew to a close, for there was still a strict Sabbath observance and the race could only begin on Monday. At a couple of minutes past midnight, at the crack of the pistol, the twenty-eight riders were off on their long ordeal. There were several British riders, specialists in this kind of long-distance event, but most of the riders were little-known Americans.

The six-day race was a world of its own, a mad, dramatic, colorful, demanding, and sometimes brutal arena with its own inner logic and rhythms. The riders circled the tiny track hour after hour, "like squirrels in a cage," stopping only when they absolutely had to sleep or eat. The task of the early hours was to pile on as many miles as possible, and the Irishman Teddy Hale quickly went into the lead, although Taylor was close behind him in second place after six hours. Ned Reading, from Omaha, Nebraska, covered 260 miles in 14 hours without once getting off his bicycle.

Nobody thought Taylor would last very long in the race, and when he first appeared on the track, the crowd "laughed at him and chaffed him." But he quickly won them over with his fast riding and his many aggressive sprints, and when they discovered that there was nobody in the race who could sprint like him, he became the favorite. "The star of the race thus far is Major Taylor," reported the *Worcester Telegram* on Thursday, after three days of riding, "and truly the little Negro is a marvel. He is as black as coal and has a fine, intelligent, laughing face. No one rides more gracefully or with less waste of energy than he. He is careful about fouling and he doesn't take any unnecessary chances. He has done more sprinting than all the others put together. He works on a system, eight hours of riding and one hour of sleep. He has followed it. The sprinting he has done ought to have killed him long ago." By the end of the third day of continuous riding, Taylor had covered more than 900 miles and was lying in ninth position, with Teddy Hale, the leader, a much older, more experienced man, about 100 miles ahead of him.

With his schedule of one hour of sleep for every eight hours of riding, Taylor was sleeping more than most of the other riders, but he made up for the lost time when he returned to the track. The crowd warmed to his efforts. "He really cannot help riding fast," said one reporter. "He likes the applause that he gets, and when people don't applaud him he whistles to keep himself company. He really thinks that he will finish. His popularity grows every minute." The crowd urged the riders on when they seemed to be flagging. "Men and women rose to their feet, clapped their hands and waved their handkerchiefs, while the Major showed that after covering 950 miles he could still fly like a sprinter."[8]

The crowd cheered and the band played 'Wearing of the Green' for Teddy Hale, "who's wearing about as much green as can be stretched over his lanky frame. But the tune changes to 'Dixie' in a jiffy as Major Taylor, the burned-to-a-crisp tamale from South Brooklyn, challenges the foreigner and picks him up for a sprint. And 'Dixie' it is for some time, for the black whirlwind sweeps past like a swallow on the wing."[9]

As the New York and Worcester newspapers spread the news that Taylor was still in the race and riding strongly, he was cheered by the arrival of several telegrams, one of which came from his cycling friends in Indianapolis.

As the race wore on, hunger and fatigue were the two constant demands, and at one point "two fried chickens and four and a half pounds of meat" failed to satisfy Taylor's appetite. The trainers were preoccupied looking after their men, massaging and rubbing them down, preparing food, and maintaining the bicycles. To one side of the track was an enclosure,

> ... that exhales appetizing odors which must tantalize the weary men as they flit by. Oil stoves and tin pans, jars of milk and cocoa, pots of beef tea, and a miscellaneous collection of provisions are all scattered within the place. Trainers and helpers in blue sweaters and nondescript caps cook meals for the riders with the utmost nicety and then carefully taste the products of their cookery themselves to be sure that it is not too heavy for the stomach of the racer.
>
> Eating under such conditions is rather singular. The men don't stop for a moment to obtain the necessary sustenance. A trainer stands by the track and signals to his man that he is ready to hand him his food. The rider slackens speed just a trifle, steers towards his trainer, puts out his left hand and grasps the pot held out to him. Still pushing on, the bicyclist feeds himself, and on the way round throws the pot back into the cooking space.

USA, 1896—1897

Celery tips, beef tea, broth, porridge, milk, cocoa and fruit are the things allowed the contestants while they are on the go. When the infrequent resting periods come around, they eat a tender steak or tiny chop.[10]

Taylor was supported in the race by Ellingham, his trainer, and Munger came to the track to advise and supervise. The trainer was crucial, both physically and psychologically. He was a combination of adviser, friend, masseur, cook, and doctor. He had to be firm yet sympathetic, to try to understand the ordeal his rider was going through, to encourage him, reassure him and baby him, but to insist that he get back on his bicycle and continue riding.

As the miles mounted up and the lack of sleep and exhaustion became more pronounced, the stress increased. Some of the trainers were so tired they fell asleep on their feet at the side of the track. As nerves became frayed, so tempers were liable to rise. The struggle, as the race continued, was to keep the riders going by any means possible. "There is a good deal of activity among the tents now," a reporter scribbled in his notebook.

Men are going to and from them all the time. The air reeks with the pungent odors of embrocations. You can hear the slapping of hands on solid flesh. The floors are piled high with food, bandages, linament and padding, all in great confusion.

The riders are becoming peevish and fretful. The wear and tear upon their nerves and their muscles, and the loss of sleep make them so. If their desires are not met with on the moment, they break forth with a stream of abuse. Nothing pleases them. These outbreaks do not trouble the trainers with experience, for they understand the condition the men are in.[11]

As the race continued relentlessly into the final two days, and the weaker riders dropped out, the prolonged exertion and fatigue, and especially the lack of sleep, produced delusions and hallucinations in the now pathetic riders. This was the part of the race that most attracted the voyeuristic instincts of the crowd, and the place was sold out. The price of admission was doubled to one dollar, but still the people lined up at the door day and night. Ironically, as the suffering increased, the race itself grew more monotonous, because the riders were now incapable of exertion and circled around the track in a state of semiconsciousness.

USA, 1896—1897

Taylor had a crying fit in his tent early one evening and was determined to quit until his trainers managed to get him out onto the track again. But then he became irrational. "You fellows want me to stay here until my leg drops off so you can sell it to the doctor," one reporter heard Taylor shout to his trainer. Then he suddenly stopped, "got off his wheel, leaned it against the fence, walked across the track, sat down on a low rail and went fast asleep. About a thousand people yelled to Taylor to wake up. He didn't hear. His trainers made a rush for him. It took ten minutes to arouse him. Then he rode like a streak."[12]

On another occasion, said the *Bearings* reporter, Taylor dismounted from his bicycle. When urged to go on, he said, "I cannot go on with safety, for there is a man chasing me around the ring with a knife in his hand. ... Taylor created much amusement seated there, astride a box, eating a large beefsteak and drinking from one of the funnel-shaped cans the men were fed with on their wheels, his face thin and emaciated, and his naturally large lips, larger still with the condition of his face."[13]

By Saturday night, with Teddy Hale firmly in the lead, the race was drawing to a close, and the condition of the remaining fifteen bicycle racers had become truly pitiable. They limped around the track now, spending more time off their bicycles than on them, succeeding nevertheless in adding miles to their totals. The spectacle, the sensation, was of course exactly what the huge crowd was waiting for, and on the final evening "more than 12,000 persons screamed and howled with the maddest enthusiasm as the end neared. It was a race until the very last hour. The end saw twelve human wrecks. Never did men finish a long-distance race so terribly exhausted. Some of them were raving lunatics."[14] The people who lapped up such a spectacle were the rowdy, low-life elements who went to boxing matches and cock fights. They were a crowd full of violent emotions, who came to satisfy their coarse appetites.

Hale left the track at 9 o'clock, certain that Rice, the second-place rider, could not overtake him, but the crowd shrieked for him to do another 10 miles, and he went back on the track once again, with two little flags, one British, one American, clenched between his teeth. "He looked like a ghost. His face was like the white face of a corpse and he stared in front of himself, his eyes terribly fixed. ... His mind was no longer there on the track, he had lost all signs of life and self-possession."[15]

As the gun for the end of the race was fired at 10 P.M. on Saturday night, no one was on the track; all of the riders had resigned themselves to their positions in the mileage totals. Hale, the winner, had covered 1,910 miles, beating the previous six-day record by 310 miles, and Taylor was eighth with 1,732 miles. He had also broken the old record. When it was all over, Hale was showered with bouquets and flowers and bottles of champagne, the people giving a rousing shout for Taylor, "whose game riding won for him many friends among people ordinarily opposed to the colored race."[16]

Hale won $5,000 for the week's arduous work and then went on to make another $1,000 from a theatrical engagement, which capitalized on all the publicity. Taylor won several hundred dollars, and a newfound fame and prominence. One sensationalized report appeared in a New York newspaper claiming that Taylor had dropped dead at the end of the six-day race. Utterly exhausted, he was taken back to Brooklyn by his trainers for a sound sleep. But it did not take long for his young body to recover, and he was soon up and about, apparently none the worse for his grueling experience. And he attended the awards ceremony at the Hotel Bartholdi in New York the following Monday.

Some people thought it was demeaning for Taylor to begin his professional career in such a race and that the effect would be to destroy his sprinting abilities. There was also severe criticism from newspapers, some journalists calling it such a disgraceful display that it should be banned by the police. They argued that it was not a sport when a dozen pathetic, half-crazed cyclists were reduced to human wrecks as they crawled around an indoor bicycle track. The French cycling newspaper *Le Vélo* called it "a cruel sport" and regretted "the lamentable scenes of horror which marked the final hours of this indescribable spectacle."[17] Another French writer thought that the race was "one of the worst tortures that one could possibly ask a human being to undergo."[18]

For someone his age and with his limited experience, it was incredible that Taylor had finished the race at all. It showed once more his extraordinary inner strength and determination. He received an invitation to ride in another six-day race in Chicago and was besieged with offers from promoters willing to back him in short-distance races.

USA, 1896—1897

His sprinting abilities had now been witnessed by an experienced crowd of managers and riders. He had certainly arrived on the professional scene.

But he would never again ride an event of that length. Speed, not endurance, would be his strength as a rider. The victory over Eddie Bald in the prologue races was really much more significant for his future career than his finishing the six-day race. Bald himself was impressed with Taylor's victory, although he was not too pleased with its repercussions. He had, he told a reporter, been "pestered to death by allusions to it" from everyone he met and in letters he had received. Taylor had earned a reputation with that win in the half-mile handicap that would last for some time.

TAYLOR AND MUNGER returned to their usual routine in Middletown and Worcester. But now there was a difference. Taylor's defeat of champion Eddie Bald and his strong showing in the six-day race had made him a celebrity. As an eighteen-year-old rider with such a stunning success for his professional debut, he was certainly someone special in Worcester.

When the *Worcester Telegram* reporter went looking for Taylor, who he called "the plucky little colored champion cyclist," he found him "the central figure in a group of local wheelmen," all anxious to hear firsthand every detail about the big six-day race in New York, and how Taylor had felt about having to keep riding for 142 hours. "The greatest difficulty that the plucky little rider met with during the race," he said, "was that of keeping his eyes open. His physical condition was good, but the lack of sleep troubled him so much that several times during the last nights he was obliged to leave the ring for a nap."[19] The Worcester cyclists showed their appreciation by holding "a testimonial as an acknowledgment of his excellent work in the big six-day race," to which all the cycling clubs of the city were invited.

That winter of 1897 Taylor continued his duties for Munger. The money he had earned in New York gave him a little freedom, and even after he sent $55 to his family in Indianapolis, he still had several hundred dollars to spend on himself.

Meanwhile, under Munger's guidance and supervision, Taylor continued to train at the Worcester YMCA. Munger had no doubts about Taylor's speed and agility or his motivation as a competitor. The six-day race had proven that he had the guts and determination to succeed. Munger's gamble had paid off. The impression Taylor had made on the New York promoters and the media, as well as the crowds of spectators, had made him a recognizable name and a presence in the world of bicycle racing. What Taylor needed now was more strength, more muscle and weight, to realize his potential as a champion.

The 1897 bicycle racing season in the United States was, according to reports in the press, the most successful and hotly contested in its 15-year history. It was also the year Taylor became the first black cyclist to enter bicycle racing as a full-time professional. As a result of the bicycle boom of 1895 and 1896, more and more people were riding bicycles, and the growing public enthusiasm for the sport meant more races, better box office takings, and bigger prizes. Promoters were more inclined now to take the financial risk of putting on races, and manufacturers were willing to invest more of their money to sponsor racing teams. The sport was in a very healthy state, and the quality of the riders and their performances were improving all the time.

"Cycle racing occupies as prominent a place in the estimation of the ever-vacillating public as any sport recorded on the calendar," said *Spaldings Official Bicycle Guide for 1898*. "The season of 1897 will be long remembered as the greatest racing season ever known in the memory of the oldest critic. ... Racing as an art has been practiced more regularly this year than ever before." [20]

EARLY IN THE SEASON, Taylor joined other Boston-area professionals in training sessions at the Charles River track in Cambridge, across the bay from Boston. Prominent among them were the famous Butler brothers, Nat and Frank, and Eddie McDuffie, who were all white, of course, so that he was highly conspicuous in their midst. But all the riders knew about his victory over Bald at Madison Square Garden, and they knew he was Munger's protégé. Most of the Boston riders welcomed him to the track. In one newspaper picture, Taylor is sitting crossed-legged on the ground, smiling happily amid a group of a dozen white riders.

Out of these training sessions Taylor earned a place in the five- man Boston pursuit team which was preparing to compete in a 5-mile race against a team from Philadelphia, another hot bicycle racing city. Taylor was selected after rigorous trials against the clock on the Charles River track.

"Each team is composed of five of the best men that can be pick-ed from the city they represent," said the *Boston Daily Globe.* "In both teams are men who have established a national reputation in the racing world. ... To be a member of an intercity team is an honor in itself as the riders have to pass through a most trying ordeal. Day after day the men who desire to go on the team go out on the track and grind off the miles at a killing pace. ... Their time is kept and the men who make the best average are selected for the team."[21]

Taylor thus earned his place on the team on the basis of his speed, and the other riders on the Boston team, Nat and Frank Butler, Burns Pierce, and Eddie McDuffie, accepted him and agreed to work with him. They were all established stars and liberal in their thinking. If Taylor was among the five fastest men to be found, they had no reason to object. He had proven himself at the trials; that was good enough for them. This Boston pursuit team, though a short-lived one, was a pioneering integrated sports team, certainly one of the very earliest in organized professional sports.

The team pursuit race, run at the Charles River track under new electric lighting on July 21, was the finale to a regular evening's racing. It attracted an enthusiastic crowd, many of whom had never before seen a bicycle race. The two teams started on opposite sides of the track, and each aimed to overtake the other. Each lead rider put in a short burst of maximum effort before swinging out to let the next man take his place. Taylor pulled the team very fast for much of the first mile before he dropped back, exhausted.

Gradually the Bostonians caught up with the Philadelphia team and then overtook them, with MacDuffie speeding along in the lead. The excitement mounted and "not a person, either in the grandstand or the bleachers, was seated at the finish of the match, when the Bos-ton flyers passed the men from the city of Brotherly Love at the finish of $4^1/3$ miles. ... The spectators went fairly wild with delight; hats went up in the air, and the crowd rushed on to the track and cheered again and again for the plucky men who had won the race."[22]

A photograph of Taylor published in *Bearings* at the time of the in-tercity match, posing with his Boston teammates, reveals both his physical condition and his mental alertness. It shows the eighteen-year-old as a slight but sinewy athlete, what weight he did have, ap-parent in his thighs. The later, much admired thinness and shapeli-ness of his calves and ankles are much in evidence, but his chest and shoulders lack the heavy muscular development he would have built up five years later.

The harmony of Taylor's athletic build is very much in evidence. His ability as a sprinter was based not on weight and muscular strength, but on agility, suppleness, and a high level of overall fitness. In the photograph he holds himself erect and with pride, without a trace of posturing in his stance or in his face. He had every reason to feel humbled or even overwhelmed by this experience of being suddenly in the company of world-class bicycle racers as their athletic equal. Yet, the photograph shows a remarkably self-possessed young man.

THE ROUTINE competition of professional riders was on the national circuit, where national championships were contested throughout the racing season in a series of events selected by the Racing Board of the League of American Wheelmen. It was on the circuit that professional reputations were made, and that was where Taylor would measure himself against the best men in the business – Eddie Bald, the 1896 champion, Tom Cooper, Arthur Gardiner, Earl Kiser, Frank and Nat Butler, Owen Kimble, Orlando Stevens, Fred Titus, and others.

"The national circuit derives its chief prestige, interest, and claim upon public attention from the fact that it is national in the fullest sense of the word," said the *Referee*.

> It is the arena in which the pick and flower of American speedsters daily measure their relative standing in the racing world. It is the great cycle-racing university, to enter which is the fondest ambition of every young racer. Every novice looks forward with keen anticipation to a day when he will regularly follow the circuit, knowing that it enlists the services of the cream of our racing talent and that to win its laurels is to attain the supreme pinnacle of racing fame. Without it, cycle racing would be sporadic and local in character and national fame would be well night impossible in racing circles. The national circuit is the supreme court of racedom."[23]

TAYLOR THUS BEGAN the traveling and racing that would be his entire life for the next eight years. At Manhattan Beach, near New York City, on June 26, he won the quarter-mile race "in a blanket finish. There were only five men in the heat, and at the tape not half a length separated the foremost man from the rear one. Taylor's victory over Sims was one of inches, but the judges agreed in picking the colored rider, who was cheered to the echo by the crowd in the grandstand."[24] Later in July, Taylor "proved a great favorite" at the races at Providence, Rhode Island, where he won a first and a second, both important victories. A reporter commented that "this would seem to put aside all talk to the effect that his finishing in the six-day race at the Garden last year has ruined his speed." The same reporter also revealed that "a wealthy colored Bostonian has taken a liking to the youngster, and is aiding him to become one of the cracks of the racing path."[25] In Harrisburg, Taylor set a new one-mile track record at a race put on by the Pennsylvania Colored Wheelmen's Association, calling all the time to his pacemakers during the race to "let 'er out!" because he knew he could go faster.[26]

In other races in Pennsylvania, Taylor also made a fine showing. In Philadelphia on August 6, at the big LAW meet that coincided with their annual convention, Taylor won his heat in the 1-mile race, "one of the most popular wins of the day," but was beaten in the final, the most important race of the meet, by Earl Kiser, Eddie Bald, and Tom Cooper. Wrote *Bearings* : "The big three managed to show to the front in the great mile race, and Major Taylor, the darkey, hissed by a few, but cheered by the majority, took a good fourth. Taylor showed during the day by his many hard finishes in the heats, semifinals, and finals, that he is not misplaced when given a position among the top notchers of the year."[27]

Taylor's rivalry with Bald was one of the hottest attractions of the season, and the upstart young black rider taking on the reigning champion made for an especially large box office draw. At Reading, where an unusually big crowd of 4,000 attended, "The colored wonder, 'Majah' Taylor, was the cause of much comment and he captured a nice sum of money. In all his races he made a good showing against his white brethren." For his win over Bald and William Becker, Taylor earned $40. At Wilkesbarre the next day, he won $150 when he beat Nat Butler in the 1-mile race and was second in the half-mile. Once again, he was the star of the show.

At Manhattan Beach again, on August 15: "The sympathy of the crowd was with Major Taylor. ... He simply went in to win," and did! At Portland, Maine, on August 20, Taylor was "the star of the afternoon, winning two firsts and one second and winning $195 in cold cash." The track at the Rigby Park Fairgrounds in Portland was in poor condition, "being owned by the horsemen who have no love for the wheelmen, and trotting races were run up to within half an hour of the bicycle races. The track was left in the rough state." But Taylor was used to all kinds of conditions and was "the hero of the meet." Once again, he was wildly cheered by the crowd. "That Taylor's win was a popular one was evinced by the hearty applause he received. The colored boy was escorted to the judges' stand and introduced as the winner of two firsts and one second in three events. Taylor seemed somewhat abashed as the applause was renewed and, bowing to the crowd, hurriedly left the stand."[28]

At Springfield, Massachusetts, between September 14 and 16, Taylor and Bald engaged in another series of fiercely contested races, showing once again the remarkable ability of the young rider. The two had become hot rivals by then, although there was never a suggestion that Bald had any racist animosity towards Taylor. In one race, the final of the one-third mile, Taylor "started to sprint with the speed of a greyhound, and it looked as though he would be a national champion. Suddenly Bald wound up his big gear and with a jump that electrified the crowd, was in a moment on even terms with the colored mascot. The struggle between the two was so great that all interest was lost in the other contestants. It looked like Taylor up to 20 yards from the pole, when Bald let out again and won by inches."[29]

WHAT WAS VERY EVIDENT as soon as Taylor began to travel on the circuit, and to appear before paying crowds, was that his growing reputation had preceded him. Wherever he went, the crowds loved him. Everyone noticed him just as they had at the six-day race in Madison Square Garden, and there was never any doubt that most of the spectators were routing for him. Some in the crowd were shocked when they saw him competing with white riders, especially on the track, where he was more conspicuous than in road races. However, there was rarely any sign of hostility towards him, and he knew how to please the crowd as he sprinted for the finishing line in a tremendous burst of speed. The crowds wanted action and drama and a strong whiff of danger, and the struggle between Taylor and his white rivals was basic and easily understandable, like a young David taking on several Goliaths at once – full of an unstated but obvious racial symbolism.

USA, 1896—1897

On the track, when Taylor first appeared, he was poised, dignified, and impeccably dressed in his woollen racing outfit. But when the race began, he became an absolute demon – aggressive and tough, fast and agile. Off the track, he was a shy and mild-mannered young man. But by dint of talent, perseverance, and an unassailable personality, he had slipped through a crack in the high wall of prejudice that had kept black people out of competitive sports, as well as every other activity in American society.

His appearance on American tracks was, at the same time, a surprise and a shock. Here was a black man winning big money with panache and predictable regularity at a time when his brothers were expected to doff their caps and step aside for any white man in the street, when only a handful of blacks occupied anything other than the most menial service-related jobs, when blacks were still being lynched in the South for even the suspicion of committing petty crimes. Major Taylor was certainly a novelty, and he aroused people's curiosity and stimulated their imagination.[30]

Appearing suddenly in this relatively new sport of bicycle racing, Taylor was controversial right from the start and caused immediate debate. Since the LAW had ruled in his favor by allowing him to register as a professional, he occupied a unique and pioneering position, a very exposed one, and everything that happened to him, everything he did, became a test case of racial attitudes.

The white riders, particularly those whom he constantly beat, had great difficulty accepting his presence. Most of them were furious at being beaten by a man they regarded as their social inferior. The reactions of the white riders went the full range, from admiration, such as that of his Boston pursuit teammates, to extreme verbal and physical hostility. So, on the national circuit, he prepared for the worst.

A S THE SUMMER OF 1897 wore on, the competition for the sprint championship heated up. Bald was in first place, closely followed by Arthur Gardiner, Tom Cooper, and Earl Kiser. Taylor, who had been enjoying a successful season and was hardly ever out of the first four places in any of his races, was in the top ten of the championship and threatening to climb rapidly to number one. The opposition from the other riders now grew more intense. "The position of the negro is a trying one," said *Bearings* in the middle of September, "for every rider is anxious to top him, owing to his color, and the battle to beat him is waged fiercely day by day."[31]

The first acts of outright physical hostility began in late August and early September. On August 31, in Taylor's adopted hometown of Worcester, Bald beat Taylor in a tremendous sprint in the final of the 1-mile race. "When the twelve riders swept into the home stretch a good-sized horse blanket would have covered the entire push. The dark form of Major Taylor shot to the front and as the tape was neared, Bald made a great spurt and fought it out with the little colored rider of Worcester. Their wheels lapped as they shot across the tape, having made the fastest mile ever ridden on the track in competition. ... The struggle between them for the first place in the final heat was magnificent."[32]

But in one of the heats of the 2-mile race that followed, Taylor had a disastrous experience. "In the last lap he was crowded into the fence, as he was rounding the back stretch, and when the riders began to spurt for the finish, his wheel struck one of the posts, and he was thrown heavily to the ground. His arms and legs were severely torn and his front wheel broken so that he could not ride it. The plucky little rider picked up his wheel, however, and rolled it over the finish."[33] Taylor entered a protest against C. S. Wells for foul riding, and Wells was disqualified from any of the other races.

At a national circuit meet in Newark, held at the Waverly Park track as part of the New Jersey State Fair in early September, Taylor shone again in the qualifying heats, and in the 1-mile sprint event he managed to beat the 'cracks' Al Newhouse, Floyd MacFarland, and Louis Callahan in a hectic finish. Major Taylor Beat the Cracks. the Colored Cyclist Wins the Mile Open at the Waverly Fair by Two Feet, read the headline the next day. "Thousands cheered the cinnamon-hued boy ... when he crossed the tape a fraction of a length to the good. Without any question, Taylor was the star of the show, and he won all the prize money. Most of the men in the final had entered into combinations to help one another and freeze Taylor out. They did work together, but the little black rider was tacking on at every opportunity and 'skinned' them all in the homestretch."

Heated words were exchanged following this race and threats made against Taylor. When the riders were called out for the final of the 1-mile handicap event, for which Taylor had qualified, his trainer announced that he was sick and wanted to be excused from the other events. The referee refused, suggesting that a little more exercise might cure him.

"Then the trainer told the real reason for the withdrawal," the reporter wrote. "The white riders were threatening to take the Major's life if he went out again and he was scared pale. There were rumors of deliberate attempts to spill and ride over him, and the darkey didn't want to take a chance against such big odds. The referee said: 'Bring me some evidence and I will have one of the cycle cops ride with you' or something to that effect. Taylor rode, but he was nervous and his head was bobbing about from side to side watching the other riders. He won nothing more."[34]

BECAUSE OF the nasty accident in Worcester a few days before, Taylor knew the white riders meant business, and he was not going to take a chance on another crash. But his stunning win, followed by consultations with the referee while the white riders looked on contemptuously, and then his failure to make any effort in the following race were obvious indications of what was happening on the track. It was a sufficiently public display of threat and hostility, and the press sat up and took notice.

The New York Sun, siding with Taylor, was particularly outspoken in its criticism of the rough treatment he was getting from the other professional riders on the circuit, which, the paper thought, justified calling for an investigation by the LAW Racing Board. "Taylor rides in all his big races in deadly fear of his racing companions," The *Sun* reported. "Taylor was recently thrown at Worcester and badly bruised in a race, and it was charged that the accident was the result of a conspiracy. ... The situation calls for prompt action on the part of the Racing Board. Taylor now ranks among the fastest men in the country, but the racing men, envious of his success and prejudiced against his color, aim to injure his chances whenever he competes. This conduct robs Taylor of many chances to secure large purses and endangers his life."[35]

The *Worcester Telegram,* aware of the interest in their hometown racer, picked up the story and reprinted it under a dramatic headline: MAJOR TAYLOR'S LIFE IN DANGER. NEW YORK PAPER SAYS THERE IS A COMBINATION AGAINST HIM. CONDUCT OF RACING MEN SHOULD BE INVESTIGATED. SUBJECTED TO CONSTANT THREATS OF INJURY.[36] Taylor's Worcester friends had no doubt that the threats described in the story were true, having witnessed the way he had been fouled during the race there.

The *New York Journal* suggested that he had not really been so badly treated and that Taylor himself was to blame for many of the problems he was encountering.

> Possibly there may be a little ground for complaint by Taylor, but in all the races in the metropolitan district in which he has competed he certainly has not been sinned against. The colored rider has a dangerous habit of crowding in on the pole, no matter how narrow the opening is in the finish down the straight, and on a couple of occasions the possessor of this desirable position has upheld his rights with a bit of 'elbow work' that was provoked by the offender.

> The success of the colored boy – and he has done some excellent riding – was sure to arouse opposition and feeling among the other riders, but officials at meets have been particularly vigilant in seeing that Taylor got all that was coming to him. In baseball and fistic circles the color line has caused any amount of trouble, and the same difficulty is now being experienced in cycling. One prominent rider declined a match with Taylor, not because he was afraid of him, but simply through his unwillingness to be singled out in a competition with one he considered his social inferior. For Taylor, it must be said, however, that he is one of the most modest and retiring youngsters with which his race was ever favored, and if given an inch, he does not take a yard. It is among the possibilities that a well-known former star of cycle racing will take Taylor on a European tour.[37]

When a reporter from the *Worcester Telegram* asked Taylor for his reaction to their story about him, Taylor agreed that it was substantially true.

> I have a dread of injury every time I start in a race with the men who have been on the circuit this year. They have threatened to injure me and I expect that before the season is finished they will do so. The cause of the feeling against me is this. Most of the races are not ridden by the men individually but by combinations. I am not a member of any combination and have necessarily ridden every race unassisted. Hard work has been rewarded by a good many victories ... and these victories have incensed the combination riders and they have threatened to fix me so that I cannot ride.

> That these threats have been made is a fact not unknown to men in charge of meets where I have ridden and the conduct of my enemies

USA, 1896—1897

has been closely watched. I know of no reason why the boys should be against me. I try to do clean riding without receiving the advantage of anything or from anybody. I only ask from them the same kind of treatment which I give and am willing to continue to give.[38]

It was not the "big men," one reporter commented, who were against Taylor, so much as the "cheap riders who are out for fractions of the purses that they can steal from the big fellows." It was the referee's job, he suggested, to see that such behavior was not tolerated.

The League of American Wheelmen, which professes to control racing, draws the color line, and only white riders are allowed in amateur races. … That is a violation of good sense, but if the L.A.W. permits Taylor to start in the professional races, it should protect him. Public sympathy is with Taylor every time, and if some rider gets killed trying to do him, very little regret will be felt. The L.A.W., among the many other things it has got to do to make itself felt, must keep the dirty professionals off its tracks.[39]

THE HOSTILITY directed at Taylor came to a climax on the second day of a two-day meeting in Taunton, Massachusetts, on September 23. He was physically attacked and choked into unconsciousness by William Becker, a white rider from Minneapolis, after an extremely close finish in the final of the 1-mile race. The winner, Tom Butler, was the Boston rider who had been Taylor's teammate in the inter-city pursuit race against Philadelphia earlier in the year. Taylor was second. Becker, the third-place finisher, came up behind him, grabbed him around the neck, pulled him off his bicycle, and threw him on the ground while maintaining a stranglehold around his neck. The police had to interfere to restrain Becker, and it was a full fifteen minutes before Taylor recovered consciousness. The crowd, agitated and angry at Becker's attack, threatened him, and only the police presence prevented the already ugly incident from getting out of hand.[40]

Becker claimed that Taylor had forced him into the fence during the race, but the source of the hostility was much deeper than this one alleged foul. Becker had been on the circuit the whole season and had seen Taylor's popularity with the crowds. There was professional jealousy as well as racial hatred behind his disgraceful behavior.

Becker was not arrested, but the incident was a sharp reminder of the aggressive feelings that were aroused by Taylor's challenge to white superiority in a sport previously dominated by whites, as well as in society in general. The two could not be easily separated. Becker's behavior was one of the first public demonstrations of the racial feeling directed against Taylor. What most people only thought, Becker had acted out.

There was widespread comment in the press and unanimous condemnation of Becker for his unjustified attack. *Bicycling World* called the incident "one of the deplorable features of the racing season of 1897. It would have been sufficiently disgraceful had the participants been of the same color; the fact that the alleged 'victim' was a colored man, and the only one now prominent as a racing man in this country, but complicates the difficulty. It is such incidents as these that bring discredit on a sport whose promoters have strenuously endeavored to keep it clean and honest."[41]

Nonetheless the writer also suggests that Taylor is somehow to blame for the hostility directed at him by white riders, that he himself is really the cause of all the trouble. Becker will undoubtedly be punished "with a lengthy term of suspension, which he richly deserves, but the colored man, the cause of the unpleasantness, will remain just where he was, with the added halo of martyr to stimulate the already hearty ill feeling which prevails against him among his rivals." Of course, the writer continues, Taylor has a perfect right to be where he is, but it is "unfortunate that he has seemed to make use of his peculiar position as the only one of his color on the track to obtain the sympathy of the public. ... It remains a fact that Taylor has participated in scarcely a meet this year where he has not put in a plea of ill treatment at the hands of competitors, and where similar charges have not been made against him.[42]

The end of the incident was not exactly a victory for Taylor. When the notorious case arrived before the chairman of the LAW Racing Board, Albert Mott, who was expected, at the very least, to impose a long suspension on Becker, he handed out instead a mere $50 fine. Mott was afraid of the backlash from the other riders if he was too hard on Becker, but also took into account Taylor's alleged fouling of Becker. But the practical effect of the small fine was to exonerate Becker. He had lost his temper and overstepped the limits of normal behavior, Mott seemed to be saying, but he had been provoked and his anger was understandable. A few white racing men took up a collection and helped Becker pay the fine. "The riders insisted that their action was not a proof of their enmity toward Taylor because of his color," said *Bicycling World*, "but on account of their belief that his foul riding caused Becker to lose his temper and act as he did at Taunton."[43]

Black people, however, did not forgive Becker's attack on Taylor as easily as the LAW official. "This rider was always marked by the colored people," said a Boston newspaper in reviewing Taylor's career in 1900, "and many times after he narrowly escaped injury at their hands."[44]

The Taunton attack did not intimidate Taylor. Two days later he was in Cleveland, where "his appearance upon the track was the signal for a storm of applause" and where "the colored crackerjack was the bright, particular star of the meet."[45] Taylor easily won the 1-mile and the 2-mile races, showing that he had lost neither his nerve nor his popularity.

However, the remainder of the 1897 championship season would be lost to Taylor because the national circuit extended into the South during the months of October and November. Southern audiences got a chance to see the stars of top-class professional bicycle racing, and the riders got a chance to extend their earnings. Of course, the results from all these races counted toward the final championship ratings.

For this two-month Southern Extension, as it was called, two special railroad cars, the *Iolanthe* and the *Pickwick*, were chartered to take all the racing men, together with their equipment, their trainers and managers, and even some journalists, on the long journey from city to city. The trip extended as far west as Illinois and Wisconsin, then dipped into the deep South through Kentucky and Missouri, and ended in Georgia and Florida. It was an ambitious promotion and a risky undertaking.

In spite of warnings that "the southern meets would never stand his entry and would refuse it peremptorily," Taylor set out on the trip from Trenton.[46] The relationship between him and the other riders was extremely tense as the tour began. Birdie Munger was involved in various ways in the organization of the tour and was keeping a watchful eye on his protégé. Perhaps it was Munger's presence on the train that made it possible for Taylor to be there at all.

On October 1, in Detroit, one of the first stops on the tour, Taylor was, as usual, in the final of the 1-mile race along with all the other top riders – Eddie Bald, Tom Cooper, Nat Butler, and Earl Kiser. There were eleven riders lined up for the race and Taylor was in the tight, jostling group that crossed the finish line, though he did not win a place. But at subsequent cities where races were scheduled – Indianapolis, Louisville, New Albany, Indiana, and St. Louis – just as had been predicted, Taylor's entries were either rejected by the promoters, or the white riders refused to ride with him. Feelings were much stronger in the South than in the East, and public opinion was more solidly behind the white riders.

Taylor was thus effectively barred from continuing his challenge of Bald and the other top riders for the national championship honors. After he had been hovering between fourth and seventh positions in the standings for several weeks, his name was suddenly dropped from the list of competitors. The prediction of one journalist earlier in the season had been confirmed: "Major Taylor will not be able to make a fight for the championship of the season," he had written, "as the circuit extends through the South, and his entry will be refused by all Southern race meet promoters, who say that it would be folly for a colored person to compete with the white riders in the South."[47]

Taylor had to make the difficult decision to abandon the Southern Extension and to return to Worcester. The pressure on him became too great in Louisville and St. Louis. Louisville, after all, had been the instigator of the LAW's racist policy and was dead set against him or any other black bicycle racer. There was nothing he could do under the circumstances except to bow out. *Bearings* reported his departure from the championship struggle without editorial comment: "Major Taylor has not ridden on the circuit for a long time. He is being steadily forced down by those who gain in points, and if he should stay off the circuit much longer, he will have no opportunity for a good position in the tables." Two weeks later, the magazine reported that "Major Taylor is dropped from the tables this week and will be unable to appear again this season. ... Taylor held his own on the track and his speed was admired by all the crackajacks."[48]

Eventually, the Southern Extension was stopped in Atlanta by a yellow fever plague, and the riders dispersed to their homes. That year, Eddie Bald was once again the national sprint champion of America.

DESPITE HIS SETBACK because of the racism of the white racers on the national circuit and in the South, Taylor's 1897 season was a remarkably successful one. He had competed in an integrated team in Boston. He had beaten Eddie Bald, the reigning national champion on several occasions and pushed him to extremely tight victories on others. He had rarely been out of the top four finishers in races against all the top professionals. He had won several thousand dollars. He had become a favorite with the crowds because of his combative, plucky riding. Promoters and managers were eager to back him. All in all, it was a pretty good start. He was undoubtedly the discovery of the season and had arrived firmly at the top of American bicycle racing. That his potential was enormous was understood by anybody who knew anything at all about athletic matters. That his position was unique was equally obvious.

One East Coast newspaper commented on the novelty of Taylor's arrival on the scene:

> Major Taylor, the colored cyclone, is really the surprise of the year. Never before in the history of the cycle sport has it been known that a colored man was of such account as a racing man. Many attempts have been made, but none was successful until Taylor came out and proved himself a wonder. Taylor, it might be said, was raised and brought up by 'Birdie' Munger. He was early initiated in the racing game and was always inseparable from his wheel.

It is Munger, the writer suggested, who was responsible for giving Taylor the social poise that had made it possible for him to be accepted at all by the white riders:

> Munger trained Taylor in the way that he should go. He taught him to know his place and it is that training which has made the lad more or less popular with the circuit men, probably more. He keeps his place and knows his place. In August, Taylor won $475. He started in ten races on the National Circuit, securing four firsts, two seconds and one fourth. ... This is a record which any white man might well be proud of. His position was earned by hard, clean riding and good sprinting powers. He is the first and the only colored man to ever achieve success on the circuit.[49]

Another newspaperman wrote a column that had the full force of Boston's abolitionist tradition, appealing to reason and moderation:

> Because Major Taylor's skin happens to be darker than that of the men with whom he races in Boston and vicinity, because he is an American citizen born of colored parents, is no valid reason why he should receive any different treatment at the hands of racing men, spectators or offi-

cials. ... Major Taylor is a quiet, honest gentleman. He is better educated than the majority of men whom he meets in the professional ranks. He is deserving of at least fair treatment.[50]

One long and revealing end-of-the-season article in *Bearings* persisted in the insinuation that Taylor himself was to blame in various ways for all the unpleasant incidents: "Major Taylor has placed himself in a difficult position, and it will be hard for the colored boy to extricate himself," the article began.

> Taylor himself brought on much of the trouble, for he had a nasty habit of cutting in on the pole in places where he had not the slightest right. His request to be let through was not granted any more than it would have been granted to any white man. Consequently, he was often run over the pole and when this occurred claimed injustice at the hands of the white riders. Referees took the position that Taylor was 'up against it' and frequently allowed him to start in finals of races for which he did not qualify. ... Favoritism was quite naturally claimed by the white men, and out of this favoritism a sentiment grew up against the darkey among the men of the party in whose veins courses southern blood. ...

> Taylor is now most anxious to right himself with the men against whom he must compete, but how to go about it he does not know. Failing in his laudable efforts, it is his intention to follow good advice given him last spring and go to France, where a colored man is never looked down upon. . . .

> The white men claim that it is not fear of his prowess and ability that brings about the present opposition, but a doubt exists if the white men are wholly honest in this. Taylor is a great rider, of that there cannot be the slightest doubt. He is also a daring rider and the first of his class to ever show championship form in the present day fast company and there is a fear that his presence in the races may excite other colored riders to such admiration that more of his race will want to compete. Taylor's trip to France would end the discussion, and no one appreciates this more than the colored man.

> One thing is certain, the meet promoters will regret his going, for he proves an excellent drawing card and his entry is eagerly sought.[51]

The best solution to the problem, almost everyone agreed, was for Taylor to disappear, go to Europe, get out of everybody's way, to remove the source of irritation. But Taylor had other plans. He wanted to stay and fight. He was not ready to give up his career as an American bicycle racer – *a black American bicycle racer*. He would not be intimidated and excluded as easily as his enemies hoped. He would be back again in 1898.

USA, 1896—1897

6

NEW HORIZONS, NEW OPPOSITION

IN A SMALL pocket notebook in which Major Taylor jotted down his expenses and people's addresses in 1898, there is a page on which are recorded, in his neat, legible handwriting, two events that touched his life deeply. The first entry refers to the death and funeral of his mother the previous year. About this sad event he wrote simply "Saphronia Taylor, June 10, 1897," which was either the date of her death or the date of her funeral, followed by some details of the funeral service.

His mother's death, which occurred shortly after his first big successes in New York, but before his career was firmly launched in 1897, drew Taylor back to his family in Indianapolis for a simple Baptist funeral service. Although he had spent a great deal of time away from his mother while he was growing up, first at the Southard's house and then as Birdie Munger's employee, and had then left home for the East Coast when he was only sixteen, Taylor was nevertheless profoundly attached to and influenced by his mother.

It was his mother, Taylor remarked on several occasions, who instilled in him his firm religious convictions and taught him to respect and observe the Sabbath. She also encouraged him in the fair and honest Christian behavior which he always advocated and tried his best to live up to. In his autobiography he describes how he rushed home to his mother after his first victories, eager to show her his prizes, to see the joy on her face, and to receive her congratulations. After his six-day race success, he had sent $55 of his prize money to her in Indianapolis. Evidently, it was a close and loving relationship, which continued to influence him even after her death.

While his mother was sick, with her death imminent, Taylor promised her that he would lead an upright Christian life. So, when she died, he reexamined his own religious beliefs. Beneath the details of her funeral in his notebook he wrote a few words full of profound impact: "Embraced Religion, Friday, Jan. 14, 1898." It was a reminder of this important date when he decided to commit himself to the severe, uncompromising Christianity of the Baptists.

It was a private act of faith, but probably he also made a public declaration of his commitment at an evening meeting held in the small wooden building of the John Street Baptist Church in Worcester, established shortly before by its minister, the Reverend Hiram Conway. Taylor affirmed his trust in Jesus and his resolve to follow His teachings from then on.

This affirmation, in 1898, of his Baptist faith would have profound consequences for Taylor's life and career. It defined the way in which he saw the world and, increasingly, how the world saw him. It was a faith he maintained steadfastly for the rest of his life and which gave him a heroic moral stature. It shaped his identity as a clean-living, hard-working, exemplary Christian gentleman, whose integrity and honesty were in stark contrast to the deviousness, coarseness, and racism of many of his white American opponents.

As Taylor's Christian personality developed, it set an example of dignity, honesty, and fairness in athletic accomplishment. His unique achievements demonstrated that a black man could be at least as good as, if not better than, a white man, using the same moral standards generally recognized in white society. He refused to be drawn into responding to the aggression and hostility directed against him, preferring to turn the other cheek, to rely instead on his athletic superiority to show the strength and righteousness of his position. As a result, Taylor was perceived as an 'uppity nigger,' who threatened to upset the natural order of white superiority. Therefore, he had to be stopped before other blacks became 'uppity' too.

Taylor's firm convictions as a strict Baptist led after 1898 to his refusal to participate in any race held on Sunday. At first, this had only occasional repercussions because most American sporting events were held on Saturdays and holidays. But when French bicycle racing promoters began to show a strong determination to lure him to France, it became more and more crucial that he be persuaded to race on Sundays. In spite of the temptation of huge sums of money subsequently offered him to race on Sundays, Taylor remained faithful to his religious principles and to the promise he had made to his mother before she died.

USA, 1898

TAYLOR'S OUTSTANDING performances during 1897 attracted a great deal of attention. From a tentative beginning he had become a thoroughly accomplished professional athlete. He had won several thousand dollars and beaten some of the biggest names in the business, including on several occasions the reigning American champion, Eddie 'Cannon' Bald. He was acknowledged in newspapers as the discovery of the season. Reporters were unanimous in their opinion that he was a phenomenally talented young athlete, obviously destined to achieve great things.

The press followed his career with fascination, and wherever he raced, he made good copy for journalists. They were alert to the uniqueness of his role as the first black professional cyclist and to the drama of the challenge which his presence on the tracks posed to white riders. The animosity of these white riders was concerted and intense. The combined opposition of the white riders and the western and southern track owners had been powerful enough to freeze him out of the 1897 championship.

The reputation Taylor established during the 1897 season was sufficient to win him a contract for 1898, and at the beginning of the year he signed on as a member of a new team, the American Cycle Racing Association (ACRA), a New York-based bicycle racing promotion company, the same group that had promoted the 1896 six-day race. They had been watching the young rider's progress and were impressed with what they saw.

The American Cycle Racing Association, headed by executives Pat Powers and William Brady, was in business to make money out of promoting bicycle racing and its stars. It was an independent group both collaborating with and partly in rivalry against the League of American Wheelmen, which, as the governing body of the sport, claimed the sole right to register riders and sanction races. In 1898, the team members were Major Taylor, Fred Titus, Edouard Taylore, a French record-breaker, and the tiny Jimmy Michael, an extraordinary Welsh long-distance rider. The team was directed by James Kennedy, and their trainer and manager was Willis Troy.

Taylor's contract was an important recognition of his promise and commercial potential. As hard-headed businessmen, Powers and Brady understood very well that the often raucous crowds would flock to see him compete, just as they had at the six-day race, that he had enormous box-office appeal. Brady, who also promoted theatrical and

USA, 1898

boxing events, had, according to one newspaper account, "expressed himself in no uncertain terms as to what he called unjust discrimination" and was prepared to stand up for Taylor's rights as well as to make good money out of him.[1] Obviously, these astute New York promoters were aware of the promise and also the controversy surrounding Taylor. They had everything to gain, in fact, and very little to lose from the publicity he was certain to generate. The biggest initial headache to overcome was to ensure that his right to compete was thoroughly protected.

Powers and Brady had sounded out Albert Mott, chairman of the LAW Racing Board, before signing Taylor. Would he be registered and able to compete legally in 1898, providing the basis for drawing up an agreement with him? The reply had been positive. Not only would the LAW definitely register him, but it would also refuse to give race meet sanctions to any track or promoter refusing to accept his entry, an application that had to be filed contractually with promoters before a rider could take part in a race.

The contract offered Taylor professional security and support in the struggles that lay ahead. At least he had secured managers who, like Munger, understood his situation and seemed to be on his side.[2] Willis Troy, his new trainer, was an important man in bicycle racing. He had been Arthur Zimmerman's trainer for several years and had traveled to Europe with him in 1894, at the very pinnacle of his success. Troy was certainly known to Munger, and it was probably Munger who advised Taylor to cast his lot with the ACRA, as the best option for his career at that point. He was certainly signing on with some very experienced men, among the very best in the business. They had great plans for him, nothing less than match races against his leading opponents and the championship of America itself.

Taylor continued his training through the winter in Worcester. He lifted weights in the gymnasium, boxed, skipped, and ran to keep in shape, but what he really needed was the warm weather that only the South could provide during the winter months. Professional cyclists had for several years set up winter training camps in Florida, on the west coast at Belleair near Tampa and at St. Augustine on the East Coast, south of Jacksonville. Here they could train on the road as well as on the track. Troy had taken Zimmerman south a few years before, and he thought the early training would give Taylor a huge advantage in his preparation for the coming season.

USA, 1898

Late in February 1898, Taylor went to New York to consult with his employers and make preparations for the trip south. Before he left Worcester, where he had been living during the winter, he went to the offices of the *Worcester Telegram*, "to thank the cycle editor for his kindness" and to say good-bye to his supporters there.

"I'm going to Florida to train for the big meetings that will be held during the summer," he told them. "I think the change to a warmer climate will improve my health. I'm out to whip the champions this season and hope to have better luck on the track, and I'll start out to make it my banner year."[3]

In New York, Troy was uncertain about the wisdom of sending him south. There were many potential problems. He would have to find a place to live and would, of course, be the only black among the white riders. His reputation as an 'uppity nigger' would precede him, and with the well-known hostility to blacks who did not 'know their place,' it was not difficult to foresee that there would be trouble.

Troy knew more about the South than Taylor, and he made inquiries about the advisability of taking him and a team of pacemakers there. The replies were discouraging. Taylor would not be welcome in St. Augustine and Belleair because white riders already there would object. So Troy decided on Savannah, Georgia, where there was a good track and where Taylor might be less conspicuous since it was one of the few cities in the South where blacks outnumbered whites. Troy telegraphed a friend there asking whether Taylor would be allowed to use the track. In spite of the uncertain reply, they decided to take a chance on the trip.

Troy went on in advance to make preparations for Taylor. He rented rooms at a boarding house near the track in his own name and then sent for Taylor, whose arrival precipitated the first of many unpleasant experiences he would have in Savannah. Discovering that the newly arrived guest was black, the other boarders threatened to leave in a body if he was permitted to stay. Other lodgings were found with a black family on Lincoln Street.

But Taylor's troubles were just beginning. When he arrived at the track at Wheelmen's Park, the owners and other cyclists would not permit him or his white pacemakers to ride. The problems Troy had anticipated were not to be easily overcome.

With the track unavailable to him and his fitness for the coming season at stake, Taylor began to train on the road. Here, too, he soon

USA, 1898

discovered, he was unwelcome. Local cyclists began to complain, especially because Taylor had no trouble leaving them all behind. It was one thing to see a well-equipped 'Negro' on a fine racing bicycle with his white pacemakers training on 'their' roads; it was another when this nineteen-year-old upstart 'mingled' with them, beat them on their home ground, and threw dust into their eyes. What began as a curious rivalry became, in the racial climate of the time, an affrontery. Taylor's presence became a provocation the white riders found impossible to ignore.

One day, Taylor was training alone on the Louisville Road, which ran northwest out of Savannah. In front of him he saw a triplet moving along at a brisk pace, exactly the kind of machine used to pace him. As he pulled up alongside the three white men, he saw that they were the best triplet team in Savannah, and they were not at all pleased to see Taylor.

As he tucked in behind them, one of the riders turned and angrily told him they had no intention of "pacing niggers." Taylor ignored him and kept on riding. More insults followed and then threats of violence. But none of the white riders was anxious to accept his challenge to settle the dispute then and there.

"Alright then," said Taylor, "if you won't pace me, I'll pace you," and with a sudden sprint he surged in front of the triplet. It was a challenge they could not reject. The training session became a race. "He led the triplet a merry chase back to the town and through the principal streets, much to the cyclists' disgust," said one newspaper account of the incident.[4] Taylor's youthful impetuosity had got the better of him, but he had provoked an unwise confrontation.

There would be no interracial training sessions in Savannah. The next morning, Taylor received a letter, which read, "Mister Taylor, If you don't leave here before 48 hours, you will be sorry. We mean business. Clear out if you value your life." It was signed "White Riders."[5] On the page was a crude sketch of a skull and crossbones. A similar letter was sent to Troy, warning him that his association with a black man would not be tolerated in Savannah and giving him the same amount of time to leave.

Taylor and Troy left Savannah at once. They had been there less than a week. They could not shrug off such a threat, especially since Taylor's behavior as a black man had been provocative. The law was a timid protector of the rights of black people in the southern states, where lynching was an almost everyday occurrence.[6] Taylor could easily have fallen victim to an 'accident' on the road.

Racial feelings in Savannah were in a particularly aroused state just at that moment because President McKinley had recently appointed a black man to the office of Collector of the Port. The American Cycle Racing Association tried to cover itself by telling the press that they had ordered Taylor home and that his departure from Savannah had nothing at all to do with the threats made against him. There was an element of truth in this claim because even before he had received the threatening letter, Taylor had been having difficulties accomplishing the training for which he had gone south. Whatever disclaimers the ACRA made, however, the message was clear.

Taylor returned to New York and awaited further instructions. He was clearly shaken up by the experience. He told a New York reporter, "I knew I had no right south of the Mason-Dixon line, but I did not think the feeling was as strong as was shown. It is useless for a colored person to attempt to get along in the South. The feeling is so strong only a race war will settle it."[7]

One Savannah newspaper took a dim view of the whole affair. COWARDLY WRITER – WRITES LIKE A MIDNIGHT ASSASSIN – SUCH ACTS NOT TOLERATED HERE – IF CAUGHT WILL BE PROSECUTED, read the headline. "What these prejudiced riders did is condemned by all who heard about it. … Taylor and his manager were not in the least intimidated by the cowardly warning."[8] Another paper, however, expressed what was closer to the prevailing attitude towards blacks in Savannah. "Major Taylor, the coon rider from the north is dead sold on the south. He does not like the way he was treated in Savannah. … It is too bad that the boys treated Taylor in such a manner. But the negro has no cause to kick. It is lucky that he was not severely handled. He forced himself on the white riders and made himself generally obnoxious. Hereafter 'Major' Taylor will give Savannah a wide berth."[9] Taylor admitted to journalists when he returned to New York that "he breathed a lot easier after he was on the boat speeding north."[10]

IN NEW YORK, Taylor continued his winter training on the safer roads of Brooklyn and Long Island and on the Coney Island cycle path. Later, at the Manhattan Beach track, where the weather, apart from the strong winds, was good enough for some intense training, the American Cycle Racing Association went to the extraordinary expense of maintaining about forty or fifty pacemakers and their machines for Taylor, Jimmy Michael, and the other team members to train behind. The pacemakers were strong, experienced racing cyclists, most of whom were ambitious to become stars themselves. They rode what were known then as multicycles, that is, quadruplets and quintuplets. Four or five strong riders working together on one of these large cumbersome machines were extremely fast and powerful.

In the search for greater speed, which began to obsess bicycle racers and spectators on both sides of the Atlantic, these strange-looking machines enjoyed a brief and dramatic period of popularity, until motor-driven pacing machines outmoded them. A race between two stars like Taylor and Michael, each paced by a succession of these huge machines, was an exciting spectacle, attracting huge crowds to the tracks. The riders hugged the rear wheel of their pacing machines, which were also excellent for training purposes, for they allowed a rider to maintain a high speed, giving him a fast, effective workout.

Taylor was now moving in a world of exciting financial possibilities. Michael, "the wonderful little midget of the cycle path," who stood just over five feet tall and had already been an international star of middle-distance paced racing for several years, signed a contract at the beginning of the 1898 season guaranteeing him $2,500 for each of nine paced races against his main rivals, including Taylor, making a total guaranteed income of $22,500, an enormous sum of money. *Cycle Age* described it as "the greatest deal in the history of professional cycle racing and in fact of all sport outside of pugilism."[11] For the few bicycle racing stars at the very top of the sport, the sky was the limit as far as what they could earn. Manufacturers were prepared to spend large amounts of money to hire star riders to advertise their bicycles and tires, and spectators lined up at the box office. Michael told a reporter he intended to make $30,000 from bicycle racing in July, August, and September of 1898.

In April, before the racing season had begun in earnest, there was another flurry of argument and publicity about Major Taylor. Tom Eck, manager of the Woodside Park track in Philadelphia, announced that he would not accept Taylor's entry forms and would bar him because of the League of American Wheelmen's general policy against black membership. "We do not do this because of any opposition to Taylor himself," Eck said, "but he must suffer with the others. Our entry blanks will be marked 'for white riders only.'"[12]

William Brady, Taylor's manager, immediately issued a statement to the press saying that Eck was merely trying to get cheap publicity and that Taylor had no need of him or his track. "I beg to assure the gentleman," he said, "that any time the Major enters a race, the American Cycle Racing Association will see that he receives fair treatment."[13] Eck backpedaled on the whole issue. He had been misquoted in the press, he claimed. "The promoter who would debar a good drawing card like Major Taylor does not understand his business, he said." It would not have been good, in a liberal city like Philadelphia, for the dispute to grow into a scandal. He decided to accept Taylor's entries.

This short confrontation was an interesting sign of new strength in Taylor's situation. Many promoters and riders were still opposed to his participation in the sport on principle. But he had become a famous rider by 1898 and had made a big impact on the crowds that flocked to the tracks to see him race. When promoters began making money out of Taylor's successes, they found they had less reason to act on their own racial feelings. It made much more sense to give the public what it wanted, the excitement and novelty of seeing this superb young black athlete pitted against the hostile white riders. Everyone recognized his athletic audacity and his popularity by then; it simply could not be denied. Bicycle racing was show business, after all, and the promoter's job was to give the public what it wanted.

Most observers agreed at the start of the 1898 season that it would be an outstanding year for the sport. "Not in years has there been such an array of first-class talent," said one newspaper writer. There were also going to be some big changes in the kinds of races presented to the public, which the same writer called "almost a complete revolution in the methods, manner, style, and quality of cycle racing in the United States."[14]

The traditional shorter sprint races, and the handicap races, were still popular and made up the core of the national circuit championship, contested all over the country. For the sake of novelty, however, there were many more specially arranged, paced races over longer distances, and these were promoted to introduce more excitement and variety. They enabled promoters to pit one star against another, to advertise personality against personality. It was good for box of-fice receipts.

These longer-distance races would be a new departure for Taylor, but there was no doubt that he would succeed at these also. "Major Taylor's debut as a middle-distance rider will be watched with a great deal of interest," wrote the author of an article headlined REVOLUTION IN CYCLE RACING. "The public has always had a considerable fondness for Major Taylor, believing that he has been unjustly persecuted by some of the riders because of his color. ... Under the management of the American Cycle Racing Association, Taylor will lack neither pacemakers nor proper encouragement to race, and if he is bound to become as much of a sensation as is promised, this summer will develop all there is in him."[15]

Taylor showed early in the season that he had lost none of the previous year's strength and speed when he beat champion Eddie Bald in the heat of the 1-mile race on a cold, blustery day in May at Manhattan Beach. Taylor and Bald "had it neck and neck clear down the home stretch, and the Major pulled ahead a scant six inches in the final ten yards." Bald, furious at being beaten again by Taylor, pulled out of the final, which was won by Tom Butler, with Taylor second. "The riding of the colored man yesterday showed him to be the peer of any of the men on the track," said the *New York Sun*.[16]

In Utica, a few days later, on another cold day, Taylor once again beat Bald and most of the other top riders in both the 1-mile race and the 2-mile handicap. "The honors fell to 'Majah' Taylor, the colored crack, who is as black as the ace of spades, and who rides like a streak," one journalist reported. "The 'Majah' is as pretty a built boy as one could wish to see and the way he sprinted past the other crack-ajacks was a caution. In the 2-mile handicap, he rode from the 30-yard mark and beat out Eddie Bald in the prettiest kind of a finish. The colored lad's sprint was a beautiful one and as he passed the champion the crowd cheered again and again."[17]

With several good wins in New York State in hand, and consistent-ly high placings against the 'Big Four' – Eddie Bald, Tom Cooper, Arthur Gardiner, and Orlando Stevens – Taylor went to Cambridge on June 17 to compete in a 30-mile paced race against Eddie McDuffie, his old teammate from the 1897 Boston pursuit team. When Taylor appeared on the Charles River track, "the band played 'The Warmest Baby in the Bunch,' and when McDuffie rode out, the strains of 'All

Coons Look Alike to Me' were heard." This was Taylor's first important paced race, and McDuffie was the winner by more than a lap of
the track, setting a new record for the distance. But Taylor's time was
also faster than the old record.

At the beginning of June, promoters at Wilkesbarre refused to accept Taylor's entry because the white riders threatened not to ride if
he was allowed to start, the familiar boycott tactic. "They are simply
drawing the color line in Wilkesbarre," Taylor told the *Worcester Spy*.
"I blame the race promoters there for not having the backbone to
allow me to ride in the race. ... You can see that back of it is the
animosity of some of the cheaper professional riders who are always
against me, but who do not always carry their point."[19] Once again,
it was clear that the angriest of his opponents were those riders he
was able to beat most of the time. "There is a lot of cheap sporting
blood in certain of the cycle racers," commented the *New York Journal* on the incident, "and it never has showed more clearly than in
the case of Taylor, who, as a rider, is really superior to most of them,
and as a peaceful, well-behaved athlete gives far less trouble to his
managers than others who feel themselves so much superior to
him."[20]

On Saturday, July 17, Taylor celebrated his biggest victory of the
season at the Tioga track in Philadelphia, winning the 1-mile championship race from Bald, Cooper, and Howard Freeman and placing
second in the 1-mile handicap. SHOWS HIS WHITE BRETHREN JUST HOW
TO PUSH A WHEEL, announced one newspaper headline, while the
Philadelphia Press reported that "a crowd of about 7,000 people saw
Major Taylor, the unassuming colored wonder, fairly ride the champions off their feet and win with comparative ease a title which all
the crack riders were anxious to win, the 1-mile championship of
America." [21]

The animosity of the white riders was aroused by Taylor's splendid
victory, which "had made him the idol of the meet and caused the
crowd to for once forsake Bald and applaud the effort of a hated
rival." In the final of the second big race, LAW chairman Mott, who
refereed the meet, saw Taylor jostled and crowded off the track by
the combined efforts of the white riders, almost forcing him into a
collision with the press enclosure at the side of the track. In spite of
the foul, however, he succeeded in placing second, ahead of Bald
once again. Manager Brady was indignant at the way his rider was

USA, 1898

treated. He was going to turn Taylor into a world beater, he said, and would put up $1,000 to match him against any other rider. "Leave the boy alone, and he will land a winner every time," he said. "Unhampered, Taylor is the fastest man on the track today. Think of the odds he has worked under. Of course, it is humiliating to have colored boys win, but he does the trick honestly, and in racing parlance, there isn't a whiter man on the track. He's game to the core, and you never hear him complain."[22] But many of the riders Brady would have liked to match Taylor against in two-up races, like Bald and Cooper, refused to meet him, afraid of being beaten in that exposed, unarguable way by the young black man.

The season was developing, as expected, into a triumph for Taylor. At Asbury Park, New Jersey, where the circuit races were held at the end of July, he was welcomed as a guest at Arthur Zimmerman's house. On that occasion, it was Zimmerman who met Taylor at the train station as the visiting star, reversing their roles of five years earlier, when Taylor had ushered the great champion from the station in Indianapolis to Munger's house. Then, Munger had told Zimmerman of his hopes for the fourteen-year-old boy, and Zimmerman had encouraged and inspired him. By 1898, at Asbury Park, Taylor had arrived in the front ranks of American bicycle racing and was well on his way to fulfilling Munger's expectations.

After giving Taylor advice about where to begin his final sprint on the Asbury Park track and firing the starting pistol, Zimmerman witnessed Taylor's progress in those five years. In front of the great champion, who in 1893 had inspired him and set an example of modesty and humility, as well as athletic brilliance, Taylor beat his most dangerous rivals, the 'Big Four' – Bald, Cooper, Gardiner, and Stevens – in the final of the $^1/_3$-mile sprint.

"Of all the ovations that I ever received," Taylor wrote, "the one that crowned my efforts at the Asbury Park track on this memorable occasion will remain fresh in my memory forever. I can hear it now. I honestly believe that Mr. Zimmerman got as much pleasure out of the ovation as I did myself. I have never seen a more happy man in my life than Zimmerman as he shook my hand warmly after the race. 'Our friend Birdie Munger was right,' he kept saying." When they left the track, Taylor and Zimmerman went straight to the telegraph office to wire the news of his victory to Munger. He was firmly among

USA, 1898

MARSHALL TAYLOR.

Above: 1. Major Taylor at age sixteen
Below: 2. The start of the *Worcester Telegram* road race in 1896

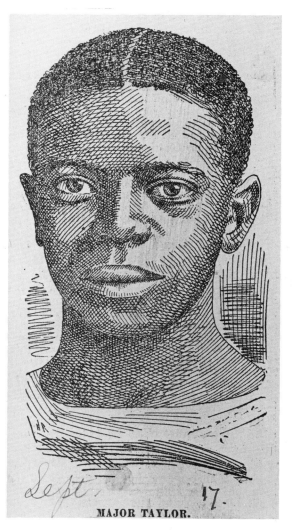

MAJOR TAYLOR.

": Majah " Taylor.

Above: 3.Taylor at age eighteen

Right: 4. About 1896, when he first arrived in Worcester, Massechusetts

Facing page, top: 5. Racist caricatures that appeared in 1898

Bottom: 6. The integrated Boston pursuit team of 1897

"MAJAH" REPENTS AND IS FORGIVEN

"MAJAH" BREAKS SOME RECORDS

THE BOSTON TEAM.

FRANK BUTLER.   "MAJOR" TAYLOR.

BURNS PIERCE.   NAT BUTLER.   E. A. M'DUFFIE.

LA VIE AU GRAND AIR

ABONNEMENTS :
PARIS...................... 8 fr.
PROVINCE.................. 9 fr.
ÉTRANGER................ 12 fr.

Paraissant le 1er et le 15 de chaque mois.
Rédaction et Administration, 106, boulevard Saint-Germain, PARIS

1er Novembre 1898. — N° 15

LE " NÈGRE VOLANT " MAYOR TAYLOR, SURNOMMÉ LE " PRODIGE NOIR "

QUI A BATTU CETTE ANNÉE TOUS LES COUREURS AMÉRICAINS ET QUI DOIT VENIR EN FRANCE LA SAISON PROCHAINE. (Voir les Échos.)

Facing page: 7 and 8. Riding the chainless bicycles used to establish
world records in 1899

Above: 9. By 1898, Taylor was an internationally famous star. This photo
appeared on the cover of the premier French sports magazine

Left: 10. Publicity photo, at the peak of his American success in 1900

Below: 11. The house Taylor bought on Hobson Avenue in Worcester, causing an uproar amongst white neighbors

Top right: 12. Louis
Munger, Taylor's
mentor

Top left: 13. Arthur
Zimmerman (on the
bicycle), America's
first cycling hero,
inspired Taylor

Right:: 14. Caricature
by the French
cartoonist O'Galop in
1901

MAJOR TAYLOR

Doué d'une voix remarquable, on peut le surprendre quelquefois à l'hôtel Males-herbes où il est descendu, s'accompagnant au piano. Notre photographie le représente au moment où il chante « *Hullo my Baby !* » chanson américaine qui fut fort goûtée durant l'Exposition.

Above: 15. "A remarkable singing voice." Taylor as an amateur entertainer in Paris, 1901

Facing page, top: 16. Taylor's first European race in Berlin, April 1901

Facing page, bottom: 17. With Henri Fournier, the famed race car driver and former cycling champion

LA VIE AU GRAND AIR

ABONNEMENTS

PARIS ... Un an 14 fr. | ÉDITION DE LUXE
DÉPARTEM.ᵗˢ — 15 fr. | FRANCE... Un an 30 fr.
ETRANGER. — 20 fr. | ETRANGER — 40 fr.

10 Mars 1901. — N° 130

Rédaction et Administration : 370, rue Saint-Honoré, PARIS (1ᵉʳ Arrᵗ).

PUBLICITÉ

PAGES DE COUVERTURE, la ligne. 1 fr. 50
LA PAGE . . . . 800 fr. »
ENCARTAGES . . . . . . 500 fr. »

MAJOR TAYLOR

Le célèbre sprinter noir, champion de vitesse d'Amérique, qui arrivera à Paris dans quelques jours
pour se mesurer avec les plus fameux coureurs européens.

18. To the French sporting press, Taylor's European tour was front page
news

LA VIE ILLUSTRÉE

LE MATCH JACQUELIN-MAJOR TAYLOR AU PARC DES PRINCES

AVANT LE MATCH. — MAJOR TAYLOR ET JACQUELIN PÉNÉTRANT SUR LA PISTE.

19. Press photographers in attendance, Taylor and Jacquelin appear on the Parc des Princes track

Left:20. Training in Paris, 1901

Below: 21. With Jacquelin at the start, May 16, 1901

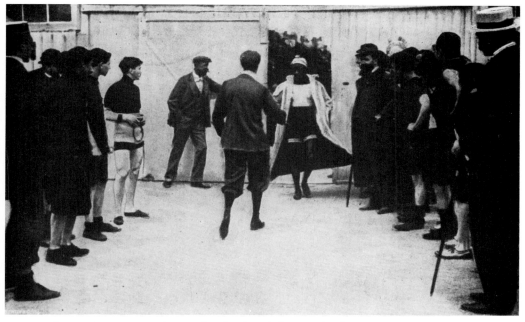

Above: 22. Leaving the track after his defeat in the first race against Jacquelin

Below: 23. With Jacquelin and trainer Buckner at the revenge match

Above: 24. With journalist Maurice Martin and painter Delancey-Ward, May 1901

Below: 25. The crowded stands at the Parc des Princes velodrome at the revenge race against Jacquelin

Facing page, top: 26. With oponents Bourotte and Grogna at Arras, 1902

Facing page, bottom: 28. Against Meyers and Ellegaard, Paris, 1903

Center: 27.
Typical track race
at Parc des
Princes
velodrome, Paris.

Top left:: 29. With Woody Hedspath in Paris, 1903

Bottom: 30. Nighttime race against Ellegaard at the Buffalo track in Paris

the top contenders for the championship honors following this race, fourth, in fact, behind Gardiner, Cooper, and Bald.

Back in Worcester, Taylor called, as he always did, to talk to the reporter from the *Worcester Telegram* and to give his impressions of his season up until then. "He says that it is rather an uphill game," the reporter wrote, "and he has yet to contend with the ill feeling with which he met last year among the cycling men. They have not yet got over the fact that he is of a darker hue than the rest of them, and while they are not so open in their dislike of him as they were last year, still they continue to make things unpleasant for him."

"I am having my troubles, if any one should ask you, and the fact that I do not look so white as some of them is yet evident," Taylor confided to the *Telegram* reporter:

I am riding faster this year than I was last, and that has saved me a good many times. I simply ride away from the rest of the bunch and do not give them a chance to pocket me, which is so disagreeable to a rider and makes it impossible to win a race. It always falls to my lot to set the pace, and this I always do to save any mixups which might occur if I remained in the bunch and gave someone else the chance of setting the pace. And it is not always pleasant to have to push out in the lead, for though I am stronger than I ever was, still it tells on a rider at the finish and takes a whole lot of strength. But it cannot be helped, and it must be done if I want to win, and by that you see I ride the race from the crack of the pistol till the finish. ... That is the way I have won all my races this season. There are some of the riders who have shown me more consideration, but the rest are just about as bad as they ever were.[23]

At the beginning of August, Taylor raced in Indianapolis, where the League of American Wheelmen Convention was meeting that year. It was the first time he had raced there since 1896, when he had returned home with Munger to break records on the new Capital City track. Naturally, the hometown crowd was rooting for him, and his rivals did everything they could to prevent him from winning in his own city.

Taylor did not, in fact, win any outstanding victories at the Newby Oval, a brand new track built especially for the occasion, and had to be content with consistent second and third places. The extra points he earned for these places were enough, however, to elevate him to tie for second position in the championship standings. In Indianapolis,

USA, 1898

he was warmly welcomed by his old employers, Hay and Willits, and Hearsey. The black community of Indianapolis feted him one night at a 'smoker' at the Herculean Club, and another night,the See-Saw Cycling Club gave a dinner-dance in his honor and presented him with a medal worth $90.

At Green Bay, Wisconsin, where all the crack racers competed after Indianapolis, Taylor made a clean sweep of the two races he entered and slipped securely into second place in the championship ratings. "Major Taylor, the little colored wonder, who has caused such a stir in the cycling world," said a newspaper report, "never rode better in his life than this afternoon, when he made a double win of the $1/3$ - mile and 1-mile professional races. The colored whirlwind brought out a round of hearty applause when he won. The southern race problem did not seem to be in it in the bicycle races."[24]

A T THE END OF AUGUST, Taylor and the Welshman Jimmy Michael, probably the best paid professional cyclist in the world that year, met in a special paced match race at Manhattan Beach, consisting of the best of three 1-mile heats, paced, from a standing start. It was promoted by his own employer, the American Cycle Racing Association, and both riders made a concession in agreeing to meet the other. Michael was a far more experienced pace follower but usually over long distances, while Taylor was a much stronger sprinter who had very little experience at paced racing.

It was the first time Taylor competed against an established international star, and his defeat of Michael on that occasion was the first stepping stone to his own international career. Taylor called the race one of his greatest achievements. Not only did he beat Michael resoundingly in two of the three heats, winning $1,000 in the process, but he twice established a new world record for 1-mile, with a standing start. The faster of his two record rides, 1 mile in 1 minute $41^2/5$ seconds beat the old record of 1 minute $43^2/5$ seconds, a speed of 34.81 mph.

As the two riders prepared for the final deciding heat in the dusky light of the early evening, "the onlookers almost held their breath as the lumbering machines came flying down the track prepared to pick up the riders, who stood motionless at the line. Michael looked cool but pale, like a monarch who realized that a crisis was at hand and that a supreme effort must be made to protect his crown of state and glory. The chocolate-colored skin of Taylor fairly shone in the dim light, his splendid muscular development being particularly noticeable. While not a big fellow himself, Taylor looked almost a giant compared to his little hundred-pound opponent, who had been the cycling king for so long."[25]

It was an astounding performance, news of which was immediately wired to Europe, and it elevated Taylor to a new level of prominence. For the first time he was now internationally famous.

Almost all the important daily newspapers in America carried the syndicated story about the record-breaking rides, hailing them as spectacular and astounding. And a glow of pride in Taylor's achievements was evident for the first time. TAYLOR IS A WONDER. PHENOMENAL PERFORMANCE IN A BICYCLE RACE, headlined the *New York Journal*. TAYLOR SMASHES WORLD'S RECORD. FAMOUS COLORED CYCLIST GOES THE FASTEST MILE EVER RIDDEN FROM STANDING START, said another newspaper. "Taylor's victory over Michael has been the chief topic of conversation among wheelmen since the race was run on Saturday," a third newspaper reported, "and it is safe to say that no more popular win upon a cycle path has been recorded since Zimmerman's days. ... For the first time in the history of cycle racing a colored lad enjoys the distinction of premiership among American racing men, of having smashed the world's record for the one mile."[26]

This victory and the resulting publicity gave a huge boost to Taylor's morale and popularity, a fact which one of the East Coast newspapers was quick to point out. "Coming as it has, just after the successful efforts of certain race meet managers to debar Taylor from their tracks," it said:

> Taylor's victory on Saturday has probably done much to convince many cyclists that there was much truth in the boy's charges against his fellow riders, for it is safe to argue that a chap capable of such speed as he has recorded against Michael should long ago have stood at the head of the list of circuit riders. ... The demand from many sources that the Racing Board take steps to stop any such injustice in future will, no doubt, now be more urgent."[27]

Immediately after this sensational victory, Brady issued a new challenge to match Taylor against Michael at any distance up to 100 miles for a prize somewhere between $5,000 and $10,000. The public announcement of the challenge "was received with tumultuous shouts

USA, 1898

by the assemblage, and the dusky victor was lionized when his record time was made known."

In gratitude to his two teams of white pacemakers, Taylor divided his prize money with them. He understood that any one of them could have affected the result of the race by failing to give his maximum effort. "All of my pacemakers against Michael were white, while I was black," he wrote, "but color evidently was not a drawback in this instance. Those fine sportsmen, who paced me in that epoch-making race against Michael, admired me as an athlete, respected me as a man and gave their utmost ... that I might achieve victory."

Taylor's new status, the fact that at the tender age of nineteen he was the holder of a world record and was evidently standing on the edge of athletic greatness that summer of 1898, was remarked by many of the journalists who reported the world record rides. Many of the accounts described him as "phenomenal" and "a wonder."

"If you fail to recognize Taylor by his baptismal name, Marshall, think of him as Major Taylor and as the possible bicycle champion of America," said one writer in an article entitled MAJOR TAYLOR, THE EBONY STREAK.

> With his great bursts of speed, it is by no means impossible that Taylor may become the all-round champion of the United States, possibly of the world. He is as sound physically as a good dollar, and would rather ride a race than eat. The white men had better keep an eye open or their colors will yet be worn by the streak of ebony."[28]

The brilliant success of Taylor's world record rides gave rise to a dispute about money with his manager and backer, William Brady. Taylor felt that his contract with the American Cycle Racing Association did not adequately compensate him because he was responsible for paying the large expenses for the maintenance of his pacing teams. Taylor was so incensed by Brady's refusal to raise his earnings that he returned to Worcester and prepared to negotiate with four or five other professional teams interested in promoting him. The disagreement was temporarily patched up, however, when his employers made financial concessions and gave him better terms. But his relationship with them was not very secure for the rest of the year.

The season moved inexorably toward its conclusion, and the race for the championship, with Taylor in second place behind Bald, was more fiercely contested. At Springfield, in early September, Taylor beat

Floyd MacFarland and Arthur Gardiner. At New Haven he won $200 and a first and a second place, the other riders trying desperately but unsuccessfully to 'pocket' him throughout the racing.

In Philadelphia, on September 17, Taylor won both the $1/3$-mile and the 2-mile races – $300 for an afternoon's work –, while his fiercest rival, Bald, suffering from the effects of a recent crash, could only manage fifth place in one race. In spite of the threats directed at Taylor that day, he was surprised when all his white rivals showed up in his dressing room to congratulate him for his wins that day. "It was the first time in my career that any of the so-called 'big' competitors had ever congratulated me for any of my achievements on the tracks," he wrote. "It was the first manifestation of good sportsmanship on the part of my opponents. I felt that their action was a demonstration of their admiration and respect for me as a man."

With almost a month still to run in the championship contest, Taylor's superiority seemed almost unassailable. "The unbeatable colored boy ... won over the best fields of the season," said a report of these Philadelphia races. "Taylor was as superior to his rivals today as was Zimmerman superior to his in the days of long ago."[29] If he continued in such incredible form, it seemed inevitable that the championship would be his.

BUT EVENTS were brewing once again in the organization of professional racing. After years of continual disputes, the tension and animosity between the riders on the tracks and the League of American Wheelmen bureaucrats in their office in New York City finally reached a breaking point. The disputes were rooted in the basic fact that an organization established by and for amateurs in the early days of cycling found itself involved twenty years later in the day-to-day regulation and administration of a huge and complex professional sport which, in the short space of five years, had grown dramatically. The LAW Racing Board had an extremely difficult, if not impossible, job trying to satisfy all the different interests in a complicated, far-flung network of clubs, riders, track owners, and promoters.

The professional riders declared open war on the League at the end of September. In Trenton, where they had gathered to contest one of the final crucial race meets of the 1898 national circuit, feelings were running very high. The grudges the riders had against Albert Mott, the Chairman of the Racing Board, were becoming more vocal and in-

USA, 1898

tense. The fact that Mott had allowed Taylor into the sport for a second season and that the black rider was at that moment poised in second position, threatening to beat Bald and all the other riders for the championship title, aroused and disturbed them more than any other grievance. If Taylor won enough points in the remaining races, the rest of the riders would suffer the disgrace and indignity of having been defeated by this upstart black nineteen-year-old. The fault was the Racing Board's, they reasoned, for having admitted him in the first place.

As soon as all the racing men arrived at Trenton on the special train that brought them to the races from all over the country, they assembled at the Trenton House hotel for an important meeting. The scene on the evening of September 25 was a lively one, reported a correspondent for the *Philadelphia Press.* "Cycling champions, their friends and admirers were flying about like so many busy bees. The sole topic of conversation was the formation of the new association, and many were the sarcastic remarks passed about the L.A.W."[30]

Eddie Bald, three-time sprint champion and leading rider in the championship tables at that moment, was elected chairman of the conference. Taylor was there, together with all his rivals: Tom Cooper, Floyd MacFarland, Orlando Stevens, Arthur Gardiner, Owen Kimble, and Nat Butler. The official grievances against the LAW were discussed, a petition drawn up and signed by the majority of the riders present, and an agreement reached on the formation of a new organization to be called, provisionally, the American Racing Cyclists Union (ARCU).

"We, the undersigned, professional bicycle riders and trainers of America," the petition read, "band ourselves together for mutual protection and the furtherance of our interests." A crucial item in the petition was that "where local opinion permits, there shall be racing on any day of the week," a statement in favor of Sunday racing, which the LAW had firmly resisted.

Taylor listened to the proceedings with curiosity and apprehension. He understood very well the objections his white rivals had to many of the policies of the LAW. But he realized that there was a hidden agenda to the proceedings, one directed at him and designed to interrupt the championship process. He knew how intensely most of the white riders detested him and how angry they were at the LAW

USA, 1898

for having admitted him and for allowing him to climb so high in the sport.

What would be the consequences for him if he were to throw in his lot with the rebellion? After all, the LAW had treated him well. The Racing Board had agreed to register him and to include him in the professional ranks. Chairman Mott had in fact been particularly solicitous of his interests that year.

Taylor refused at first to sign the petition . He was not alone in his hesitations. Titus, Kimble, Freeman, and Nat Butler – all top riders – also refused at first. A *Worcester Telegram* reporter, who was at the Trenton meeting, asked Taylor why he had refused to join the rebels. "Why should I?" he replied:

> They say that they are hanging together, and that I should be with them. They have hung together so well that they have shut me out of tracks. They went to the promoters and said, "We will ride if you don't let the nigger ride" and now they ask me to join them against the League. The League has ... opened the tracks of Baltimore and Washington and other southern cities to me, and I just stick by the League. ...[31]

After the races at Trenton, which were interrupted and spoiled by torrential rain, the riders moved on to Philadelphia where they held another meeting on September 28, to solidify their rebellion. By then, Taylor had done some soul-searching. It was a difficult and threatening situation. He had been supported and protected by the LAW and would be accused of disloyalty if he left it. But if the rebel movement succeeded and he refused to join it, he would have no more opponents in the championship. The League would certainly award him the championship title since Bald had gone over to the rebels, but the victory would be a hollow one.

"Had I remained in the L.A.W., I would surely have gained the top of the ladder," Taylor told a reporter from *Cycle Age*, "but everybody would have laughed had I won the title against mediocre men, and I couldn't stand that."[32] Nearly all his main opponents were deserting the LAW, and they were the men he was most interested in racing against. So Taylor changed his mind and applied for membership in the new organization. After a long discussion, he was accepted.

Despite the underlying logic to his decision, it was an unexpected change of direction, considering the animosity of his white rivals. And he was soon to discover that there was a devious and divided strategy behind his election into the rebel movement. A few of the white riders wanted to see him continue in the sport, recognizing his athletic abilities and his right to compete, but the majority were trying to lure him away from the shelter of the LAW in order to separate him from its support and backing. In fact, they had the specific intention of renewing their harassment of him in the new organization.

The white riders were determined, at any cost it seemed, to exclude him from professional bicycle racing. That is what most of them wanted. Though there were certainly many disputes going on between the riders and the LAW, the threat of Taylor's dominant position at the end of the season of 1898 was at the very center of this turmoil within the sport. Newspaper reports strongly suggest that the white riders were prepared to take the risk of tearing apart the structure of the sport rather than see Taylor emerge victorious as the first black champion of America. The feeling against him had never been stronger. The white riders would not accept him as a peer. It was unthinkable to them that he should win the championship.

Whatever hopes Taylor might have had that his situation within the new association would improve were soon dashed. Far from improving, it became rapidly worse, fulfilling his worst fears and proving to him that he had made a big mistake in deciding to go over to the rebel movement. Soon it became clear to him that he was now at the mercy of an organization made up almost entirely of his rivals and enemies, against whom he had no redress.

His problems intensified as soon as the riders left Philadelphia for the two final race meets of the championship, in St. Louis and Cape Girardeau, Missouri, which were being held under the auspices of the rebel organization. Going into these final races, Taylor was still in second position, only a few points behind champion Bald, but not so far behind that he could not overtake him with several victories and thus clinch the championship.

St. Louis was the city where Taylor's 1897 championship chances had come to an end when his entry form had been refused because of the 'color line'. Once again, in 1898, he encountered bitter racism and discrimination. He was unable to find hotel accommodation and was forced, therefore, to stay "... with a colored family, and even though I was on a very strict diet, I did not feel free to ask my hostess to rearrange menus in my favor. Instead, I made a long trip three times a day for my meals which I secured for several days in a restaurant at Union Station. After several meals at this location, the restaurant manager very rudely informed me that I would not be welcomed henceforth and so instructed the head waiter who was one of my own color. This, however, the waiter refused to do and was promptly discharged for that reason."

Despite these difficulties, at the races held on October 8, Taylor won his heat in the 5-mile event. But the final was delayed by rain that day and could not be run off in the darkness of the evening. Riders and officials decided to extend the racing into the next day, Sunday, even though Taylor and several other riders objected strongly to racing on Sundays.

Taylor had in fact been promised by the rebels when he agreed to join them in Philadelphia that there would be no Sunday racing, and this decision in St. Louis was an obvious and immediate betrayal. It was the first serious test of his religious principles and Taylor was adamant – he would not break the promise he had made to himself. He did not race in the final of the 5-mile race that Sunday and thereby gave up his chance, on that occasion, of drawing level with Bald in the 1898 championship. "The colored champion does not say in so many words that the American Racing Cyclists' Union took this action to freeze him out of taking a big slice of the honors," said a Chicago newspaper about the incident, "but that he believes as much cannot be doubted."[33]

Taylor was so disgusted with the St. Louis betrayal that he was ready to pack his bicycle and return to Worcester, when Henry Dunlop, the promoter of the forthcoming races at Cape Girardeau, about 100 miles south of St. Louis, approached him with an offer. Dunlop told him that he himself owned the hotel where the riders would be staying in Cape Girardeau, and that he personally guaranteed that Taylor would be welcomed there. On the basis of this promise, Taylor reluctantly signed the entry form for the event and went on to Cape Girardeau with the white riders.

Dunlop was especially interested in having Taylor at his races because the black residents of Cape Girardeau, who had been denied the chance of seeing him the year before, had promised to contribute $400 in prizes on the condition that the color bar be relaxed and Taylor allowed to start. But when he arrived at the hotel, Dunlop told him that he had made arrangements for him to stay with a black family nearby. Taylor reminded Dunlop of their agreement, but he refused to honor it. Taylor decided that since Dunlop had broken faith with him, he was no longer obligated to participate in the championship races the next day.

Disgusted and disheartened, Taylor decided to leave as soon as possible, to abandon the races at Cape Girardeau and his Championship chances. Early in the morning, he went to the railroad station to buy a ticket for Indianapolis, only to be met there by Dunlop and several of the white riders.

Dunlop was caught in a trap created by his own double-dealing and by the confusing and complex racial animosities of the time. He had set out to stage a race meeting including Taylor, in an atmosphere that was basically hostile to the idea. He wanted the prize money the black people of Cape Girardeau had offered because they wanted to see Taylor compete, and therefore he needed Taylor urgently at that moment. He knew that the prize money would be withdrawn if Taylor left and that his whole promotion would be threatened with collapse.

"They told me," wrote Taylor later of the heated encounter at the railroad station, "that if I failed to ride in the races that afternoon they would see to it that I was barred forever from the racing tracks of the country." He told them firmly that he would not race and did not care about the consequences. And he left Cape Girardeau for Indianapolis. The disappointed black people of the town withdrew the $400 they had promised and the riders were forced to compete for much reduced purses, which ruined Dunlop's promotion. Taylor had broken an important contractual agreement with the ARCU, however, and this particular conflict would return to haunt him and create a very serious problem in 1900.

To Taylor it was becoming more and more clear that the object of all the machinations against him was, quite simply, to harass him whenever possible and, thus, to exclude him from the profession.

"As time went on," he wrote, "I became convinced that the color line was drawn against me in St. Louis and Cape Girardeau by hotel proprietors, when in reality the strings were pulled by my co-racers.

They evidently felt that I was a good enough rider to land the championship out on the track and that the best way to ensure one of their number corralling the honors was to have me kept off the race course through some ruse. I was suspicious that this plan was afoot following my experience in St. Louis. When the brazen Cape Girardeau trick was pulled on me, I became convinced of their diabolical plan and made up my mind that I would never ride in another race."

TAYLOR LEFT Cape Girardeau in disgust. It was a bitter disappointment, the low point of a tremendously successful season. Shortly before his twentieth birthday, he had been deprived, for the second season running, of the chance to become champion of America, and he had been much closer than in 1897. The riders and western promoters had treated him with contempt. The racist tricks and dishonesty had been even more blatant than the previous year.

He had been manipulated into leaving the League of American Wheelmen and then excluded from the rebel organization, the American Racing Cyclists Union, as well. The attempts of the white cyclists to leave him completely stranded, without professional affiliation, had temporarily succeeded. "The affair is greatly to the discredit of the outlaws and will do more to hurt their cause than anything else that has been done," said a League official from New York to a reporter from the *Worcester Telegram*. "Taylor was induced to desert the League and join the insurgents in order that he might be thrown down on both sides. I have heard it said that it was a case of 'anything to *do* the nigger.'"[34]

The championship was in a state of chaos at the end of the 1898 season. The breakaway movement had caused unresolvable confusion. With two separate organizations vying for control of the professional sport and each running its own races, it was impossible to decide the championship. The four leading contestants – Bald, Taylor, Gardiner, and Cooper – all advanced good claims, and Tom Butler, who had remained faithful to the LAW, was in the end declared the 1898 champion. But the championship process had been fatally and irreparably disrupted.

The only thing that could be said with absolute certainty was that Taylor had been prevented from having the opportunity to emerge as a clear winner at precisely the moment when he had the best chance of all the contestants to do so.

From Indianapolis, Taylor wired Chairman Mott, asking to be readmitted to the LAW, which Mott agreed to as long as he paid a $150 fine. The ARCU, the 'outlaw' movement, vowed at the same time to blacklist him permanently for what they claimed was his failure to fulfill his contractual obligations to Dunlop, the promoter at Cape Girardeau. Even Taylor's relations with his employers for most of the season, the American Cycle Racing Association, appear to have been in a state of collapse at this time. It was a bureaucratic nightmare for the young sprinter. Instead of praise and encouragement for his outstanding achievements during the season, he was experiencing confusion and rejection as his reward.

TAYLOR WAS rescued from this predicament by the well-known Waltham Manufacturing Company, whose 'Orient' bicycle he had been riding for much of the season, and by Harry Sager, the young owner of the Sager Gear Company, of Rochester, New York, who had collaborated with the Waltham company in the development of a chainless bicycle. Since September 1898, in fact, Taylor had been testing the Sager chainless bicycle in some of his races and was the first professional racer to use it in competition.

Sager agreed to pay the $150 fine to have Taylor reinstated in the LAW and made him a business proposition. He wanted him to test and promote his invention by breaking records on it. In the intense competition for technological development in the bicycle industry and the battle for the American consumer's dollar, the chainless bicycle offered a bright new possibility, and there was extended discussion in the cycling press about its advantages and disadvantages. The main benefit it offered, at a time when roads were dusty and muddy, was a totally enclosed transmission, which would not become clogged and damaged by dirt or need constant cleaning.[35]

With the backing of the Sager Gear Company and the manufacturers of the 'Orient' and with a new manager, Mr. Ward, Taylor went again to Philadelphia's Woodside Park track, "accompanied by a complete battery of pacing artillery." For nearly two weeks, in the calm but cold, often freezing, November weather, where trainers and officials stood around in overcoats blowing on their fingers and the pacemakers "huddled together in a small dressing room, hugging the stoves," Taylor succeeded in establishing a series of new world records for distances from a quarter mile to two miles, paced by fifteen of the best and fastest pacemakers in the business, including his former Boston teammates, Nat Butler and Burns Pierce.

The most coveted record was the 1-mile flying start, which was then held by the French rider Edouard Taylore, with a time of 1 minute 32 $^3/_5$ seconds. Sager promised Taylor $10,000 if he could bring the time

USA, 1898

for the mile down below 1 minute 30 seconds. Twice, Taylor reduced the record, first to 1 minute 32 seconds, and then on the last day, he succeeded in taking another $^1/_5$ second from it, riding the fastest mile in the history of cycling. With the temperature close to freezing, Taylor "gave a really marvelous exhibition of riding and astounded the hundreds of spectators and officials," wrote *Cycle Age*. He was never shaken from his pace, and no matter how ragged the pickups might be, he closed again and again gaps which would have been impossible to other record holders."[36] He did not get below the 1 minute 30 second mark, however, and many of the people who watched the speed trials and heard him shouting for more speed from his pacemakers concluded that only a motorized pacing machine could give him the additional speed he was capable of realizing.

"Like the breaking of daylight from the darkness of night, the dawn of the mile-a-minute bicycle has appeared," said the *Philadelphia Press.*

> On a chainless wheel, which the cycling hosts cried down in its infancy, that wonderful racing man, Major Taylor, yesterday brought the world's figures for the mile down to a minute, thirty-one and four-fifths seconds. This remarkable feat of cycling, which a short while since physicians of note and the know-alls of cycledom stamped as an impossibility, was performed yesterday afternoon. ...
>
> Several hundred spectators witnessed the grand race that little Major Taylor made against Father Time, and everyone agreed that he is the most wonderful cyclist of the age. It was speed, the like of which has never before been witnessed, ... and as the little colored boy followed the terrific pace set by the crews on the multicycles, it was evident to everyone that no human pace is fast enough for him."[37]

Taylor was deluged with telegrams after he succeeded in breaking the 1-mile record for the final time on November 16. The world records were athletic feats which no white riders or bureaucrats could take away from him. Newspaper reports were full of superlatives. A Wonderful Rider of Unknown Possibilities, said one headline. Major Taylor is a Cycling Wonder, said another. "His riding at Woodside stamps him as the fastest man in the world. No one knows what speed possibilities are concealed within those lithe limbs of the colored boy."[38]

USA, 1898

Once again, Taylor had shown that he had the athletic ability and tenacity to fulfill the hopes and expectations of his sponsors. Breaking world records with fifteen pacemakers – three teams of five riders, all of whom had to be fed and housed – was not cheap. In addition, mechanics and masseurs had to be hired and the rent of the track paid, not to mention Taylor's salary of $100 a week and a prize of $500 for the 1-mile record itself. It cost between $3,000 and $5,000 for the record rides in Philadelphia.[39]

When Taylor arrived home in Worcester from Philadelphia, he was a local hero. He enjoyed the enviable reputation of being officially the fastest bicycle rider, the fastest self-propelled human being, in the world. The *Worcester Spy* called his end-of-season triumph "the greatest series of record-breaking rides ever undertaken by any cyclist," adding that "... the colored lad from this city has fairly astounded the cycling world by his two weeks' work in Philadelphia."[40]

By the end of 1898, Taylor held seven world records, at distances from $1/4$ to 2 miles, including two of the most prestigious, the 1-mile, paced, standing start (1 minute $41^2/5$ seconds) and the 1-mile, paced, flying start (1 minute $32^3/5$ seconds). He was also the most hated, the most admired, the most controversial, the most talked about, quite simply, the most famous bicycle racer in America. He had become the most prominent black American athlete, and one of the most celebrated black Americans.

Taylor's career was propelled forward by a seemingly unstoppable momentum. At the age of twenty, he was undeniably a world-class athlete, the fastest bicycle racer over short distances in America, and one of the two or three fastest in the world. Racist opposition had constantly threatened him and slowed his progress. The uncompromising deviousness of his white rivals had denied him, for two consecutive years, the possibility of becoming champion of America.

But his phenomenal speed, his courage and determination, and his warm but confident personality had made him into an extremely popular, highly marketable, star in the show-business world of bicycle racing. There was no shortage of businessmen in the bicycle world prepared to back his career. Major Taylor had weathered the worst waves of the storm of racial opposition and was evidently in the sport to stay.

USA, 1898

7

THE FASTEST BICYCLE RIDER IN THE WORLD

THE FAME Major Taylor had won for his 1-mile world records in November 1898 was an asset his sponsor, Harry Sager intended to make good use of in publicizing his chainless bicycle. Sager decided to send the famous black rider around the country during the winter months to promote the much-discussed new departure in bicycle technology. Taylor would help the company establish dealerships, become in fact a traveling salesman, carrying with him for display the actual bicycle on which he had broken the records. Sager had high hopes for his invention in the coming year and great faith in Taylor.

In Waltham, Massachusetts, the Waltham Manufacturing Company gave away 1,000 photographs of racing cyclists and 1,000 handsome hat pins to the men and women who visited its store on Moody Street. There they advertised a GREAT EXHIBITION OF CYCLES AND PLENTY OF MUSIC, and promoted Taylor's presence. Their publicity proudly announced, "The famous rider arrived here yesterday and is demonstrating the merits of the Famous Sager Gear Orient Chainless. Friday and Saturday he will exhibit the Sager Gear to the ladies in the Ladies Department."

In Worcester, the chainless bicycle was exhibited at the Casey Brothers store on Main Street, and a large crowd showed up for the opening. The shop window was decorated with potted plants and flowers and the interior hung with the red and purple colors of the Orient Company. Taylor was, of course, the center of attraction, explaining the good points of the Sager gear with such skill and affability that it was clear the manufacturers had gotten themselves a topnotch salesman as well as a world-class rider.

In January 1899, on his way back to New York from the important Chicago Cycle Show, Taylor stopped off in Indianapolis for a few days to visit his family. There he exhibited the Sager bicycle at the shop of his old employer, Harry Hearsey, where, just a few years before, he had taught bicycle riding to beginners. Questioned by the *Indianapolis Sentinel* about his plans for the upcoming season, Taylor said he intended to go after records in America and perhaps go to Europe in the fall. If he went abroad, he said, it would be in quest of European records at shorter distances, but he would not race in France because "all the cycle racing is done on Sundays, and one thing that I shall never do is race on the Sabbath. I am not a religious crank nor anything else excepting a man who has his own ideas as to right and wrong, and who, believing as I do, that cycle racing on Sunday is not right, will refrain from taking part in any contests on that day." Taylor complained bitterly about his treatment at the hands of what he called "the outlaw crowd" the previous fall and their betrayal on the question of Sunday racing. Their behavior, he said, "satisfied me that the sooner I got out and back to the L.A.W., the better for me, and now that I am back I'm going to remain where the sanctioning body and racing board is strong enough to say a thing and stand by it." [1]

Taylor's most prominent public appearances during that winter were at the two big bicycle trade shows held every year in Chicago and New York. These shows were a central event in the world of bicycle manufacturing and bicycle racing. Here all the commercial energy and brainpower of the industry were concentrated for a few days, with every important company in the industry setting up booths to display their latest models and products. There was an intense exchange of ideas and information, each company vying with its competitors to produce something new, better, and different. Thousands of catalogs were given away, contracts worth millions of dollars were signed, and the cycling press brought out luxurious editions of their publications filled with advertisements that explored the smallest details of bicycle technology.

It was familiar territory to Taylor, who had been attending shows with Birdie Munger since the winter of 1895. As the crowds passed by Harry Sager's booth, they offered Taylor their congratulations and he showed off the chainless bicycle. He also wandered among the colorful booths, greeting old friends and avoiding some old enemies too. And, reunited with Munger, his friend and mentor, he had a chance to talk over some of the more serious problems of his painfully complicated and disorganized 1898 season and how he might avoid falling into new traps in the future. It was gratifying to be among

USA—CANADA, 1899

friends and supporters, but both he and Munger understood very well that the problems of being the only black professional cycling champion in America would not simply evaporate overnight just because he was now the world record holder. What was most important was to make careful and serious plans for the future.

During his travels that winter, Taylor was also welcomed and entertained by black social clubs in many of the cities he visited. They were all anxious to meet the famous cycling star. "Every colored man and woman is proud of Major Taylor, the champion bicyclist," said the columnist for the "Afro-American Notes" in the *Pittsburgh Press*. "About 45 members of the Loendt Club had a very gala time Thursday evening. Major Taylor was the guest of honor, and he had a shake all around with the boys." [2]

Black people, of course, understood very well the prejudice that Taylor was encountering and the abuse directed at him. His youth and education and his stand on Sunday racing made him all the more attractive to his own people. Blacks admired him intensely and cheered him frantically at races. They followed newspaper reports of his struggles to establish himself in bicycle racing. To them he was a hero. Like other black sports champions much later – Jack Johnson, Joe Louis, Jessie Owens, and Jackie Robinson – Taylor set an example of courage and determination that inspired them. He demonstrated that a black man could excel and make his own way in the world. This perspective was not, of course, reported in the white press, but wherever the black community congregated, Taylor's name was on everyone's lips. In a world where few blacks ever emerged from anonymity, his bicycle racing feats and especially his world records were a unique achievement. Among people of his own race, he enjoyed flattering praise and encouragement.

But socializing at smoky evening receptions was not an ideal environment for an ambitious world-class athlete, and by the time he returned to Worcester, the *Worcester Telegram* reported that he was "another member of the chubby brigade. His work for his gear company has kept him so busy that he had no time to do even light gymnasium work, and the result is that the colored whirlwind is almost elephantine." [3] Soon, Taylor was busy training as usual at the YMCA gym, working to get himself in shape for the coming season. He always insisted on the crucial importance of training and followed a meticulous and disciplined routine of lifting weights, skipping,

USA—CANADA, 1899

boxing, and running. "When the spring rolled around," he wrote, "I was in excellent condition for what was destined to be my greatest season on the American tracks."

Taylor's prospects for 1899 looked good indeed. The dreadful confusion of the year before was behind him as he now had security within the ranks of the League of American Wheelmen and Harry Sager's sponsorship. Many manufacturers were forced to limit their sponsorship of racing in the face of the serious recession that followed the boom of the mid-1890s, so Taylor was one of the few professional riders sponsored that year, and he continued to publicize the Sager gear as it was launched into the marketplace.

Taylor's goals for 1899, what he called "a heroic-sized order," were a culmination of everything he had set out to achieve in bicycle racing – to win the two most prestigious honors: the world championship, to be held in Montreal, and the American championship, which, through no fault of his own, kept slipping through his fingers. He wanted to lower the 1-mile world record to below 1 minute 20 seconds and, if possible, to persuade both Eddie Bald and Tom Cooper, two of his most bitter white rivals, to meet him in match races. He had always maintained that he could beat them, but Bald and Cooper had steadfastly refused to join him in such contests.

With competitive fitness within his grasp, the scene for the 1899 season was finally set when Taylor went to Syracuse with Munger to sign a contract with the E. C. Stearns Company, manufacturer of a bicycle advertised as the 'Yellow Fellow.' Taylor, Munger, and Sager had been negotiating a sponsorship with another Syracuse company, the Olive Wheel Company, but the deal they worked out with Stearns was in the end a better one. Stearns agreed to build Taylor's bicycles using the Sager gear chainless mechanism. They weighed about 20 pounds and had an 88-inch gear for sprinting and a 120-inch gear for longer, paced races.

Stearns also agreed to build Taylor a revolutionary steam-powered pacing tandem, behind which he could attack world records and challenge the other leading exponents of paced racing. One reason Munger agreed to add the formal management of his now famous protégé to his many other responsibilities was his excitement over the extraordinary possibilities of the rapidly developing steam- and gasoline-powered pacing machines. Since setting his own records on the old high-wheel, Munger had been thoroughly obsessed with the idea of pushing at the boundaries of human athletic potential. Like any-one who had heard Taylor calling for more speed from his human-powered pacing teams during the 1898 record attempts, Munger knew that the only way the young champion could hope to achieve sub-stantially greater speeds was through the development of a success-ful, reliable, motorized pacing machine.

Munger's decision to resume his supervision of Taylor's racing career also grew out of their long winter discussions about his 1898 problems. Munger wanted to give him a firm and fatherly guiding hand athletically and to steer him through the treacherous and still unstable political quagmire of racial hostility within the sport. With Munger as his manager, Sager promising to back Taylor in match races against anyone he chose, and the capable Bert Hazard as his trainer, Taylor had a remarkable combination of talent and resources behind him that year.

"Taylor is looking in fine condition," said an optimistic report on the signing of the contract. "He said last night that he never felt bet-ter in his life."[4]

MEANWHILE, THE GREAT political battle for the control of profes-sional bicycle racing continued. In February, at the LAW Nation-al Assembly in Providence, League officials voted to retain their control of racing despite the strength and determination of the rebel move-ment. "The outcome of the battle, for which the L.A.W. and the N.C.A. have locked horns," said *Cycle Age*, "is the absorbing feature of dis-cussion now in the cycle racing world, not only in this country but the world over. The international championships are to be run at Montreal the coming season and there has been, is, and will be to a greater extent than ever before an interchange of visits among the champions of all countries, so cosmopolitan has cycle racing be-come."[5]

LAW officials believed that it was in the best interests of the sport to have it controlled by those who were not financially involved and by an established organization with a proven national reputation. The National Cycling Association, however, a larger, alternative organiza-tion, which included independent promoters and track owners, as well as the racing cyclists who had formed the rebel group, the ARCU, accused the League of gross mismanagement through ignorance and incompetence and maintained that racing should be organized by those who were most directly involved in it.

This political struggle had proved to be much more than just a bureaucratic affair to Taylor, for it had severely disrupted his 1898 season and would continue to have an impact on him during 1899, when he was one of the few leading riders to remain loyal to the LAW. Since the 'outlaws' were barred from League races, Taylor did not race that year against many of his fiercest rivals – Bald, Gardiner, Stevens, MacFarland, Kiser, and Cooper. While he was relieved to be free of their racism for the year, the forced separation from his old rivals meant that much of the 1899 racing season was less dramatic, especially from the spectator's point of view.

At the end of May, in case there were any lingering doubts in racing circles about their feelings towards Taylor, the 'outlaw' organization, the American Racing Cyclists Union, formally announced a 'color line,' refusing to admit blacks to membership. It was a ban directed specifically at Taylor since it was likely that the LAW would soon be forced to abandon its control over racing, and Taylor would then have to apply once again for affiliation with the rebels. This announcement by a sporting organization already very much in the news was both applauded and condemned by strongly worded newspaper editorials.

In New York, the *Morning Telegraph* carried an editorial under the headline THE BOYCOTT AGAINST MAJOR TAYLOR WAS TOO LONG DELAYED. The editor was "pleased to see this emphatic assertion of the superiority of the Caucasian over the Ethiopian," although he wished the white riders had boycotted Taylor before "the black whirlwind" had defeated them all. "It is, of course, a degradation for a white man to contest any point with a negro. It is worse than that, and becomes an absolute grief and social disaster when a negro persistently wins in the competitions."[6]

The editor of the *Syracuse Telegram*, however, disapproved of the ARCU ban. Although he patronizingly suggested that "it would be well for the colored man to spend his time on the school primer instead of on the bicycle racing track," he thought that the ban was dangerous and "a display of the same feeling that incited the people of the South to burn Sam Hose at the stake." He saw the racist treatment of Taylor as one more example of the racism in American society and took a firm stand on behalf of black people:

USA—CANADA, 1899

The condition of the colored man in America is one of the great questions for us to handle. All intelligent people know that we can't benefit
the state of the colored man by denying him the privileges we enjoy.
He has been treated like a beast too long. We must first make him know
that he is a man before we can educate him.

The colored man has always been denied the right to share in the fruits
of civilization with the white man. The school door has been closed
against him for generations, and he has been allowed to propagate in
ignorance. He has been forced to toil and not to study, and that is the
reason why the ordinary negro lacks the mental power of the ordinary
white man. The colored man should enjoy the same privileges as the
white man. He should be on an even footing with the white man. Education is the remedy the negro needs. ...

Uncle Sam allows the negro to serve him. ... If the negro is qualified
he should have the same position the white man can have. If he fulfills
all the requirements his color should not weigh against him. If he can
ride a bicycle or a horse, or handle a baseball as well as a white man,
he should not be denied the privilege of displaying his abilities.[7]

THE BUILDING and testing of the experimental steam-powered
pacing machines did not happen overnight, and there were many
disappointments early in the season.[8] Taylor matched himself against
Eddie McDuffie, star of middle-distance racing since the early 1890s.
In 1899, McDuffie was sponsored by the Pope Manufacturing Company and rode the 'Columbia' chainless bicycle, a rival machine to
Taylor's Sager gear chainless.

In Philadelphia, on May 27, at a meeting to inaugurate the cycling
season, Taylor and McDuffie were scheduled to race 15 miles behind
motor-pace for a purse of $1,000. Ten thousand people crowded into
the track to see the revolutionary machines. Taylor had to borrow a
French petroleum-driven pacing tandem for the occasion, because the
steam machine promised by the Stearns Company was not yet ready.
The noisy French machine was reliable, but not quite as fast as
McDuffie's completely silent steam tandem made by the Stanley Company.

But the experimental machines were temperamental, and the crowd
was disappointed when McDuffie's broke down several times, cough-
ing, spluttering, and spewing steam dangerously over its two riders.
"It was," said one reporter, "a great opportunity lost to impress the

public with the beauties of cycling as a sport."[9] To give the crowd something for its money, the two stars rode a 5-mile pursuit race, which Taylor lost, and an agreement was made to race again in Boston.

Interest in these races was intense because most spectators had never seen motorized pacing machines before. But at the Charles River track in Cambridge, on June 17, the much-heralded 25-mile race was another farce. Taylor's petrol pacing machine went perfectly for a while, but McDuffie's Stanley steamer did not oblige. The race was started and restarted. The crowd booed and hissed. After his pacing machine also failed, Taylor set out to complete the distance without it but was stopped by the referee after $12^1/2$ miles because the frustrated spectators had swarmed onto the track. IT WAS A FIZZLE, complained a newspaper headline. THE 25-MILE MOTOR-PACED RACE DIDN'T PAN OUT.[10] Stanley announced later that some oil had found its way into the boiler of McDuffie's machine, causing the mechanical problems.

The victory for greater speed would not be won so easily. The riders were ready, but the machines were not. While Taylor was occupied with other engagements, such as racing Tom and Nat Butler on the LAW circuit, McDuffie persisted in tinkering with his pacing machines. On June 30, at New Bedford, he succeeded in clipping a miniscule two-fifths of a second off Taylor's 1898 human-paced world record of 1 minute $31^4/5$ seconds, using mechanical pace for the first time. McDuffie was throwing down the gauntlet to Taylor, whose most prized possession had been taken from him. The Taylor—McDuffie rivalry was to become one of the hottest contests of the year.

THE SAME DAY McDuffie broke Taylor's world record, June 30, the Brooklyn cyclist Charles Murphy established another record, which set the whole country talking. Taylor was, in fact, dethroned twice on the same day from his position as the fastest bicycle rider in the world. Murphy's ride, however, eclipsed McDuffie's in its daring.

Murphy rode a mile in $57^4/5$ seconds behind a train at Maywood, Long Island. It was the highest speed ever achieved by a human being propelled by his own muscle power. Murphy's sensational ride, at a speed of 62.28 mph, is recorded in history books as an extraordinary combination of courage and folly. It was symbolic of a period when racing cyclists were setting more and more spectacular goals for themselves, paced by whatever machine could push up their speed. The striving of bicycle racers for greater speed through the late 1890s and the first decade of the twentieth century contributed greatly to the wider quest for the development of speed and efficiency in other, more sophisticated kinds of transportation, first motorcycles, then automobiles, and, finally, airplanes.

Murphy's ride was foolhardy in the extreme, and he was very lucky to come out of the experience alive. Its suicidal potential and near-fatal outcome made it all the more newsworthy, of course. Murphy rode on a track of heavy wooden boards laid down between railroad tracks behind a steam locomotive owned by the Long Island Railroad. On the back of the train a special platform was built to partially surround and shelter the rider.

After several trial runs, with his wife and children and a crowd of several thousand watching, the twenty-eight-year-old Murphy succeeded in riding a measured mile at more than 60 mph on a bicycle. During the 57-second ride, the greatest danger to Murphy was the turbulence created by the train. If he had fallen far behind the thunderous bulk of the locomotive, the fierce gusts of turbulence created in its wake would have tossed him about like a helpless feather. Crashing at 60 mph on a three-and-one-half-foot-wide board track was not a pleasant prospect.

Murphy's face was contorted with agony from the effort of staying in the safety of the slipstream of the train. Struggling for control, he rode unsteadily and his bicycle wandered from one edge of the board track to the other, with spectators watching from the back of the train certain that he would crash and be killed. As he almost lost contact with the train, Murphy wrote later, "All kinds of unpleasant things passed through my mind. I saw ridicule, contempt, disgrace and a life dream gone up in smoke. ... I raised my thought to God to help me. My prayer was answered, and an indescribable feeling came upon me. It was the hand of God. New vigor and energy with each push of the pedals. I felt better and stronger. I could see myself gaining the lost ground. Oh how I suffered! It was a hot, fast, serious, life-or death contract on my hands."[11]

At the end of the mile, when he was just two or three seconds away from the end of the track, "half blinded with dust and dirt, weak and fainting from the terrible strain he had undergone, his mind wandering," his helpers on the special platform dragged Murphy aboard the

USA—Canada, 1899

train with his bicycle still attached to his legs by his toeclips and straps. "The spectacle was a most fearful one to those on the rear of the pacing train," reported the *Chicago Tribune*. "His helpers hung on to him like grim death. ... As gently as possible Murphy, who had collapsed, was dragged over the rail. He sank unconscious but safe on the platform. The climax was too much for the officials and spectators. Those in the pacing car were rushing about or sinking down, all with blanched faces, cheering madly or nervously trying to get at Murphy. ... Several collapsed and had to lie down on the floor of the car."[12]

Murphy had succeeded in accomplishing an exploit that he had been thinking about for several years. The feat was reported in newspapers all over the United States and Europe. It was one of those events which caught and held the popular imagination. Murphy told reporters afterwards that he was willing to leave future speed records of that kind to others. "Without disparaging in any degree the persistence and pluck of the bicyclist," said *Scientific American*, "the most interesting feature of the ride is the impressive object lesson it affords as to the serious nature of atmospheric resistance on moving bodies."[13] Charles Murphy was known from that time on as 'Mile-a-Minute' Murphy, and before very long, cyclists, inspired by his example, would regularly be approaching speeds like his on the track behind huge pacing motors.

Shortly before 'Mile-a-Minute' Murphy made his crazy record ride behind the train, Taylor was asked what he thought of the upcoming attempt. He replied coolly, "I should think it would be an excellent opportunity of developing speed. I don't think there is much doubt that my record of 1 minute $31^{4}/5$ seconds will be broken." Taylor and sponsor Sager talked frequently of undertaking a similar record attempt but decided it was too dangerous. Taylor was never interested in danger for its own sake, he faced plenty of danger already from the normal risks of bicycle racing and especially from his white opponents without wanting to ride at 60 mph behind a train.

M AJOR TAYLOR'S principal rival for the sprint races of the LAW national championship during 1899 was the young Boston cyclist Tom Butler. Twenty-two years old, he was the youngest of the three famous Butler brothers, Tom, Nat, and Frank, and was one of the few outstanding professionals who, like Taylor, had remained loyal to the LAW. His behavior was polite and gentlemanly compared with the racism of many of Taylor's 1898 opponents. The 1899 races were marked by much greater fairness and a recognition of his right to compete. He was also racing more often against liberal East Coast athletes like the Butler brothers and Eddie McDuffie, who regarded him as a fierce rival athletically, but had never questioned his fundamental right to be in the sport. Nat Butler, along with J. J. Casey, owner of a bicycle shop in Worcester, began to ride on a tandem with Taylor that year, a good indication of the men's friendship.

On May 30, Taylor beat Tom Butler twice on the familiar terrain of the Charles River track, winning $875 for his afternoon's work. Proved a Star. The Major Handily Takes All of His Races, headlined a Worcester newspaper. A month later, he won $800 in a match race against Tom Butler at the same track. Before the match, "there was a conference and the men would not start until the long green was brought out. Finally someone brought out a big bunch of greenbacks and the faces of the two contestants were all smiles."[14] The hard reality of the business was never far away. Riders had been cheated; promoters were absconding with the offered prize money. It was wise to make sure the money was there before making an effort to win it.

When the racers went west on the national circuit, the sight of a black professional bicycle racer who won races convincingly was still a shocking novelty. A large and enthusiastic crowd at Ottumwa, Iowa, had some difficulty knowing how to react when they watched Taylor beat Tom and Nat Butler. "Major Taylor demonstrated that he was a wonderful rider in the two days that he was here," said an Ottumwa newspaper. "He has tremendous power and his ebony legs seem to fairly fly around." But he "is a queer specimen. He is supremely arrogant and egotistical and he ... imagines that he is the whole performance. ... The sympathies of the crowd are naturally with the white riders, yet they could not help admiring Taylor's wonderful speed, his endurance, and the doggedness which made him cling on to a race as long as there was any hope." Another account of the same races reported that "Major Taylor, the far-famed negro, was a surprise to the crowd. He is a perfect wonder on a wheel and rides much easier than any other rider. ... But the crowd did not like him and they did not want him to win."[15] It was one of the rare instances when the press reported that a crowd was unsympathetic to Taylor.

Both Taylor and Munger were frustrated that Eddie McDuffie held the 1-mile world record. Work on perfecting the Stearns steam pacing

USA—Canada, 1899

machine continued, but progress was slow. It was fast when it worked, but it was unreliable, temperamental, and hard to regulate and repair. At the end of July, Munger had the machine sent to Chicago so Taylor could make an attempt on McDuffie's record at the Ravenswood track. Several thousand people gathered, but the pacing machine "sailed around the track in a slow fashion, raising a cloud of steam which hid it from the spectators ... and leaving a wet trail behind it."[16] It could not be repaired that day, and McDuffie's record was safe for the time being.

A few days later, on July 29, with renewed determination, certain that the world record was within his grasp, Taylor tried three times to capture it during a Saturday cycling festival at Ravenswood. In the afternoon, with Munger steering, the machine broke down twice, and the frustrated crowd shouted, "Fake!" and "Blow it up!" and "Give us a rest!" By the evening, it was performing well, but the electric lights cast weird and confusing shadows on the track and made Taylor so nervous that he abandoned the attempt. That same evening he was told that McDuffie had broken his 1898 record of 1 minute $31^2/5$ seconds twice that day at New Bedford, Massachusetts, setting times first of 1 minute 31 seconds and then of 1 minute 28 seconds. "That's good, I'm glad to hear it," was Taylor's characteristically simple and generous response to the news.

Anxious to overcome the frustrating problems with the pacing machine, Taylor and his teammates moved from Ravenswood to the uneven cement track at Garfield Park, and Munger redoubled his efforts to get more speed out of the machine. On the evening of August 3, they were ready for yet another attempt on the record. The evening was ideal, with hardly a breath of wind stirring. After warming up behind a triplet, Taylor was ready, and Munger, steering the pacing machine, gave the word to go. Taylor fell in behind the speeding machine to approach the crack of the pistol and the timekeepers who were waiting to click their watches at the starting line.

Finally, the pacing machine was working smoothly, and with Taylor hugging its rear wheel, tucked in behind it, it raced silently around the banked track emitting small puffs of steam. The racing triplet team circled, watching carefully, ready to take over the pacing should the motor develop any problems. But all went well, and Taylor finished strongly, his body almost stationary and his legs working like pistons as he pushed the chainless bicycle with its 120-inch gear. As they approached the finishing line, Munger screamed "Now, sprint!" and Taylor surged up alongside his pacers as they crossed the line together.

There was no doubt about it. It was a new record. Five separate timekeepers had held their stopwatches on Taylor. A cheer went up from the 400 people who were watching when the world record was announced. They swarmed on the track and surrounded the timekeepers. "Aw, yo joshin', yo foolin' me – 'tain't right," panted the perspiring rider as he came around the track to the finish at a slower rate," the *Chicago Times-Herald* reported: "But the crowd soon convinced him that he had it and his face beamed with most intense satisfaction. The fans mobbed Taylor and escorted him back to his dressing room. "I am sure I can do it in 1:20" Taylor exclaimed breathlessly, as he was being rubbed down by his trainer, Bert Hazard.

Goes Mile in 1:22^2/5, announced the *Chicago Times-Herald* on its front page the next day, an extraordinary honor, since sports news was normally printed on page 3 or 4. Major Taylor Beats World's Record on a Bicycle: "In the presence of a yelling, frenzied crowd, Major Taylor, the swift colored professional cyclist, rode a mile behind his steam motor in the phenomenal time of 1:22^2/5, thereby beating McDuffie's time by 5^3/5 seconds."[17] It was the most drastic reduction of the mile record in years, a dramatic breakthrough. Taylor had raced over the mile at a speed of 43.68 mph.

The record fever was intense. No sooner was one record broken than another attempt was planned. Within a few days, there was talk of doing a mile in less than a minute on a long, straight, flat road, wherever such a stretch could be found. But for the moment, Taylor was content with his success. That evening, he wired the great news to Harry Sager: "Won't stay here any longer," his telegram read; "Leave for Rochester tonight at 9 o'clock. No use staying here because I've got the record. New mark, 1:22^2/5. Shake. Major Taylor."

TAYLOR ARRIVED in Montreal for the world championships at the beginning of August amid the fanfare of applause for his spectacular world record ride. It was the first time he had been outside the United States. He was full of pride and confidence and was in the peak of condition. The record ride had been reported in newspapers all over the United States and in Europe. *Cycle Age* called the ride "the most remarkable speed performance in the history of the 1-mile record. ... French promoters have cabled generous offers to the

USA—Canada, 1899

colored phenomenon since the news of his latest and best performance reached the other side."[18] In Montreal, he was generally conceded to be the best rider there and the favorite for the all-important
1-mile world championship title. The fans knew his history and his
troubles and wanted to see him race – and win.

The crucial question in the days immediately preceding the championships was whether members of the 'outlaw' professional movement, the American Racing Cyclists Union, now affiliated with the National Cycling Association, would be allowed to participate. A. G.
Batchelder, president of the breakaway movement, was in Montreal
to lobby on behalf of the rebel organization's members and was allowed to make a statement to the International Cycling Association,
the world governing body of cycling, founded in 1892 in London. It
made little sense, he argued, to exclude most of the strongest American professionals because they had decided to part company with the
LAW, and he pleaded for them to be admitted to the championships.
The insecure situation in American racing had meant that many of the
top European riders had either been unwilling to go to the expense
and trouble of crossing the Atlantic or had actually been prevented
by their own national organizations from doing so. Obviously, if they
came, these riders wanted to race against all, not just a few, of the
American champions.

However, the arrival in Canada of the imposing and regal Henry
Sturmey, the British executive secretary of the International Cycling
Association, squashed the rebels' remaining hopes. No, they could
not compete, said Sturmey. There could be only one controlling body
of the sport in America, and as far as he was concerned, the League
of American Wheelmen was that body. What amounted to a pact between President Thomas Keenan of the LAW and Henry Sturmey was
sufficient to freeze out the rebels from the world championships. This
decision meant that Taylor would not be facing the full force of either
his American or international competitors. Eventually, however, the
French and Italian cycling bodies would be putting pressure on Sturmey because of what they called "the disagreeable and really in-
tolerable situation" in which they were placed by the chaos in American racing. After the championships in 1899, it was only a question
of time before the LAW would be forced to relinquish control to the
NCA.

USA—CANADA, 1899

THE 1-MILE WORLD championship race was of crucial symbolic importance to Taylor. "All through my racing career, my one outstanding motive was to win the World's Championship," he wrote later, "and the same desire inspires every rider to his greatest efforts at all times. ... So keen was the interest of the public in the meet that thousands of enthusiasts gathered at the track daily to watch their favorites going through their training preparations. In the breast of every one of that contingent of riders burned the desire to win the world's championship title, and take the crown back to the country under whose colors he rode."

On Thursday, August 10, 1899, at the Queen's Park track, in front of a crowd estimated at close to 12,000 and with hundreds more outside unable to get in, the final of the 1-mile world championship was run. The heats had been held, the finalists selected. A moment of dramatic solemnity settled over the vast crowd as Taylor and his rivals stripped off their warm-up suits and took their positions on the starting line. His strongest opponents, the Butler brothers, were formidable tactically and knew how to work together to defeat an opponent. "They worked with clocklike precision and understood each other so perfectly that no signals or secret codes were necessary," wrote Taylor.

After some jockeying for position on the first lap, the race began in earnest. "Fast and furious they came around the last turn," said the *Montreal Gazette*, within sight of the white line, the colored rider crouched lower than ever over his mount and made a finish that would have caused the most sensational of them all to turn green with envy. Major Taylor fairly lifted himself and his wheel across the line a tire's width ahead of Butler. Thirteen, for that was his number, was for once a lucky one." [20]

The Butler's tactical scheming was no match for Taylor's sheer speed, and he won the championship title from Tom and Nat Butler and the French rider Courbe d'Outrelon in what he called "a clean-cut and decisive triumph." WORLD BEATER, shouted the *Boston Globe*, MAJOR TAYLOR WINS MILE CHAMPIONSHIP. LANDS VICTORY BY QUICK JUMP." [21]

"How the great throng did roar. It was indeed a glorious thrill," wrote Taylor.

> I shall never forget the thunderous applause that greeted me as I rode my victorious lap of honor around the track with a huge bouquet of roses. It was the first time that I had triumphed on foreign soil, and I

USA—CANADA, 1899

thrilled as I heard the band strike up the 'Star Spangled Banner.' My national anthem took on a new meaning for me from that moment. I never
felt so proud to be an American before, and indeed, I felt even more
American at that moment than I had ever felt in America. This was the
most impressive moment of my young life and I was a mighty happy
boy.

EVEN THOUGH TAYLOR was three months short of his twenty-
first birthday, he felt that he had at last accomplished his life's
greatest ambition, the highest honor he could achieve in the cycling
world. The victory was not only a statement of his personal athletic
prowess, but also a demonstration of the potential and promise of his
race. It gave him the outstanding and pioneering honor, at this tender
age, of becoming the first black world champion bicycle racer, the
second black world champion in any sport.[22] Nine years before the
notorious Jack Johnson won the heavyweight world boxing championship, and nearly half a century before Jackie Robinson was integrated into the Brooklyn Dodgers, Major Taylor had officially arrived
at the top of the most popular spectator sport of the time, after an
epic struggle for acceptance and recognition.

Yet, like the great Zimmerman who had inspired him five years
before, Taylor was an unassuming, modest, and mild-mannered world
champion. "Though rather small, he is finely proportioned and taken
all around, is probably the best developed man on the track," commented a Montreal newspaper reporter. "He is a very pleasing looking boy when he smiles and his skin, though dark, looks soft and
smooth as velvet."[23]

Taylor's success in the 1-mile championship and his popularity with
the crowd did not guarantee fair treatment, however, nor any change
of heart in the majority white riders and officials. The prominence and
importance of the four-day championship meet did not protect him
from routine and predictable harassment. "Perhaps this very success
made the other riders and some of the officials envious," suggested
the editor of Cycle Age, who alleged that Taylor had received the shab-
biest kind of treatment at the championships.[24]

The nastiness began on the first day when Taylor was in an extremely close sprint finish with Charles McCarthy in the final of the
half-mile race. The two riders were a tire's breadth apart on the line,
and in a decision which today would be made by electronic means,

the judges gave the first place to McCarthy. The crowd of thousands reacted angrily, booing and hissing and shouting "Dead heat!" and "Give the colored man a chance!" Even the mayor of Montreal protested against the decision, and Taylor was cheered again and again. The protests continued for half an hour, and the police were called in to prevent a violent demonstration.

Taylor himself was stunned that the decision was against him. He was sure he had won and went to the judges' stand to press his claim. When they refused to change the decision, he said calmly, "Well, all right, if that is your verdict, gentlemen, I shall have to abide by it. I have no complaint to make, but I believe that I won." Never ruffled or allowing himself to be provoked into an angry response, Taylor showed on this important occasion how much self-control and poise he possessed.

Nonetheless, he could also assert himself and hold his own when he had the power to do so. When he refused to race the winner of the amateur world championship, the English rider Tom Summersgill, in a traditional race of amateur versus professional for which there was no prize, Taylor asked for a prize of $500 to be put up, claiming that he had everything to lose and nothing to gain by matching himself against Summersgill. He was severely criticized by the officials, including the ICA Secretary Henry Sturmey and some members of the press, who said he had "developed a grand streak of yellow" and accused him of bad sportsmanship.[25]

Taylor disagreed. "I felt that it was a matter of principle. ... On top of that I was somewhat peeved over the way I had been 'gypped' out of first place in the half-mile race, and the fact that the prizes for such important races were exceedingly low. Winning the world's professional title at this meet netted me a paltry $200, despite the fact that there was a capacity attendance at the event," he wrote later.

The editor of *Cycle Age* supported Taylor. "After the bad treatment he received throughout the meet," he said, "it is unjust to censure him for being unwilling to get up and ride merely for the amusement of the crowd and an utterly empty honor." A race between an amateur and a professional was a farce anyway, he asserted, and proved nothing, since the two riders were of a totally different class. Instead of being criticized, he said, Taylor "should be given credit for being one of the best conducted racing men who ever followed the circuit and for showing less obtrusive conceit over his undoubted speed and ability to win races and break records."[26]

The world championship victory of 1899 was both a triumph and a disappointment for Taylor. While he had won the official title against strong opponents, his white rivals and critics in America pointed to the absence of the best 'outlaw' and international riders because of the ongoing war against the LAW and thus denigrated his victory. The pressure on him to meet the leading European national champions became insistent from that time on. The world championship title, once gained, had to be defended and legitimized over a period of time.

Sadly, this was the only official world championship Taylor would ever contest in his prime. In future years, the championships were always held on Sundays in Europe, and from 1901 to 1903, his answer was always the same. No, he would not race on Sundays even if the world championship was at stake. Only in 1909 would he again compete in the world championship, but by then he was far past his peak and did not even make it into the final after being beaten in his heat.

T HE LEAGUE of American Wheelmen and the rival National Cycling Association continued to sponsor separate circuit races all through the summer of 1899 for two parallel American championships. The LAW races, though fiercely contested, did not have the same excitement and drama as previous years, and the crowds were smaller. The cyclists' war was definitely bad for the sport; some commentators believed that it was being irreparably damaged.

During the remainder of the season, Taylor's most consistent rivals were Tom and Nat Butler, and he competed in many tight races against their tactical cunning. As a black world champion and world record holder, Taylor was a doubly marked man. The white riders, led by the Butlers, continued to pocket and obstruct him. They restricted his freedom of movement on the tracks, hoping – sometimes plotting – for a white victory. Most of the time they stopped short of fouling him physically, but they posed the same old severe tactical problems. Whereas the white riders could always find an ally, could hope to spring a surprise jump, Taylor was always alone, a closely watched and marked man.

It was no longer the naked racism of previous years, and riders did not contest his right to be in the sport, but they certainly did not intend to let him win easily. The fiercely tactical nature of a race with more than two contestants always had the potential to develop into a racial battle. And when his opponents did actually violate the rules by obstructing him, the judges were quite likely to turn a blind eye.

At the League championship races in Boston in August, just after Taylor had won the world championship, the plotting was especially intense. ANOTHER POCKET. BUTLER BROTHERS HAVE IT IN FOR THE MAJOR, headlined a Worcester newspaper. TAYLOR SHUT OUT IN EVERY EVENT, said another paper, OTHER RIDERS POCKET AND OTHERWISE PREVENT MAJOR'S SCORING.[27] After receiving a tremendous ovation from the spectators, Taylor wrote, "the entire field violated every rule of the track at my expense, as the fans howled their disapproval of the underhanded methods adopted by my rivals. The officials did not so much as reprimand those who had fouled me in such a dangerous manner."

In spite of the intense opposition, Taylor went on winning and enjoyed a commanding lead as the American championship races drew to a close. He won in Taunton, Massachusetts, and he beat Tom Butler three times in one day in Peoria, Illinois, where he had ridden his very first race as a fourteen-year-old boy in 1893. In Indianapolis, where he went to train for a few days in October for the Peoria races, he was so famous by then that large crowds gathered at the track just to see him train and to admire the beauty of his style.

The Peoria races clinched the national championship for Taylor. With nine first places, four seconds, and one third in the season's qualifying events, he was ten points ahead of Tom and Nat Butler, and the title was his. Whatever his critics would say about the inadequacies and unrepresentativeness of this problematical championship, Taylor had triumphed once again. He had finally completed a championship season and was the official LAW American sprint champion for 1899. The gold medal was his. Tom Cooper, his longtime enemy, won the rebel NCA championship, but that year the two archenemies did not meet to dispute the title of overall champion of America.

IN INDIANAPOLIS, where he had gone hoping for a few days well-earned rest after the Peoria races, Taylor had an urgent telegram from Harry Sager. Eddie McDuffie had just cut more than a second off Taylor's 1-mile world record in Brockton, Massachusetts. He had set a new record of 1 minute 21 seconds, a speed of 44.44 mph. Mc-

Duffie had now gone to the Garfield Park track in Chicago, where he was going to try to lower the record still further, to score a resounding victory before retiring altogether from bicycle racing. Sager was coming immediately to Indianapolis with a pacing machine and two mechanics, he told Taylor, and then they would go together to Chicago to challenge McDuffie, who would be riding the same Columbia chainless bicycle made by the Pope Manufacturing Company he had been using the whole season. Sager was determined that his commercial rival would not steal a late-season world record, giving the Columbia a tremendous publicity scoop throughout the winter.

"Major Taylor dropped serenely into town," said *Cycle Age*, "with his Stearns Sager gear and steam tandem. ..."

> Whenever his white rival makes any meritorious ride, it is his intention to go out and eclipse it. He will even appear at the track simultaneously with McDuffie and when the latter goes for a speed record, the dusky shadow will go for the same distance under similar conditions. If these intentions are carried out, Chicagoans will be treated to a remarkably interesting and amusing spectacle, not the least of which may be a final mixup in which the Bostonian will seek revenge through his arms instead of his legs.[28]

Between November 9 and 16, a tense late-season battle was fought in Chicago, in freezing, sometimes stormy, weather, between two fierce rivals, the two fastest short-distance racing cyclists in the country. McDuffie had fitted some strange windshields to the rear of his pacing machine to give him more protection and speed. Because he did not want to concede any advantage to his opponent, Taylor decided to fit them too.

Day after day Taylor tried for the record, working constantly to coax more speed out of the bright yellow pacing machine. But it refused to work as well as McDuffie's. "It was a fickle piece of mechanism which acted like a wayward child," said a reporter. "It seemed human in its perversity."[29]

On November 15, Taylor tried twice for the record, but still the steam tandem refused to produce the necessary speed. After a vigorous rubdown in the training quarters, he came out on the track determined to make one more attempt, and on this occasion the machine worked flawlessly. "It flew around the track with the speed of an express train, but as noiselessly and smoothly as a steamship glides through the water," said *Cycle Age*.

USA—CANADA, 1899

The crew sat motionless with their feet on the rests, and the exhaust steam rolled in miniature clouds on the track. Through these the colored boy drove his Stearns machine fitted with the 121-inch gear with marvelous rapidity, though with apparent ease. ... Taylor stuck behind his shield like a postage stamp to its envelope, and without a break in the motion flew over the tape two seconds sooner than any man had ever done before.[30]

It was another world record, 1 mile in 1 minute 19 seconds, at a speed of 45.56 mph. Taylor had finally produced the ride he and Sager had been waiting for. The ecstatic Sager immediately began to talk to the press about that long flat stretch of road where Taylor would be able to ride a mile in 55 seconds, beating 'Mile-a-Minute' Murphy's record. But first they needed a bicycle with a higher gear, he said, and the pacing machine had to be redesigned.

Eddie McDuffie was a disappointed man when he left Chicago. He had intended to retire from bicycle racing for good to go into the motor business, and he had desperately wanted to establish a world record, "so that his fame would live through the winter at least," said the *Chicago Daily News*, "but the weather and Major Taylor spoiled his calculations." [31]

Newspaper reports glowed with praise for Taylor after he climaxed a phenomenal season with the new world record in Chicago and his convincing display of superiority over Eddie McDuffie. TAYLOR HAS AN ENVIABLE RECORD, headlined one paper, THE COLORED CYCLONE CAPTURED TWENTY-TWO FIRST PRIZES IN TWENTY-NINE STARTS BESIDES ESTABLISHING MANY NEW RECORDS. "If he didn't have it before," said another review of his season, "Major Taylor has this year gained the title of champion cyclist of the world. It would be presumptuous for anyone to question his standing. The last year has undoubtedly been the best one in Taylor's years of professional riding." Articles referred to him as "the black whirlwind," "the black cyclone," "the dark wonder," or just "the great colored rider," and the *Chicago Times-Herald* talked of "the colored boy who has astonished the world of cycling by his great feats of speed on the track," and printed a complete list of his season's victories.[32]

AFTER HE returned to Worcester on the express train from Chicago, local correspondents, always interested in this source of good copy, interviewed Taylor at length. They produced long and reveal-

USA—CANADA, 1899

ing articles about the successes of Worcester's cycling celebrity, directed at an audience hungry for news of their hometown hero's activities. CYCLONE GETS HOME. MAJOR TAYLOR, THE WONDER, IS NOW BACK IN WORCESTER, said the *Worcester Spy*. OUT FOR A 1:10 MILE. MAJOR TAYLOR TO RIDE FOR THAT NEXT YEAR, said the *Worcester Telegram*.[33]

Taylor was his usual modest self in talking to the journalists and was not at all inclined to boast. He tried at first to brush aside his remarkable performances, but was gradually drawn into conversation about them. The *Telegram* reporter reminded his readers how some people had laughed at Taylor the previous year when he had said he would be able to ride the mile in less than 1 minute 20 seconds, but he had lived to fulfill his prediction. And, Taylor assured the reporter, he had not yet ridden as fast as he was capable of riding. "If I go out for the records next fall, as I have done this year and last, you will see me riding in faster time than ever. I am confident the maximum speed on the bicycle has not been reached. Give me the pick of track and day ... and you will see me reel off a 1:10 mile, and no mistake. In fact, I feel confident I can shade a minute on a straightaway course whenever I make the attempt.[34]

What about his plans for the future, the *Telegram* reporter asked Taylor. He had no special plans, he said, except to stay at home for several weeks and have a good rest to recuperate from his exhausting record rides. And there was no truth at all in stories that were being published about his intention of leaving for Europe shortly. "It is just the work of some of those bicycle paragraphers," he said, "who always get together some great stories about me whenever they think they see a lull for me ahead. They are always making me married or contemplating a European trip. ... If I was married, I don't know when it happened, and Worcester people know well enough that I am not going to Europe, because it would necessitate Sunday racing, and they know my views on that question."

Yes, there had been some disappointments to his season, Taylor confessed, especially the harsh decisions made against him by judges at the LAW meeting in Boston and at the world championship. But he was not disappointed with his earnings, he said, smiling quietly, which he would not be drawn into discussing. The *Telegram* reporter estimated that his income for the season from all sources – his contract

USA—CANADA, 1899

with Sager and prizes from championship races and world records – "should run up to $10,000."[35]

Taylor told the *Spy* reporter a similar story of the year's successes and disappointments. He talked at length about his November world record contest with McDuffie. "Newspaper reports say you kept calling for more pace in that 1:19 mile," suggested the reporter. "Yes, I could have gone faster," said Taylor, "if the motor had gone faster. I did not find the slightest trouble clinging to it." The one thing he had needed most during the season, he added laconically, was "a competent bill collector." He had been cheated out of nearly $2,000 in prizes, he said, which the management of various tracks 'forgot' to pay him.[36]

Taylor talked easily with his reporter friends, but his honors were never totally secure. The LAW hesitated over whether to accept the November 1-mile world record, debating the legality of the windshields Taylor had used, though they had not questioned McDuffie when he had first used them. Then in December, Taylor quarreled with the Associated Cycling Clubs of Worcester over whether or not there would be any objections to his appearance at an exhibition at a Thanksgiving bazaar. He told the *Worcester Evening Gazette* that if there was any more rudeness, he would publish their heated correspondence to "let the public judge for themselves whether all the prejudice against the colored man is confined to the South."[37]

THAT SUCCESSFUL 1899 season was the first of Major Taylor's three years of professional bicycle racing when he achieved all of his goals without severe setbacks, and without being excluded from the American championship by the plotting of his white rivals. It was without doubt an astounding season. People who were unable to acknowledge a black man's dominance said that the world championships and even the American championships had been a farce because Taylor had not competed with the strongest riders. But the world records were impossible to dismiss, and the truth was that Taylor was the unrivaled bicycle racing star of 1899. No other American rider had come close to his consistently fast performances and the range and variety of his victories: twenty-two first places in major championship races all over the country, the League of American Wheelmen Championship on points, world champion in Montreal, and the defense of his own world 1-mile record in two strenuous record-breaking campaigns. It was a phenomenal season's work.

No other American athlete in any sport could boast of such an accomplishment that year. It was a startling and unique phenomenon for a black man to attain such a peak of athletic excellence and to become an international celebrity. It was the first time that a black American athlete had ever entered the mainstream of any sport. Taylor competed regularly against whites in front of paying audiences, he enjoyed protection from cycling's governing body, the LAW, and he was sponsored and promoted by two important businesses for advertising purposes. He was the first black athlete to have struggled and won the right to compete in his chosen sport in this thoroughly modern way.

USA—CANADA, 1899

8

CHAMPION OF AMERICA AT LAST

BY THE END OF 1899, Major Taylor was an international cycling celebrity with a rapidly growing reputation. In France, the European country most passionately involved with bicycle racing, the fans longed to see the new world champion, a figure with an air of mystery about him, as well as an extraordinary athletic record. The French press had been spreading rumors of his arrival in Europe since the end of 1898, when he had first broken world records, and a handsome photograph of him was published on the cover of *La Vie au Grand Air*, the most important weekly sports magazine in the country. French racers who had visited the United States and witnessed Taylor's racing feats considered him the strongest attraction French race promoters could procure. He was, in fact, the best known of all the American sprinters.

Such a big star with a proven ability to pull in crowds was an obvious money-maker, and late in 1899 the offers began to pour in. One representative of a French promoter called on Taylor in Worcester with a tempting contract in his hand, offering an astonishing amount of money. But the one big stumbling block to Taylor's accepting such a contract in France, or any other European cycling country, was his refusal to race on Sundays. For Taylor, the Sabbath was a day of rest. REFUSES $15,000! MAJOR TAYLOR WON'T RIDE ON SUNDAY. OFFER FROM FRANCE TURNED DOWN, ran the headline in the *Worcester Telegram* on November 30, 1899. "As all his Worcester friends know, Taylor is unequivocally opposed to Sunday racing. He has refused ever since he began his racing career to ride on Sundays, and he is as steadfast as ever to confine his racing to weekdays."[1]

In mid-December, another offer was made to him when a party of leading European professional cyclists arrived from Paris to take part in the six-day races in New York and Boston and to tour the United States. Among them were George Banker, an American with several years' experience of racing in France, and Tommaselli, the Italian champion, winner of France's most prestigious bicycle race, the Grand Prix de Paris, in 1899. Managing them was Victor Breyer, a dapper, good-looking young Parisian bicycle racing impressario and journalist, who would play an important role in Taylor's future European career. Breyer was one of the managers of the famous Buffalo track in Paris and a writer for the Parisian daily cycling newspaper, *Le Vélo*. He had grown up in England and thus spoke fluent English, and he was an important man in the cycling life of the French capital, always on the lookout for new talent to promote in the flourishing Parisian bicycle racing scene.

One of Breyer's most important missions on his winter trip to America was to meet the new world champion and try to persuade him to sign a contract to race in France during the coming season. The Paris International Exhibition would be taking place in 1900, with visitors coming from all over the world, and important races would be held on a specially constructed indoor track. All the leading European sprinters would be there.

Taylor was as enthusiastic to meet Breyer and the European party as they were to meet him. As soon as he heard that they had arrived in Boston for the six-day race, he sent them a wire and went to their hotel the next day to welcome them. They responded by inviting him to dinner. Breyer was immediately charmed by him and wrote in *Le Vélo* that his meeting with "the enigmatic black cyclist" was probably the most interesting thing about his stay in Boston. "We met the negro at last!" he exclaimed.

> He is a lad of about twenty-three, very well behaved and with very correct manners. His bearing is in striking contrast to that of the majority of negroes one encounters in America. He is of moderate height, rather on the small side ... He is burning with such a strong desire to come to France that we have high hopes of persuading him to overcome his religious scruples about racing on Sundays."[2]

At his dinner with Taylor, Breyer and the other racers were amazed to find that the black champion was a strict teetotaller, and they had a good-natured laugh at his blunt refusal to take even a sip of wine or brandy.

After dinner, they adjourned to the Charles River track, where Taylor and Tommaselli had a short running match, which Taylor won. When they parted, no definite decisions had been made, no contract signed, but the invitation was firmly in place, a relationship had been established. Breyer had great expectations for the future.

Once Breyer and his party had left New York, Taylor was annoyed by rumors published in the *New York World* and the *Worcester Spy* suggesting that he was weakening in his stand against Sunday racing and had, in fact, capitulated to Breyer's terms. He had no intention of changing his mind, he told the *Worcester Telegram.* "I stand today just where I stood a year ago and hope to stand a year hence. I am irrevocably opposed to Sunday riding and you will never catch me in a Sunday race anywhere. I have never ridden on Sundays and I do not propose to begin at this late date."[3]

But Breyer's contact aroused excited discussion in the French press about the possibility that Taylor would be crossing the Atlantic. A long follow-up account of Taylor's life and career was published in *Le Vélo,* written by Marc Braun, a German journalist who was the paper's Chicago correspondent. "Major Taylor can certainly be considered the best American bicycle racer," wrote Braun, "and, if he does come to Paris in 1900, he will certainly be seen as a worthy successor to Zimmerman." [4] The line between reporting and promoting was a thin one. The French promoters were waiting anxiously for the arrival of the new American star, a rider with a mystique and the ability to capture the imagination of the public and set the crowd on fire.

Robert Coquelle, another influential writer and promoter and a colleague of Breyer's at *Le Vélo* and at the Buffalo track, also contributed to this premature boosting of Taylor's European visit. In an article in *La Vie au Grand Air,* he called Taylor 'le nègre volant' (the Flying Negro), the nickname by which he would often be known in Europe in the future.[5] In his and other foreign observers' descriptions of Taylor, there was a change of tone and emphasis from the coverage he had gotten in the American press. They were curious about Taylor as a personality. What kind of a person was he? What did he say and do? What were his physical characteristics? Since the American Negro culture was foreign to them, Frenchmen felt that there was something mysterious and enigmatic about him. Taylor's mystique was certainly a useful promotional gimmick. They did not see him through the same prejudiced eyes as so many Americans. The French were neither afraid of nor threatened by Taylor.

A T THE END of January 1900, Taylor decided to buy a house. He had cash in the bank, and he had seen a house he liked on Hobson Avenue in Columbus Park, a choice new development in a select, affluent, white neighborhood on the north side of Worcester. He could not buy the house in his own name because the developer who owned Columbus Park, Charles King, would never sell to a black man. So Taylor instructed a real estate broker, John Maher, to negotiate a deal without revealing his identity. The dialogue between the two agents and subsequent events were reported later in a local newspaper.

"You know the requirements of purchasers in that neighborhood," said the Columbus Park man. "They've got to be of good character and American citizens."

"My customer meets all your requirements," said Maher, "and he has money to pay in cash."

"I must see your man," said King. "What does he do and where is he?"

"He's a traveling man, going around the country all the while on business, you know, and isn't here much of the time," replied Maher, "But he's an American, born and bred of respectability. His name is M. W. Taylor."

After several days of negotiation and further hesitation from King, a certified check for $2,850 was finally handed over and the deed to the house exchanged.

When Taylor moved into the large house on Hobson Avenue with his sister Gertrude, King soon discovered that he had been tricked. The white residents of Columbus Park descended angrily on his office, demanding an explanation. King told his visitors to calm down and asked what the trouble was.

"Trouble, sir," roared the spokesman, "there are colored persons, sir, a whole house full of them, sir, right in the midst of our neighborhood. You have sold your house to a colored man, and, worse than that, sir, to a sporting colored person! We are going to sue you for damages."[6]

COLUMBUS PARK MUCH TROUBLED. ALL BECAUSE MAJOR TAYLOR BECOMES ITS NEIGHBOR, announced a headline in the *Worcester Telegram*. "Charles King, builder and real estate man, is decidedly unpopular because he sold a house at the park to Major Taylor, the ebony cyclone of the professional bicycle riders of the country."[7]

USA, 1899—1901

The event prompted more than just local interest. In Boston, Taylor was well known, and his purchase was one more example of his determination to assert his full rights as a black American. Major Taylor Shocks Society. Colored Cyclist Buys a House in Swell Section of Worcester and Will Live There, read the headline in the *Boston Post.*

> The dusky whirlwind, as he is known on the circuit, is one of Worcester's four hundred, so far as owning and occupying his own home goes, but the other three hundred and ninety-nine are making a tremendous fuss over having him for a neighbor, and all because of his color. In private life, Major Taylor is one of the most quiet and gentlemanly men in the country. He is polite and deferential to a fault, but this does not appease the Columbus Park residents. They do not want a colored man for a neighbor.[8]

With the deed signed, there was not much King could do about the situation, which, as several newspaper writers appreciated, had its comical aspects. The white residents of Columbus Park, determined to keep their neighborhood lily-white, offered to buy back Taylor's house for $2,000 more than he had paid. But he refused. "The cycling champion was obdurate," said the *Boston Post,* "and the battle closed with the enemy in possession of the field." [9]

Because he had bought the house in such a controversial way and was noticed in Worcester stores buying nearly a thousand dollar's worth of furniture, some of the curious began to speculate that Taylor was actually married. Others guessed more accurately that he was simply buying the house for himself and his sister. Taylor felt that he was under no obligation to explain publicly every move he made, and in fact he rather enjoyed keeping people guessing about his intentions. "I don't know why I haven't as much right to buy a little place and get some furniture for it as any man in town, without having every man I ever knew and a lot whom I never saw before informed as to my intentions," he told a Worcester newspaper reporter, who was pestering him for information.[10]

The editor of the *Worcester Spy* called the whole affair "a tempest in a teapot," and stood up for Taylor's rights. "Worcester is not the South," he said, "It was the soil of Massachusetts that was first watered with the blood of the patriots of the Revolution because they protested against tyranny and stood out for equal rights and human liberty. The color line should not be drawn so straight as it appears to be drawn here. Major Taylor is a young man, and so far as reports from those who know him best tend to show, of irreproachable character. He has made money in spite of all obstacles thrown in his way and by sheer force of native ability. The public will watch developments in the case with curiosity."[11] There were no further developments. The 'tempest' blew over and exclusive Columbus Park was gradually able to accept, even to respect, its distinguished black resident, who lived there for twenty-five years.

Taylor had a very pressing practical reason for refusing to bow to the pressure to part with his newly acquired house. His younger sister, Gertrude, who had been living with him in Worcester and attending Worcester High School, had been seriously ill with tuberculosis since the previous September. He had nursed her through the winter, but her condition had worsened. She would enjoy only a few months in the new house on Hobson Avenue, and her grave health was another reason why Taylor had not jumped at the chance to cross the Atlantic in February.[12]

TAYLOR CONTINUED to vacillate over whether or not to go to France for the season's racing. It was a difficult decision to make. The discussions he had had with Breyer and the visiting European riders were encouraging. They had assured him that he was the best-known American rider in France and that enthusiastic crowds were waiting to welcome him with open arms. But the issues of Sunday racing and whether it would be worth his time and effort financially to race only on weekdays made him hesitate.

He had another long discussion with Breyer and the French ex-cycling champion and motorcycle racer Henri Fournier at the beginning of February, just before they left the United States for Paris. Afterwards, he told the *Worcester Telegram* that he had finally made up his mind. He wanted to see the world and had decided 'to cross the big pond.' "The Paris racing fever has struck him with full force," said the newspaper, "and he believes he sees gold and glory awaiting him in the pilgrimage to Paris."[13]

The foreign riders had time and again emphasized that Taylor would be a popular idol as soon as he landed upon French soil, and they ridiculed the idea that he would experience any difficulties because of his color. They also assured him that he would make plenty of money even if he refused to race on Sundays. Taylor said he thought he would go to France as an experiment, as a freelancer, without a big contract to tie him down. He wanted to see for himself what bicycle racing was like there.

"I am not going to Paris with any kind of expectation of making a mint of money," Taylor told the *Telegram* reporter. "That is not my purpose. I want to see the Exposition and perhaps do a little traveling in other parts of Europe, and I have figured it out that I can just about make expenses. Were I willing to ride Sunday, I would have no doubt about my ability to bring back a good part of the purses." He was also confident that he was in fairly good condition. "The man who looks out for himself," he said, "who does not dissipate, and whose system is not full of liquor, tobacco, or dope, can come to his speed in a very short time. The change in the climate is the only thing to which I am giving any thought."[14]

But Taylor did not leave Worcester, as he had intimated. He still had problems at home to settle. Paramount was his professional standing in the ongoing war between the League of American Wheelmen and the National Cycling Association. He did not want to be hounded by bureaucratic problems while he was thousands of miles away in France. When the LAW held its 1900 convention in Philadelphia at the beginning of February, the control of racing was the burning item on the agenda. The problem had been argued and reargued many times, and everyone acknowledged that the conflict between the two rival organizations was extremely damaging to the sport. Even the International Cycling Association recognized the weak position of the LAW and put pressure on it to stand aside. It was prepared to recognize the NCA as the de facto governing body in the United States.

At the LAW convention, it took the assembled delegates less than five minutes to find a peaceful resolution to the battle that had disrupted the sport for a year and a half. "The speed and facility with which that vital matter was disposed of savored of the manner in which a hot potato is popularly supposed to be dropped," said *Cycle Age*. "Anyone who heard the hearty cheer which followed the announcement of the vote (it was practically unanimous) would have imagined that the assemblage had at last rid itself of an incubus that was fast sapping its vitality."[15]

Suddenly, after battling through the whole of the 1899 season, determined to retain its control, the LAW relinquished its authority over bicycle racing and handed its responsibility for the sport to the National Cycling Association, a federation of cycling organizations, which had as one of its members the 'rebel' bicycle racers' group, the American Racing Cyclists Union. These two organizations would now have the responsibility of registering and licensing riders and the right to accept or reject membership.

Taylor was not taken entirely by surprise by this dramatic turn of events, but he now found himself without the fatherly protection of the LAW Racing Board and his allies there. He had been suspended for life from both the NCA and the ARCU, and now he was literally out in the cold, without affiliation in a professional cycling organization.

LOST IN SHUFFLE! MAJOR TAYLOR IS AT MERCY OF HIS ENEMIES, said the *Worcester Spy* :

> In the shuffle, scuffle and settlement of the cycle race control question, Major Taylor, the fastest of them all, has been the victim of a game of freeze out. Unless race control officials change their attitude towards him, the Worcester boy will be forced to retire permanently from cycle racing and to gain his livelihood by other means. Taylor and his friends have realized for months that something was to drop before long. The drop came last week at Philadelphia. It hit Taylor, and hit him hard. The League of American Wheelmen, when it voted to give up race control, gave Taylor's chances of ever racing again, either in this country or in Europe, a black eye.[16]

Things were especially serious for him in view of the entrenched hostility of his white rivals, especially the bitter experience he had had when he briefly joined the ARCU in the fall of 1898. The racist clique of Bald, Gardiner, Kiser, Kimble, Cooper, and MacFarland, who controlled the ARCU, had shown on many occasions that they detested Taylor and would do anything in their power to damage his career. Now they had him exactly where they had always wanted him, with complete control over his destiny. Taylor was faced with the humiliating prospect of having to petition the ARCU to lift his life suspension and readmit him. If it refused, as seemed quite likely, he might be banned from competing on American tracks.

The press understood the gravity of this sudden turn of events. LITTLE HOPE FOR MAJOR TAYLOR. APPEARS TO BE PERMANENTLY BARRED FROM ALL RACING, said the *Worcester Telegram*, whose reporter stayed close to Taylor during this difficult period.

USA, 1899—1901

Major Taylor's chances for readmission into the N.C.A. are just about one in a thousand. With a determination born of desperation, he is playing the single chance to win, at the same time realizing that almost certain defeat stares him in the face. If favorable action is not secured, Taylor's career as a racing man is ended, and Major Taylor, who has astonished the world by his great feats of speed upon the track ... will never again ride a wheel in sanctioned competition. The cycle field will not offer to Major Taylor the opportunities that were once open to him and he will be forced to seek a livelihood by other means.[17]

To be willing to readmit him, his old white rivals and enemies would have to experience a change of heart, or some extraordinary pressure would have to be exerted. It is not surprising then that Taylor gave up his plans to go to France until this crisis was resolved.

A S IF TO UNDERLINE the awkward timing of this upheaval in his professional status, yet another offer came from France. In March, Marc Braun, the reporter from *Le Vélo,* dropped by to see him at his new house in Worcester on his way back to Chicago from France. Braun had been sent personally from Paris by Victor Breyer and Robert Coquelle to try again to persuade Taylor to sign a contract. He had been commissioned to make all the necessary arrangements and was authorized to offer him the princely incentive of a $10,000 payment for his appearance at a stipulated number of races in Europe, plus whatever prizes he could win. It was an enormous amount of money, far more than any other American bicycle racer was offered at the time. Braun represented a consortium of bicycle makers, tire manufacturers, and racing promoters. The promoters and track owners, he pleaded, were desperate for a firm commitment because they wanted to plan their schedules, and they needed new blood, a star attraction to offer the spectators. Braun insisted, however, that there would be no contract unless Taylor agreed to race on Sundays.

Braun spent two days with Taylor in Worcester in long and animated discussions. Taylor explained why he was not able to accept the contract: Sunday racing, the most serious stumbling block, his difficulties with the ARCU, and his sister's illness. It was just not the right moment for him to leave. Braun told a reporter that his offer "remains open and Major Taylor may cable at any time and they will deposit the money when he has fulfilled the conditions of his contract. He may do this at any time up to the middle of the summer."[18]

USA, 1899—1901

It was, of course, the money that interested the press the most. TAYLOR REFUSES $10,000. HE WON'T RACE ON SUNDAYS, declared the *New York World*. "There was not the slightest hesitation on the part of the colored rider in rejecting this offer of a small fortune for one season of work. He had made up his mind in advance, having previously rejected the same offer by mail. "I cannot and will not ride on the Sabbath Day,' he told Marc Braun."[19]

Why was he so opposed to Sunday riding? Taylor was asked a little later by a group of cyclists and journalists, who were all incredulous that he had turned down such a lucrative offer. "It is a matter of conscience," he replied. "It makes no difference how many ministers you quote me, it is the way I feel and believe about it. You want to know why? I reckon it is because of my early teaching. I still haven't outgrown what I was taught. It's the same in other things besides Sundays. No one ever knew me to take a drink. I am the loser on the money, maybe, by not racing on Sundays, but I don't believe I could win a Sunday race." But why was he so religious, they persisted in asking him. "I believe in the saying that "a mother's prayer will last forever,' and I honestly believe it's my mother's prayers that are standing by me now," he replied.[20]

Taylor's stand on the Sunday racing issue was widely reported in the American press. In refusing to work on the Sabbath, he was taking both a personal and a political stand. He was determined to be true to his own Christian conscience, but he also wanted to set a good example, to prove to the world that a black athlete did not have to be an unpleasant, dissolute character, as many of the black boxers were supposed to be, but could be a fine, upstanding, moral person. He wanted to exemplify this strong Christian element in his culture and race to the rest of the world.

His stand, though greeted with astonishment by some, was also applauded and respected by others. "Many satirical remarks have been made concerning the resolve of Major Taylor not to ride on Sunday," said *Cycle Age* later in the season, "but the speedy colored boy must be given credit for having withstood a hard temptation for the sake of his principles. While great races have been contested abroad, the ebony flyer has remained at home to whip men hardly in his class. Think of the possibilities for Taylor in the Grand Prix of the Exposition! All of the great sprinters rode – all but he, and it is probable he is the greatest of all." [21] In fact, the winner of the Grand Prix had carried off a magnificent $2,000 prize that summer.

When an admirer from Whiteface, New Hampshire, wrote Taylor a letter congratulating him for his stand, Taylor's reply was published in a local newspaper, along with the editor's commendation.[22] Taylor wrote, in part:

> Your letter brought much encouragement and just at the right time too; for sometimes it comes to me so forcibly that it seems as a mountain to overcome. I am laboring under the greatest temptation of my life, and I pray each day for God to give me more grace and more faith to stand up for what I know to be right. ... I have no fear for the future, for I feel that I will be taken care of, although things seem very cloudy at present. ... I am having considerable trouble to get reinstated, and my case will be brought up for action at Louisville on April 3, and if I am not reinstated I am all through with racing and will seek for other means of earning a livelihood. ... He signed his letter, "Yours in Christ, Major Taylor."

As a first step towards opening a dialogue with the hostile forces of the National Cycling Association and the American Racing Cyclists Union, Taylor enlisted the help of William Allen, vice president of the NCA, who lived in Worcester. Allen was sympathetic to Taylor's cause and offered to take up his case with the NCA authorities in New York, to see if he could pave the way for a reconciliation, at least get some negotiations under way. "I don't know what I can do for Taylor," he told the *Worcester Telegram* reporter who was closely following the story of the star cyclist's predicament. "I have not yet planned my line of action. I should be glad to help the fellow in any way I could, for he is a Worcester rider, and a fast one, and his presence would give added interest in any meet. Personally, I should like very much to see the N.C.A. readmit Taylor, but I fear my sentiments do not meet with favor in the minds of the majority of the officials of that body."[23]

Allen wrote about Taylor to F. Edward Spooner, chairman of the ARCU Racing Board in New York. The reply, while somewhat harsh in tone, did not reject completely the possibility of negotiating a settlement of the conflict. Taylor and Allen then lodged a formal appeal for his readmission to the ARCU and asked for a date to be set for the consideration of his case.

The busy riders of the ARCU executive committee procrastinated and kept promising a hearing. First, they said they would discuss the matter at their annual meeting in Louisville in the middle of March, but they postponed the meeting twice. While some of the members – Cooper, Kiser, and Spooner – were somewhat favorably disposed towards readmitting Taylor,others – MacFarland, Stevens, Freeman, and Hardy Downing – were against him and played a filibustering role by finding excuses to be absent from meetings when Taylor's case was on the agenda. As far as they were concerned, the longer the decision was delayed, the better. For Taylor, the delays were extremely frustrating because he could make no plans for the season, and his career was in suspension. His worst fear was that the ARCU would simply put off making a decision until the season was almost over, making it impossible for him to compete in 1900.

The NCA met in Buffalo at the end of April and decided that it had no objections to registering Taylor as long as he was able to resolve his disagreement with the ARCU. The complex bureaucratic muddle was beginning to work itself out. ACTS ON TAYLOR ! said the *Worcester Telegram* on April 24. N.C.A. TAKES VOTE FAVORABLE TO MAJOR. HE MUST PACIFY THE RACING UNION.[24]

Taylor's popularity as a person and a star performer was of critical importance in determining the outcome of the struggle. Throughout the four months that he was stranded, like a stateless person, his popularity with the general public was his biggest asset. They loved his style of winning and the excitement he generated on the track, and they were eager to see him race again. The track owners and promoters, too, understood in terms of dollars and cents how good he was for the sport.

His most influential supporters were perhaps the writers on cycling magazines and daily newspapers, who watched the development of the affair with keen and sympathetic attention. They understood that the conflict was more than just a bureaucratic struggle within a sporting organization. They appreciated that Taylor stood at the center of an ongoing social debate and that his fight with the white cyclists was a test case of the right of blacks to participate on terms of equality with whites in other aspects of life.

Of the many reports of Taylor's predicament that were published in the press during the first half of 1900, one article, published in both the *Cycling Gazette* and the *Worcester Spy*, underlines the strength of the public support for him.

USA, 1899—1901

Major Taylor, colored whirlwind, world's record holder, world professional 1-mile champion, and for two years bone of contention in cash prize racing circles, is again in the deep mullogatawny, floundering wildly about and gasping for help. ... Treason is the charge against him and permanent suspension the threatened verdict. But he will not be permanently suspended.

The riders have drawn the color line; it is unconstitutional, un-American, unsportsmanlike. It is wrong in the abstract, unrighteous in the concrete. It is indefensible, particularly at a time when you are dealing with something other than theory, and all the more so since the color line will not be accepted by the American public as a valid excuse for the ruling off of a champion.

Major Taylor is a stern reality. He is here in flesh and blood, and he must be dealt with as a human being, entitled to every human right. His case cannot be decided on the color question, but on its actual merits, and we believe the riders so agree. That being the case, the question arises, "What punishment does he deserve?"

In answering this query, the judges must be unprejudiced. To gain for themselves the hearty esteem of the public, it is required that they make due allowance for the unique and trying position Taylor has always held and take into consideration the admitted shortcomings of his race. If they would win golden praise, they will temper justice with mercy and then turn in and prove, if they can, his inferiority as a racing man by beating him fairly and squarely in the championship competition.

Taylor is no angel. His faults are probably no fewer than those of the average racing man. But he has always been the subject of a natural prejudice and at all times ... he has felt himself an unwelcome competitor. Had he felt at home among the professionals, he never would have deserted, a fact not to be overlooked. Then, also, while Taylor displayed weakness in deserting the riders' cause, malice on his part has not been proved, and this, too, must be considered. Furthermore, he should be dealt with in a spirit of consideration for his inborn shortcomings.

We might go still deeper into this matter, but we feel that there is little necessity for it. The racing men have triumphed and, as victors, they can afford to be merciful. Not one of them wants it said next fall that he is champion because Taylor was barred. ... The committee will, we believe, be even more lenient to Taylor than its members would be were he a white man. If for no other reason than to disprove the public

USA, 1899—1901

suspicions of unfair play and to prove their manhood and their confidence in their ability as racingmen. ...[25]

Another newspaper expressed its opinion in even stronger terms. "If the American Racing Cyclists Union wants the endorsement of every fair-minded lover of sports in this country, it had better strike out that word 'white' in its rules ... and strike it out quick."[26]

Remarkably, Taylor took it all in his stride. With his fate and future as a professional cyclist hanging in the balance, he made a convincing attempt to be nonchalant. When asked what he would do if the riders refused to reinstate him, he said, "Well, I have other talents besides an ability to ride a bicycle, and I will use them. They can't prevent me from going to work, can they?"[27]

Finally, on May 28, 1900, the white bicycle racers who made up the executive committee of the American Racing Cyclists Union were forced to come to terms with the issue. They were training at the Vailsburg track, near Newark and after finishing their daily workout, they met in executive session at the Continental Hotel. Seven of the nine members of the committee were present: Earl Kiser, president; Tom Cooper, first vice president and treasurer; Orlando Stevens, second vice president; Howard Freeman, secretary; John Fisher; Jay Eaton; and F. Edward Spooner. Taylor had gone to Vailsburg on the advice of his old friend and trainer Bob Ellingham, so he was on hand, but was not invited to the meeting.

In the days preceding the meeting, there had been some hectic lobbying against Taylor's reinstatement by white bicycle racers who were not on the committee. Californian Floyd MacFarland was especially active in opposition, and there was a lengthy and heated debate. Taylor's rivals had to decide between their own aversion to the black rider and his popularity with the general public.

What were the main offences with which Taylor was charged? The principal one was that he had broken his contract to appear at Cape Girardeau, leaving promoters, riders, and spectators in the lurch. Another was his desertion of the ARCU for the LAW, which delayed the demise of the League. Taylor had, indeed, broken a contractual agreement, but the life suspension had been out of all proportion to the seriousness of the offense, more an indication of the racist feelings and spitefulness of the riders than a legitimate response. Thus, he felt no loyalty to the ARCU or its plans to oust the LAW.

Relunctantly, Tom Cooper, the professional champion of the NCA in 1899, made the motion to reinstate Taylor. Fisher seconded it, and with deceptive ease, by a unanimous vote, Taylor was reinstated, with a fine of $500 – $100 to the ARCU for having left the organization in 1898 and $400 for the prize money which had been lost when the black residents withdrew it at the Cape Girardeau race.

The white riders were forced in the end to capitulate to public opinion. They were extremely sensitive to the accusation that they were cowards, that they were trying to oust Taylor because they were afraid of being beaten by him. They also knew that his presence in races swelled the gate receipts, made the promoters happy, and meant larger cash prizes for them. Thus, practical considerations overrode their fundamental racism. Ironically, they were right, that by voting him back into the sport in May 1900, they were setting themselves up for certain defeat.

In the end, they were allowing Taylor back into bicycle racing not because they liked him, admired him or respected him, but because the public wanted to see him, and because they did not want it said that they were afraid of him.

The *Worcester Telegram* reported: "The arguments advanced at the meeting in favor of Taylor's reinstatement were that such action should be taken for the general good of the sport. The members were called on to act favorably in line with good sportsmanship. Cycle racing needed Taylor, they agreed, and would receive a new impetus by the addition of his presence in the ranks fighting for the championship.

"Taylor's color, which caused all the trouble, was in large measure responsible for his return to the fold. Public sentiment was with him. The life sentence imposed by the A.R.C.U. would not stand the light of public opinion, and the men realized it. There has been a vast amount of comment on the point by newspapers in all parts of the country, and all agreed that such action was too harsh." A member of the ARCU committee admitted that "had Taylor been white, we would never have acted in this way. His case was reprehensible and almost unpardonable. But public sentiment was with him. ... I think that people will realize that the riders have acted most sensibly and for the general good of racing."[28]

What the decision said to the world at large was that, although the white riders did not like having to say yes to him, Taylor had become

USA, 1899—1901

a much too important athlete to exclude from the sport. The white riders did not overcome their own prejudices, but were forced to admit him into their midst on terms of equality.

Taylor had won a resounding victory against the deeply rooted prejudices of his white rivals. As a test case, it was a pioneering moment in the history of American sports. He had insisted on his right to compete on equal terms and had won. There would be no further challenges to his right to register in any American cycling organization, although there would continue to be many racial challenges in fierce battles on the tracks.

TAYLOR'S OLD TRAINER, Bob Ellingham, and Ellingham's employer, Fred Johnson, of the Iver Johnson Arms and Cycle Works, saw a bright commercial opportunity. Although he had not as yet competed in a single race, the extensive press coverage of Taylor's affairs had made him the most publicized bicycle racer that year. It was an ideal moment to sponsor the dynamic young bicycle racer. Johnson paid the $500 fine and agreed to sponsor Taylor for the rest of the season.

Early in June, Taylor and Ellingham went to the Iver Johnson factory in Fitchburg to see about making some new bicycles. They decided that Taylor should give up riding the chainless bicycle, which was good for fast high-gear riding behind a pacing machine but inappropriate for the short-distance sprinting he would concentrate on during the remainder of 1900. Thus, Taylor returned to riding standard chain-driven bicycles, which were now painted in the brilliant trademark colors of blue and red, and he wore a matching blue racing suit with the company's name blazoned across the front of his jersey. Once again, Taylor was supported by some of his most ardent and reliable allies, that group of liberal white bicycle manufacturers of New England who recognized his genius and honored him as an athlete.

The decision to sponsor Taylor was a coup for the well-known Fitchburg bicycle manufacturing company. IVER JOHNSON'S SURPRISE. UNEXPECTEDLY REENTERS THE RACING GAME. TAYLOR EMPLOYED AS THEIR STAR, headlined *Bicycling World*. "The surprise comprises an unexpected reentry into the racing game with no less than the redoubtable Major Taylor comprising the Iver Johnson 'team,' and few will dispute that the colored wonder is a whole team to himself. ... Coming just at this time, when the trade with few exceptions has set itself against support of racing teams, the Iver Johnson move is in the nature of a clever stroke that will stand out and increase the advertising effects that will result." [29]

As had happened several times in the past, Taylor's athletic fortunes took a sudden turn for the better. From the nadir of a life suspension hanging over his head, he had soared to a position of almost unassailable dominance in the sport. Suddenly released from bureaucratic and financial worries, he had another chance to win the American sprint championship. France would have to wait another year. He would be worth even more if he crossed the Atlantic as the unchallenged champion of America.

For the first time in 1900, Taylor stood on firm ground. The year had been an emotional roller coaster for him, from the personal anguish of his sister's death in April, to the difficulties of dealing with the enticing offers from France, to the settlement of his dispute with the ARCU. With the problems behind him, he could get down to some serious work, and he was soon training at one of his favorite haunts, the Charles River track. Once again, he had overcome opposition and adversity and looked forward to a promising year.

THE SETTLEMENT of the dispute between the LAW and the NCA and Taylor's reinstatement were good for the sport of bicycle racing. There was general relief that things were at last back to normal and that spectators would once again be able to see the best talents pitted against each other. Taylor would be in the field with many of his old white rivals – Cooper, Kiser, Stevens, MacFarland, Newhouse, Freeman, Downing, Eaton, the Butler brothers, and others. And there would be one hot new rival, too, Frank Kramer, from East Orange, New Jersey, the outstanding young amateur champion of 1899, who had just turned professional and was widely touted as the man to watch.

Overcoming a slow start, while he was recovering his form, Taylor met Kramer, at the end of June, at Manhattan Beach, in the first of their many bitterly fought match races. "When Kramer and the Major come together, the spectators will see two of the most graceful riders in the world," the *Worcester Spy* predicted. The race excited a great deal of interest, and the 'black whirlwind' disposed of his young blonde rival in two straight heats and won the $500 prize. "Taylor is a fine figure of a racing man," said the Wheel. "Usually the crowd does not enthuse much over a man of the off color; but Taylor's character is fine and it shines through his face. ... He is distinctly liked by the crowd." [30]

A few days later, Taylor beat Jay Eaton, considered one of the best sprinters in the NCA ranks, for another purse of $500 at the Vailsburg board track. He seemed to ride effortlessly, hardly needing to exert himself to win. He rode alongside Eaton "with a cheerful, infectious grin on his dusky face. He won this heat with ease and as he got off his wheel the crowd cheered him lustily." Eaton sat up on the homestretch, so badly was he beaten. One reporter said, "Major Taylor showed very plainly why the professionals of this country took such good care last season not to permit him to try his mettle against them." [31]

Taylor's desire to win in front of the enormous crowd of fans in his hometown of Indianapolis on July 18 was enhanced by the presence of his father. "My father, who was a veteran of the Civil War," wrote Taylor, "had as his guests on the occasion a number of his comrades in the Union Army. It marked the first time that he had ever consented to see me race and made me doubly desirous of giving one of my best performances."

Although Taylor was beaten by the Louisville rider Owen Kimble in his heat of the one-third mile championship race, one of his rare defeats that year, he went on to score a resounding victory in the 2-mile handicap. After the races were over, Gilbert Taylor came to his son's dressing room to congratulate him, but with a surprised look on his face. "Well, son," he said, "there is one thing I don't understand. That is, if you are the fastest bicycle rider in the world, as the newspapers say you are, why don't you beat those white boys out further at the finish line?"

"Well, I won by a couple of lengths, didn't I?" replied Taylor.

"Yes," his father responded, "but I expected to see you leave them so far behind that you could get dressed and come out and see the rest of them fight it out for second and third money."

"The innocence of old age," commented Taylor when he wrote about the incident in his autobiography. "This was my father's idea of how fast his boy could ride a bicycle, and of what I was up against because of my color."

USA, 1899—1901

Taylor's dominance of the season continued. He won in Buffalo and New Bedford. He was laid up for a few days following a nasty crash in Hartford and had to suspend racing on the advice of his doctor, but he recovered quickly and was soon back on the tracks. In Milwaukee, a match race with one of his fiercest rivals and antagonists, Tom Cooper, the NCA champion of 1899, was finally arranged, with an unusual prize of $1,000, but it was canceled at the last moment when both riders agreed that the track on which it was to be held was much too dangerously constructed.

By midseason, with the departure to France of three of his keenest opponents – Cooper, MacFarland, and Stevens –, Taylor's competition was depleted. Manager Ellingham, determined to defend the prodigious reputation of his rider, insisted that his match races with individual rivals be on the basis of winner-take-all, leaving no share of the purse to the loser. So dangerous was Taylor as a sprinter, so difficult to beat, that he found himself with a shortage of opponents willing to meet him on these severe terms. "Major Taylor, the dusky whirlwind, has reached a point where he is in a class by himself with no one eligible to give him battle," commented a newspaper columnist. "In consequence of all the crack riders practically acknowledging that Taylor is the fastest rider on the track, which is the opinion of most good judges, he finds himself at a loss for matches."[32]

In August, at the opening of a splendid new track, the Coliseum, in Worcester, Taylor was "the attraction who stood head and shoulders over all his competitors." He demanded and received a hefty appearance fee from the track manager, Charles Culver, and then established a track record of 1 minute $37^1/_5$ seconds for the mile behind a motorcycle pacer under the yellow glare of the brand new electric lighting. "The crowd had never seen a motorcycle before," said the *Worcester Telegram*, "and they went wild over its speed."[33]

The heated rivalry between Taylor and Kimble was a racial powder keg, which no official recognition of the black rider could calm. Kimble's hometown of Louisville was the heartland of opposition to integrated bicycle racing. In Indianapolis early in September, Taylor was in such a close finish after a hectic shoulder-to-shoulder sprint with Kimble in the $^1/_3$-mile championship race that three of the five judges ruled a dead heat and asked them to ride the race over again. Both refused. Taylor claimed that he had won and that the judges were prejudiced against him. Kimble claimed that he had been fouled.

USA, 1899—1901

At a conference with the judges, a fight almost broke out between them. Finally, they agreed to rerun the race another evening for the original prize of $200, with an added $100. At this race, on September 11, where his old employer Tom Hay was one of the announcers and the Indianapolis military band played a rousing concert program, Taylor beat Kimble the second time around and made sure there was no question about it. "I never in my life found a man so hard to beat," Taylor told the *Indianapolis News*, "for when he gets up on his wheel against me, he seems to ride like a fiend."[34]

In his autobiography, Taylor expanded on the tense feeling that existed between him and Kimble.

Kimble, being a Southerner, did not like me because of my color," he wrote.

> He was naturally imbued with all of the old traditions relative to that perpetual color prejudice and race hatred that are so typical of that section of the country. Kimble felt that in order to uphold those inherited ideals of his forefathers, he was obliged to hate me with a genuine bitterness and to do his utmost to defeat me every time we met. Because of this intensity of color hatred for me, Kimble always seemed to be able to develop an extra degree of speed when battling it out with me that he never displayed against any other rider in the world.

Taylor also beat Kimble and Kramer in Indianapolis in an intense three-man battle in the final of the 2-mile championship race, which put him securely in the lead in the overall championship standings. Kimble and Kramer worked together to try to spoil Taylor's chances. Taylor talked constantly of the threat of such 'combinations.' He was up against what he called "that almost fiendish desire on the part of a field to humble a champion in his native city. ... Just enough of that 'color business' was injected into the race to rouse one's sporting blood, giving it just the right 'pep' and the public an extra run for their money." Neither of his opponents offered congratulations on his victory, but, thought Taylor, "The wonderful ovation given me by the sports lovers of Indianapolis ... again demonstrated that the public always likes to see the best man win." Taylor's pleasure in such victories was acute. It was not just the fact of beating his opponents and crossing the line first that thrilled him. "The real climax," he wrote, "was the glory of vindication and the joy of retribution following each success, which was always indeed a personal triumph, because of their prejudice and unsportsmanlike methods."

USA, 1899—1901

There was no cliff-hanging climax to the championship season of 1900. Taylor fought his way securely through the remainder of the qualifying events, beating Kramer and Kimble in Terre Haute, Erie, and the other circuit cities. He made a strong impression on spectators and the press in Erie, where he had not raced before, paying an expensive bill for the best room at the Liebel House Hotel. "The Major is a rare exception to his class generally," remarked an Erie newspaper.

> He is fairly modest, conservative and not overly proud or stuck up. ... He is very white for a colored man. Taylor has other qualities that should recommend him to the public. He never drinks, chews or smokes tobacco; does not use profane language; will not ride on Sunday and goes to church regularly. The Major looks the part. He is not as light as George Dixon, the boxer, but he is a dandy in dress and has a muscular development the envy of all the slim jims that see him.[35]

By the end of September, Taylor was the clear winner of the 1900 championship, with a decisive lead of 40 points over Kramer's 20 and Kimble's 18. Kramer's performance was a remarkable one, considering it was his first season as a professional, but Taylor had finally realized his fondest dream, becoming the sprint champion of America in open competition. After a hesitant start to the season's racing, he had triumphed over the best of the American sprinters and was uncontestably the fastest of them all. It was, said *Cycle Age*, "an almost unbroken string of victories, culminating in a flawless win of the American championship."[36]

Taylor was thrilled, and so was Fred Johnson, who had pinned his faith on Taylor to advertise his company's bicycles. "I must own," the New York representative of the company told *Cycle Age*, "that I was rather skeptical at first at this, for us, very radical departure in advertising. We gave the new departure, however, a fair trial. Not only did we make the Major's victories prominent in our display advertising, but we kept our agents constantly informed on his successes on the Iver Johnson bicycle. I am now absolutely convinced that his riding of our wheel was a most profitable advertising investment."[37]

THERE WAS TALK of Taylor going after more motor-paced records, benefiting from his end-of-season strength and fitness to attack the prestigious 1-mile world record, as he had done at the end of 1898 and 1899. But instead of undertaking the stress and strain of more record breaking, Taylor embarked on a new career. Capitalizing on his success and fame as champion of America, he decided to go into vaudeville.

Vaudeville was the popular entertainment of the day and part of Taylor's everyday experience. He liked to strum on the mandoline and played ragtime on the piano and had a fine singing voice. A bicycle racer was, after all, also a popular entertainer. Contracting with Charles Culver, manager of the Worcester Coliseum bicycle track, Taylor agreed to ride indoor races on the 'home trainer' against the famous 'Mile-a-Minute' Murphy. Home trainers were machines consisting of a number of rollers, upon which the cyclists balanced and rode their bicycles on the spot. Two home trainers were set up alongside each other on the stage of a theater and connected to big dials, which showed the distance the two riders had covered by means of two big arrows. The machines were splendidly set up on stage, decorated with flags. With the firing of a pistol, the race began, the two men pedaling furiously, while the audience followed their progress from the two arrows. A 5-mile race heated to a frenzy of sprinting in front of the roaring, cheering crowd.

Culver thought the act would be an instant hit, and he was right. When it opened at the Park Theater in Worcester at the end of October, sandwiched between comedy routines, acrobatics, song and dance acts, and moving pictures, it was an instant success. The audience "cheered until it was hoarse as the race progressed," reported the *Worcester Telegram*, "bursting into wild enthusiasm when the report of the pistol marked the finish – a dead heat. The hands of the dial at the rear of the stage showed the riders' progress, and one followed them as they moved around the circle with as much interest as one would riders on a race track."[38]

From Worcester, the unusual vaudeville team of Taylor and Murphy went on to Pittsfield for a week, where they appeared between the third and fourth acts of the Herald Square Comedy Company's production of *Michael Strogoff* at the Academy of Music. Then they were off to Springfield for a week at the New Gilmore Theater. Taylor also rode a mile on his home trainer in the window of a Hartford bicycle dealer's shop in the record time of $43^3/5$ seconds, a speed equivalent to 82.5 mph. A crowd of more than a thousand people watched him.

USA, 1899—1901

Having established the success of the act, Culver contracted with Keith's Theater in Boston for the two cyclists to appear nightly on the Boston stage, and the home trainer races continued throughout December and January. Keith's was perhaps the most famous vaudeville company on the East Coast, and it was they who pioneered the idea of a continuous, revolving performance, which the audience could enter and leave as they pleased.

TAYLOR DID NOT ride in the six-day race at Madison Square Garden that winter. At the request of Fred Johnson, he turned down a surprising offer to team up with his archenemy, Floyd MacFarland, in one of the newly introduced two-man teams. Johnson preferred that Taylor stay with short-distance racing, which was always his forte. But Johnson did arrange for him to meet with another archrival, Tom Cooper, in a 1-mile match race staged at Madison Square Garden as part of the festivities on the opening night of the six-day race.

In the same place, four years before, as a brand new young professional who had just celebrated his eighteenth birthday, Taylor had challenged and beaten the reigning American champion, Eddie Bald, in a sensational race that had immediately established his reputation. By 1900, Taylor and Cooper were both famous stars, concerned not with establishing their American or international reputations, but with defending them. Taylor, world champion of 1899, LAW champion of 1899 and reigning NCA champion of 1900, was pitted against Cooper, the NCA champion of 1899, who had just returned from a successful tour in France, even though beaten by the great Edmond Jacquelin, the world champion and French champion of 1900. If Taylor could beat Cooper in New York, the victory would enhance his status as the best American sprinter and rank him as the legitimate challenger to Jacquelin's world title.

The race was so important to Taylor that he put in two weeks' special training for it, as well as continuing to work out in the home trainer races, which kept him supple and fit. He had often competed against Cooper, but never in a match race. "If there were two riders on earth that I wanted to meet in match races above all others, they were Eddie Bald and Tom Cooper," wrote Taylor. "Now, after three or four years of dickering and yearning, my opportunity to meet him was at hand." The prize was $500, and Taylor had insisted on his usual terms that season: no sharing the prize money with the loser.

USA, 1899—1901

Bob Ellingham and Tom Eck, the managers of the bitter rivals, eyed each other suspiciously as their men came out onto the track in the crowded, smoke-filled arena. Taylor later recollected the witty but bitter repartee exchanged between them.

"Well, Bob, Tom will now proceed to hand your little darkey the most artistic trimming of his young life," said Eck. "In this first heat Tom is going to give the Major his first real lesson in the fine points of the French style of match racing. Tom has a fine assortment of brand new tactics, fresh from Paris. ... However, Bob, I have cautioned Tom, in the best interest of the sport and for the good of all concerned, not to beat the little darkey too badly."

Taylor and Cooper smiled at each other as they listened to Ellingham's sarcastic reply.

"It is true, Mr. Eck," he said, "that Major Taylor has never raced in Paris and will, therefore, be obliged to ride this race on what he has been able to pick up on this side of the pond. What he may lack in track strategy he will have to make up in gameness and speed. He is always willing to learn and never lets an opportunity slip by to teach the other fellow a point or two."

The occasion was a typically raucous New York success. "Ten thousand howling enthusiasts packed the boxes, galleries, the oval and aisles of Madison Square Garden," said *Cycle Age*, "and proved that cycle racing of high degree is as popular as ever with New Yorkers."[39] Despite Cooper's recent European success, Taylor confidently disposed of him in two straight heats. There was no need for a third. MAJOR TAYLOR, THE MARVELOUS COLORED SPRINTER, UPHOLDS HIS SUPREMACY, lauded the *New York Journal.*[40] No one could say that had Cooper remained in the United States, Taylor would never have won the American championship. It was another unarguable triumph for the Major.

"Had the purse been $5,000 instead of $500, it would have been a mere bagatelle compared with the supreme satisfaction that I felt over my defeat of Tom Cooper," remembered Taylor.

> If ever a race was run for blood this one was. World wide prestige went hand in hand with the victory. Neither Cooper nor Eck offered to shake hands with me at the close of the race, nor did they utter a word of congratulation. I have never seen a more humiliated pair of Toms than were Cooper and Eck as they marched silently to their dressing room.

As a matter of fact, I was equally silent as Ellingham and I repaired to our dressing room. I had never indulged in boasting over my conquests either within the hearing of my opponents or elsewhere. I felt that real sportsmanship demanded that an athlete wear his laurels modestly. ... It is still my belief that no real champion in any line of sport could or would resort to such ungentlemanly conduct. But many times I have had all I could possibly do to refrain from handing out a bit of the old sarcasm.

Watching the crucial race between Cooper and Taylor was the manager of the European riders who had come to New York for the six-day race, Robert Coquelle, Victor Breyer's young business partner and a colleague of his on the staff of *Le Vélo*. More than ever, Coquelle was determined to persuade 'le nègre volant' to cross to France. He was enormously impressed with Taylor. He wrote in *Le Vélo* that he was built like a bronze statue and that he simply toyed with Cooper in their match race.[41] He thought Taylor would be able to beat every champion in Europe, if only he could be persuaded to sign a contract.

Taylor continued to repeat that he would not compromise on the issue of Sunday racing. Coquelle promised all kinds of money if he would agree to drop his scruples, but Taylor insisted that he would not go to France until he was satisfied that it would be profitable for him to race only on weekdays. Until then, he would take his chances on American tracks.

A fresh round of negotiations took place while Taylor was performing on stage at Keith's Theater in Boston and Coquelle was looking after his riders at the Boston six-day race on the tiny track at Park Square Garden. On one occasion Coquelle, together with two of his riders, Champion and Gougoltz, visited Taylor at his home in Worcester, where they met his father Gilbert, who Coquelle later described as a venerable white-haired man, who showed them portraits of Roosevelt and Booker T. Washington hanging on the wall and asked them how they liked America.

"Oh, wonderful, magnificent!" Coquelle replied.

"Is Paris as beautiful?" Gilbert Taylor asked.

"Oh, much better! Major will be able to tell you all about it later on because I hope very much to be able to take him over to France."[42]

Once again, Coquelle offered Taylor $10,000 for a tour that included Sunday racing. Taylor refused. Coquelle then offered $3,000 for just weekday appearances. At first, Taylor agreed, then changed his mind, saying it was not enough money. Coquelle became angry and announced that he was breaking off all negotiations. He was incredulous that Taylor could turn down the offer of such a large sum of money because he refused to race on Sundays. For a time it looked as though the deal had fallen through completely.

But a compromise was found. They agreed on a sum of $7,200, no Sunday racing. They had a contract at last! Coquelle's determination and Taylor's intense desire to race in France had finally effected a compromise. Taylor had remained steadfast to his moral principles and Coquelle had secured his rider and might still do very well promoting weekday races. It was the beginning of a long and sometimes stormy friendship and business relationship between the young French promoter and the famous black American star, which appears to have been one of mutual affection and respect. Coquelle, born in 1875, and only three years older than Taylor, had himself been a talented racing cyclist between 1894 and 1898, and a member of a star triplet team during the heyday of human-powered paced racing. Coquelle claimed later that it was he who had in fact 'invented' Major Taylor as a European star. Certainly his determination over the years to persuade Taylor to pursue his European career was a crucial factor in the unfolding saga of Taylor's life.

The *Worcester Telegram* reporter was on the spot in Boston and headlined his article: TAYLOR ON CONTRACT! GREAT SPRINTER IS TO RIDE ALL EUROPE! Taylor had finally signed a contract with Coquelle to race against world champion Edmond Jacquelin in Paris in May.[43]

Coquelle kept the wires to France humming with the good news. It was a great business coup for him personally and a great event for French bicycle racing. "Sensational news, which I can guarantee the accuracy of," he wired to *Le Vélo* on January 3. "After much hesitation, Major Taylor has finally decided to make the voyage which has been awaited for so long by every European sportsman. Yesterday evening, at 8:40 P.M., Major Taylor signed the contract."[44] On receiving the news in his office in Paris, Breyer was jubilant. The eagerly anticipated contract was signed and sealed. The American champion every French sports fan was desperate to see was finally coming to France!

9
SUPERSTAR

THE FOUR months Major Taylor spent in Europe, from March to June 1901, proved to be the climax of his athletic career. At the zenith of his physical strength and international popularity, he arrived in France at the culmination of a long period of rumors and promises of his imminent coming. Promoters and spectators were hungry for the new sensation. There would be something magical about that first visit, something that gripped the public imagination.

There could have been no more incredible adventure for this twenty-two-year-old black American. He was thrust suddenly into a totally new world, just as he had been as a child in the Southard household. It was so different from anything he had experienced in America that he was totally unprepared for the reception he was given by the cycling world and the European public. He had been told that he would be popular, but to become a superstar overnight amazed him.

In America, bicycle racing was a cutthroat affair, and Taylor had battled his way through four years of tough professional competition, succeeding in spite of intense racist opposition. Bicycle racing was also a tough and fiercely contested sport in France. And it was, at the turn of the century, well on its way to becoming the national sport, its champions revered and idolized as heroes, as they still are today.

Even though Taylor had become famous in America, respected and admired by friends, employers, and white and black spectators alike, he had never been able to enjoy his success. There had always been a new problem just around the corner. His fame had always been qualified and tinged with doubt and suspicion, limited by racial antagonism. Vehement hostility from most of the white racers and officials was never far below the surface when he came out on the track, and often it was extremely blatant. In his own country, he was a persona non grata, but from the moment he arrived in France, he was a *cause célèbre*, the long-awaited, much-publicized champion. Immediately, he was transformed into a hero, one who excited the curiosity and imagination of all who came in contact with him. In France, where prejudice was replaced by fascination, Taylor was able to grow and flourish. His athletic achievements were widely appreciated, and as the underdog who had triumphed against overwhelming odds on the other side of the Atlantic, a mystique surrounded him. Promoters and spectators alike did not try to diminish him because he was black. They welcomed him because he injected a new element of excitement and drama into the sport.

Because of France's colonial history, blacks did not have an integral place in its tightly structured culture, nor were they viewed as a threat to white pride and security. Thus, this mysterious outsider, this handsome, young, well-behaved stranger, posed no threat as an example to an aspiring black underclass. It was this unique identity, as well as his phenomenal athletic talents, that allowed Taylor to be elevated to the status of a superstar.

Paris prided itself on being the sporting capital of the world at the turn of the century, just as the French capital was the mecca for artists, writers, and composers, who made it the cultural center of the world. Only London and New York rivaled it. To compete against international rivals in Paris was to have reached the pinnacle of success. Parisian spectators were well known for their enthusiasm and sophistication. Bicycle racing was the most popular sport of the moment and thousands flocked to velodromes all over the country. What was especially interesting about the French riders and spectators was their sense of style, their understanding of the more refined and aesthetic aspects of bicycle racing. Tactics, for instance, were much more important there. American spectators wanted drama and excitement and hated what they called 'loafing,' when the riders rode slowly, watching and waiting for the others to make a move. In America, especially with a big field, there was a tendency to dash madly for the finishing line, often with a pacemaker to make sure the speed was fast and furious. In France, particularly in match sprinting, there was a greater tendency to play the watching and waiting game, sounding out the opponent, trying to affect him psychologically, then waiting for the optimum moment to surprise him and jump away.

Taylor adapted easily to the French style of racing. His own style had always been extremely tactical. He had always been forced to watch and analyze every move his opponents made.

IN THE THROES of making preparations for his departure for Europe, Taylor wrote to Coquelle in Paris. He was in excellent health, he said, and eager to get back to serious training when he arrived in France. He thought four weeks would be enough time for him to get into condition as long as the weather was not too cold, and he was sure he would be ready to take on any opponent by the beginning of April.

After saying good-bye to his friends in Worcester, Taylor left for New York on March 4. With him was William Buckner, an experienced trainer from Chicago who had been engaged for the trip to Europe. A good trainer was a crucial component of a professional cyclist's success. A combination of masseur, doctor, mechanic, and general assistant, he fulfilled an important practical and psychological supporting role, advising about training procedures and tactics during races. Buckner, who was black, was one of the most experienced trainers in the sport. There was no opposition in the United States to the idea of a black trainer, and many of the white champions employed them.

One of Buckner's responsibilities was to take charge of the large wooden trunk that contained Taylor's Iver Johnson bicycles and all his racing equipment – wheels, spare cogs and tires, clothes, and tools. The trunk was beautiful and attracted a lot of attention. Painted a bright royal blue and varnished, it was inscribed in striking red letters, MAJOR TAYLOR, THE AMERICAN CHAMPION. The bicycles themselves were finished in a brilliant black enamel, with a contrasting red head tube and rims.

Worcester was intensely interested in his adventure. Headlines in the local newspapers proclaimed: WILL MEET THE BEST! MAJOR TAYLOR GOES AFTER NEW LAURELS. WILL RACE ON FASTEST TRACKS IN EUROPE. WORCESTER STAR IN FINEST CONDITION and WORLD CHAMPION WILL SAIL TOMORROW. MAJOR TAYLOR, CYCLING WONDER, ASTUTE FINANCIER AND YOUNG MAN OF STAUNCH CHRISTIAN PRINCIPLES WILL COMPETE ON EUROPEAN RACE TRACKS – NO SUNDAY RACES ON THE PROGRAM...

When Taylor boarded the *Kaiser Wilhelm der Grosse,* one of the fastest luxury trans-Atlantic liners, capable of a six-day crossing under normal conditions, some of his New York friends were there to see him off with a large floral creation in the shape of a racing bicycle, which they carried to his cabin. Everyone on board knew who he was, and he was luxuriously installed in a first-class cabin. During the journey, he skipped and ran and lifted weights to keep himself fit, but he was not a good sea traveler and was seasick most of the trip.

EUROPE, 1901

Even while Taylor was voyaging on the Atlantic Ocean, his promoters, Coquelle and Breyer, were putting their publicity machinery into high gear. The fans were pressing them for information, and hardly a day passed without letters from readers in the local press asking about his arrival. "Major Taylor is awaited like the Messiah," wrote Coquelle in *Le Vélo*. And he wrote a long and interesting article about Taylor in *La Vie au Grand Air,* a magazine read by everyone in Paris interested in sports. At last, after three years of waiting, Taylor was on his way. The French champion, Jacquelin, Coquelle said, was the only sprinter in Europe who had any chance of beating him. Drawing on his memory of their meetings in New York and Boston, Coquelle called him one of the most splendid athletes imaginable and described his superb body and style of riding.[2]

Coquelle was not at Cherbourg to meet Taylor when his ship arrived at the docks at three in the afternoon on March 11 because he was getting married that day. But another correspondent from *Le Vélo* was there, as well as a group of journalists from *L'Auto-Vélo*, the other daily Parisian cycling newspaper.[3]

After some brief introductions, the party boarded the special train for Paris, and at one in the morning, it was met at the Gare St. Lazare by Breyer and a group of his journalist friends, merry from celebrating Coquelle's wedding. Taylor leapt energetically from the first-class compartment and shook Breyer's hand. He was pleased with the reception and told Breyer how glad he was finally to be in France, a country he had wanted to visit for several years. He wanted to see and do everything, he said, but not before he had accomplished his main purpose, his training and racing.

No bicycle racer since the great Zimmerman had been so eagerly and impatiently awaited as Taylor, wrote Breyer the next morning in *Le Vélo*, and no other bicycle racer in the world could arouse the same amount of interest on the tracks of Europe.[4]

When Taylor was asked what his feelings were about his future rival, Edmond Jacquelin, champion of France and champion of the world, he replied, "They say he's the best man in the world. Well, when I'm in form, we'll see how I measure up to him right enough. I've never really found my equal in America, and if it wasn't for all the unpleasant tricks that my American colleagues play on me, I would hardly ever have been beaten." When asked whether he would race on Sundays, he said, "Absolutely not! Before I left home I swore to

God that I would never race on the Sabbath, and I don't like the idea of going to hell!"[5] Taylor was conducted by Breyer and the merry group of journalists, fans and hangers-on to the Hotel Scribe, where he finally got to bed at three in the morning.

AMID A FLURRY of attention from journalists and photographers and recognized and stared at wherever he went, Taylor set about the business of his first few days in Paris. Everywhere, he was the center of attention. Crowds waited in the morning at his hotel to inquire whether he had passed a good night, and the press reported with amazement that on his very first morning in Paris, he had risen at 6 A.M. and gone for a walk with Buckner. Seamstresses and shop-boys hurrying to work recognized him as he tasted the atmosphere of the Parisian streets and gazed with curiosity down the length of the Avenue de l'Opéra.

Whenever Taylor went out, crowds followed him in the street, all wanting to shake his hand. A black man was still a rarity in Paris, and he wrote to a friend in Worcester that he felt like a prizefighter in the United States. The aristocracy left their calling cards at his hotel, and he was inundated with invitations to attend social and sporting events. The daily newspapers reported his every move, what he did, what he said, what he ate, what he looked like. They analyzed his racing abilities and compared him with his famous French rival, Jacquelin.

At the office of *Le Vélo,* Breyer reported, Taylor walked around the editorial rooms like an enthusiastic child, leafing through back issues and admiring photos and portraits of cycling champions pinned up on the walls. Letters continued to pour into the newspaper, demanding information about Taylor and photographs. Crowds waited all day outside the Hotel Scribe, hoping for a glimpse of him. "It really is true that Major Taylor is a king in his field," wrote Breyer, "the king of the bicycle." [6]

On his first Sunday morning in Paris, Taylor went to an English church, then sailed down the Seine in the afternoon. In the Bois de Boulogne he was fascinated by the comings and goings of all the bicycles and automobiles. Met by a journalist who wanted to take him to a café, he refused politely – "Never on Sundays," he said.

Taylor also gave interviews to visiting journalists at his hotel and waited impatiently for someone to translate the French newspapers and illustrated magazines for him. When a reporter from *L'Auto-Vélo* visited him, he sat down at the piano and without any prompting, gave him a sample of his remarkable singing talent.

One evening, the entire staff of *L'Auto-Vélo* took him to the circus to see 'Little Chocolate,' the clown, the only other famous black person in Paris at the time. 'Chocolate' referred to Taylor's presence during his performance, and all eyes in the theater were turned towards the box where Taylor sat, enjoying himself immensely.

Taylor was also taken to the Café Espérance, the cycling café on the Avenue de la Grande-Armée, where old champions like Bourrillon and Constant Huret and riders, trainers, promoters, and journalists gathered for cycling talk and a bottle of wine. There Taylor renewed his friendships with some of the European stars he had met in New York and Boston.

One afternoon, Jacquelin passed the café in his automobile and saw Taylor surrounded by a group of admirers. "That's Taylor," he cried and, jumping out of the car, ran to greet him. Within five minutes, the two champions had become fast friends. Jacquelin was surprised that Taylor was so small. A tape measure was produced, and the two men began comparing their measurements.

"You have splendid big legs," said Taylor.

"Yes, but yours are so much prettier," replied Jacquelin.

"That may be so," responded Taylor, "but yours are so much stronger than mine."

"But suppose yours prove quicker than mine? What then?" was Jacquelin's final retort.[7]

The proprietor of the Café Espérance brought out a bottle of champagne to propose a toast to Taylor's health, and everyone was astonished when Taylor refused to take even the smallest sip from the glass poured for him. Instead, he asked for a glass of water to toast his new friends and gulped it down with obvious pleasure.

At lunch with Coquelle at Sylvain's, a restaurant popular with the sporting crowd, he was, of course, instantly recognized by everyone from the chef to the busboys. Overjoyed to find himself the center of attention, Taylor stood up with a beaming smile on his face, and shook hands with everyone there, customers and staff alike.

When Taylor went for the first time to the Parc des Princes velodrome in Auteuil, a Paris suburb, to unpack his bicycles, install himself in his cabin there and inspect the track, a huge crowd followed him. "There was such a big crowd on hand I thought there was a race meet on," Taylor told a reporter. As he had grown in the habit of trusting in the number 13, he asked for cabin number 13 but found that it was full of brooms and other equipment and had not been used by any of the cyclists for a long time. So he was given cabin number 57, next door to Jacquelin. When he appeared on the track, people waiting in the stands took off their hats and shouted "Vive Taylor!" A football game that was in progress on the infield of the track was stopped, and both teams joined in the cheering. The fans insisted that Taylor take a spin around the track, and he obliged them by borrowing a bicycle and slowly riding a lap, followed by a crowd of amateur racers, all of whom wanted to ride right behind him, glued to his back wheel.

A few days after his arrival in Paris, an important editorial entitled "Black and White" was published on the front page of *Le Vélo*. The author, Paul Hamelle, probed and explored the significance of Taylor's life and career and speculated about his chances against Jacquelin. The arrival of Taylor in France, he said, "the man with a dark skin, child of old Africa and young America, champion of the world and of two races, the heroic guardian of the Sabbath," was a sensational event and could only be compared in importance with Zimmerman's visit eight years before. But there were big differences between the two champions, he said, because Zimmerman had been the uncontested king of cycling when he arrived in Europe, he was a known quantity, and he was white. Taylor, however, was black and an unknown quantity. "His reputation is as much the result of our own ignorance and the unusual nature of his career as of his own undoubted, but as yet unproven, merits. He arouses our curiosity all the more, appears more important, because he is an unknown quantity, and is surrounded by mystery because of the color of his skin."[8] When speaking of Taylor, Hamelle continued,

> ... one must always bear in mind that he is black and that he has done all of his racing in America..In order to cross the finishing line first, he has not only had to be better than each of his rivals individually, but also better than them collectively. In every one of his races, he has come up against the instinctive and spontaneous coalition of all of his white brothers....and each victory of Taylor's has been won against all the rest of the riders.

He was not exaggerating at all in saying this, emphasized Hamelle.

The Negro was the enemy who absolutely had to be beaten, against
whom his rivals had to do battle, sometimes dishonestly, always passionately. Owen Kimble, for example, full of the pride of his race, in
no way an extraordinary rider, has done some remarkable performances against Major Taylor, who always considered him as the most brutal of his opponents. Kimble was seized by a kind of atavistic rage, the
rage of the master confronted by the fact that he could be beaten by a
descendant of one of the slaves his father used to whip.[9]

Hamelle concluded that Taylor was actually a better rider than his victories would seem to indicate. Just as important as the fact of winning
was the way he won, he said. And Taylor's style was very impressive.
"Everybody remarks on the ease with which he exerts himself," he
wrote, "they admire his supple power, his skill and cunning, his jump
and his final sprint. Everybody who has seen him gets the impression
that he is not giving everything he has, that he always has a reserve
of energy. ... There is something mysterious about his power, and
this mystery is itself a potent force."[10]

Taylor was soon installed in his cabin at the Parc des Princes with
his bicycles assembled and prepared. He visited the offices of various
tire manufacturers in Paris before signing a contract with a company
that made a tire called *Le Pâris*. He was anxious to begin riding, but
the weather was bitter and icy, and more than a week after his arrival
he had still not begun to train. On March 23, he went to the track,
determined to put in some preliminary miles, but he suffered so much
from the cold weather that he sat shivering in his cabin, refusing to
respond to the pleas of his colleagues to dress warmly and get on his
bicycle. He repeated several times, "I am an African, not a European,"
when they tried to encourage him. Finally, he consented, and dressed
entirely in blue, with a large number 13 pinned to the back of his jersey, he rode onto the track amid the applause of a small crowd of onlookers.

Breyer was surprised by Taylor's position on his bicycle during this
early season training, for his handlebars were rather high and his saddle rather low. Even his racing position was much flatter than any
other sprinter at the time. "He has a very strange position on his
bicycle, rather unattractive at first sight," wrote Breyer. "He is not bent
over the bicycle, and literally lies on his machine with his upper body
almost horizontal. ... But his pedaling is remarkably supple and his

body does not move at all, even when he is making his maximum effort."[11]

Taylor's style of riding was always described as being beautifully smooth, agile, and economical. Unlike many riders, who were jerky and harsh in their movements, his upper body remained practically motionless and his legs spun with a seemingly effortless power. His superb sprinting ability was based not primarily on powerful muscular development, but on his overall strength and fitness and his suppleness and agility. Of his position on his bicycle, Taylor wrote the following:

> My racing position was made conspicuous because of the absence of any unnecessary motion of the head or body ... I reasoned that any unnecessary motions only tended to impede the rider's efforts, whereas if the same amount of exertion were employed in the only motion necessary, from the hips down, with a light, quick motion of the ankle, it would not only produce a maximum of efficiency, but by constant practice it would produce an easy, graceful celerity of motion that is pleasing to the eye. It would also conserve the rider's energy for the final lap where it is most needed.

Many of the sprinters of the 1890s used deeply plunging handlebars and were almost tilted forward on their bicycles. Taylor's position, as Breyer remarked, was different and very unusual at the time. He sat rather low on his bicycle, with the handlebars somewhat high up and extended forward, so that his position resembled that of a modern road rider. In order to ride in this position and to be able to adjust his handlebars minutely, he designed what came to be known as the 'Major Taylor' or 'outrigger',stem, seen in many of the photographs.[12]

As the weather improved slightly, Taylor relaxed and began to settle into his usual rigorous training regime, appearing in the mornings at ten o'clock and in the afternoons at three, greeted at every session by a crowd of several hundred admirers and fans who paid a few cents for the privilege of being there. They hung over the railings around the outside of the track, getting as close as possible to their hero. His style and his machines were carefully examined and analyzed by the other cyclists, and each morning *Le Vélo* and *L'Auto-Vélo* reported interesting details about his previous day's workout.

But it was still cold and rainy at times, and when he was prevented from going out on the track, Taylor skipped and boxed indoors with Buckner or hit away at his punching ball, which he said was good for

his wind and the firmness of his stomach. When the rain fell in torrents one day, he passed the entire morning looking at paintings in
the Louvre. Even the guards recognized him and nudged one another,
pointing and whispering, "You know who that is, don't you, that's
Major Taylor." When he was not training, or giving interviews at his
hotel, or visiting the sights of Paris, Taylor read and wrote letters or
played the piano or mandolin. He was also a keen photographer and
took pictures with the portable Kodak he had brought with him from
the United States.

On March 28, when a heavy snowfall made it unthinkable to train,
Taylor was invited to lunch at the fashionable Excelsior Hotel by the
Count de Dion, the pioneer automobile manufacturer, and several of
his distinguished friends, who were delighted to meet with the man
of the moment, the most famous athlete in Paris. Taylor was introduced to these important figures in the French automobile world by
his friend, Henri Fournier, the ex-champion of France, who was a
well-known motorcycle and car racer on both sides of the Atlantic.
After lunch, he visited the de Dion-Bouton factory, rode in a de Dion
automobile, had tea at five o'clock, and then posed for a photograph
– de Dion, the great engineer, and Major Taylor, the great cyclist. In
France, Taylor's color was not a barrier to meeting with such distinguished men. At such moments, his self-assurance served him well.
He was not uncomfortable or overawed and took such encounters in
his stride. He had not exactly "come out' in society, *L'Auto-Vélo* said
of his meeting with the famous count, but he had certainly had a very
interesting experience of what it meant to be a Parisian.[13]

The rhythm of Taylor's training intensified when the spring sun
began to shine through the rain clouds. "Major Taylor is beginning to
really fly," reported Coquelle on April 2; "he made a very strong impression yesterday on everyone who has been following his daily
workouts. His position is much better now than on the first day, and
his pedaling is much more relaxed."[14] The following day, Breyer reported that the hundred or so spectators who were watching Taylor's
training had been amazed by the way he had sprinted away from the
other riders. His mood improved with his condition, and one afternoon, he entertained the other riders with a demonstration of his skill
as a trick rider, riding backwards and steering with his feet, which
was much appreciated by the habitués of the Parc des Princes.

TAYLOR'S FIRST European racing engagement was not in Paris but in Berlin. He left the French capital on the night train on April 6 to undertake the first of many long nocturnal journeys across the continent during the next three months. The weather was still very cold and wet, and the intensive training he had hoped for had been seriously curtailed. Coquelle, who saw him and Breyer off at the Gare du Nord, had never seen Taylor looking so sad and gloomy.

In Berlin, at the Friedenau track, on his first appearance in Europe, Taylor was beaten in the final of the 1,000-meter sprint by Willy Arend, the young German champion, and Thorwald Ellegaard, champion of Denmark. The weather was terribly cold, and Taylor complained bitterly. Three days later, however, he took his revenge by beating Arend and Ellegaard convincingly amid a tremendous ovation. After the race, Arend gave Taylor a photo of himself, on which he wrote, "From Willy Arend, to his esteemed black colleague." A crowd of about 500 escorted Taylor from the track to the railway station. The extraordinary routine of his triumphant European tour had begun.

From Berlin, Taylor went to Roubaix, in northeast France, and Verviers and Antwerp in Belgium, where he beat the twenty-one year-old Belgian champion, Louis Grogna, on three occasions. At each city the tracks were filled to capacity, and people traveled long distances to see the sensational 'Nègre volant.' In Roubaix, Coquelle, who was traveling with Taylor, reported that he was the center of attention and aroused everyone's curiosity. He was met at the station by an elegant open carriage and rode in splendid style to his hotel, waving to the crowds who lined the road cheering him as he passed, just as if he were a visiting minister or ambassador. At the Hotel Moderne, where Taylor asked for and received room number 13, a procession of people, determined to meet the famous athlete, waited from morning to night. At Verviers he once again insisted on taking cabin number 13 at the track, which was normally used as a first aid post for injured riders.

After each race in a foreign city or a French town, Taylor returned to Paris to resume his training at the Parc des Princes and to receive mail from home. Letters arrived from the United States addressed simply "Major Taylor, Paris, France" or "Major Taylor, Champion American Cyclist, Paris, France." They had no trouble reaching him, such was his fame at that moment. In Paris he also discussed his future engagements with Coquelle and Breyer. The contract between them stipu-

EUROPE, 1901

lated, of course, that there was to be no Sunday racing, and all his races had to be carefully scheduled to coincide with national holidays that fell on weekdays in the various European countries. Coquelle and Breyer, as well as other promoters and riders, quickly discovered that successful events could indeed be held on weekdays when there was a star attraction.

Taylor's visit to Bordeaux at the beginning of May was an event of great local importance, since this French city boasted the most ardent cycling enthusiasts outside of Paris. He was booked to appear there just before the start of the famous Bordeaux—Paris road race, and processions of bicycle racing fans arrived at the Vélodrome du Parc from all over southwest France, some of them riding long distances to see the famous black rider.

Taylor was picked up by a chauffeur in a superb Dorsay six-seater automobile belonging to Henri Barbereau-Bergeon, promoter of the race in which he was to appear, and taken on a short tour of the city. When he was dropped off at the track for a training session, Taylor was greeted by a huge crowd of people awaiting his arrival.

The race meet on May 2 was almost a disaster. The Vélodrome du Parc was crowded with fans, waiting in high spirits for their first glimpse of Taylor. But the newly installed electric lights failed to work, and the riders refused to ride in the dark. After more than an hour's delay, the racing was postponed until the following afternoon. Some of the more rowdy among the fans began shouting angrily and then started ransacking the track, smashing the obstinate electrical fittings, breaking up tables and chairs, and setting them on fire. The velodrome director was forced to barricade himself in his office, and Taylor and the other riders left surreptitiously by a backdoor. The fire brigade and the police had to be called out, and the near-riot was finally quelled, the police making arrests with revolvers in their hand and sabres drawn. A Bordeaux newspaper called it a deplorable fiasco.

The promoters made sure that the illumination did not fail a second time, and at the races the following afternoon, Taylor beat the Italian champions Ferrari and Bixio in the final of the international sprint race. The crowd cheered him wildly as he rode the lap of honor, threw their hats in the air, and waved their handkerchiefs, a typical European expression of enthusiasm. He then attacked the record for the one-third-kilometer lap of the track and broke it by more than a second, with a ride of $20^1/5$ seconds, setting an unofficial world record.

EUROPE, 1901

While he was in Bordeaux, Maurice Martin of *Le Vélo* took Taylor to be examined by some distinguished doctors at the Academy of Sciences, an analysis prompted by a desire to test out the popular racial stereotypes of the day. After listening to his heart, the doctors measured and X-rayed him. *Le Vélo* reported that "they agreed unanimously that he had a wonderful and uniquely developed physique. ... They declared that Major Taylor was a human masterpiece, that he could be said to be absolutely perfect were it not for the fact that because of his bicycle racing, which has exaggerated the size of certain of his leg muscles, his thighs were a little over-developed."[15]

ONE OF THE MOST famous races of the French season, the eleventh Bordeaux—Paris road race, began the next day. Taylor was there to see the great pioneers of long-distance bicycle racing, among whom were Lucien Lesna, Andé Garin and Léon Georget, as they set out on the epic 594-kilometer ride to Paris. The competitors bustled about at the start in front of the Café de Bordeaux, making final preparations for the grueling race ahead. Taylor, who had had extensive experience in road racing early in his amateur career, watched the scene with fascination, while the crowd watched him.

Before the race began, a photograph of the competitors was taken, with Taylor standing happily and proudly among them, the peaked cap which had become his trademark set jauntily on his head. As the riders lined up, Taylor held up the rider number 13, Léon Georget of Chatelleraut, who was overjoyed to be given this honor. Amid a huge crowd of onlookers, a pistol shot rang out at 4 o'clock and the race was under way.

Taylor and Breyer followed the beginning of the race in Barbereau-Bergeon's Dorsay. After about twenty kilometers, they were forced to stop to repair a puncture, but were soon under way again. The publicity surrounding the racing in Bordeaux had spread the word of Taylor's presence, and he was easily recognizable sitting in the back of the open car.

Major Taylor was greeted with tumultuous applause all along the route. Peasants and cyclists lined the roadside waving to the American. Maurice Martin asked Taylor to sign his name on the pages of his reporter's note-book and the Major threw the sheets into the air as they passed by. The crowds were thrilled to see the famous 'Nègre volant' as he raced by them in a cloud of dust. He urged on the racers who had been left behind, and he said he would never forget the superb race as long as he lived.[16]

The descriptions of Taylor's stay in Bordeaux published in *Le Vélo* by Maurice Martin captured marvelously the atmosphere of this early classic bicycle race and the recognition and honor Taylor was accorded as a world-class bicycle racer. It was an astonishing transformation for the young black American, after all those years of struggling against racism in the United States. Emerging into the clear, beautiful air of the French spring, he mingled in Bordeaux as a champion and an equal among the great pioneer road racers, the burden of hostility and oppression momentarily lifted from his shoulders.

WITH HIS FIRST important victories in Europe, Taylor's popularity continued to soar. The daily press coverage of his races and his personal life was unabated in its intensity. Advertisements appeared in newspapers promoting Iver Johnson bicycles and the Le Pâris tires he was using. Coquelle and Breyer tended their publicity machine carefully and made sure that Taylor was constantly in the news, his name on everybody's lips. But they did not have to fabricate an identity for their star, who was a fascinating enough personality already and gave the press plenty to talk about by just being himself.

On May 4, 1901, a long, illustrated article was published in *La Vie au Grand Air*, occupying four pages of the popular sporting magazine.[17] Written by Taylor himself, it was translated into French with extensive editing by Breyer or Coquelle. Such a personal article by Taylor had never appeared in an American magazine. The article, which was illustrated by eleven photographs, described his reactions to Paris and his racing experiences. It depicted him not just as an athlete, but also as a human being, with interests, opinions, and other talents besides his bicycle racing. He spoke of his initial annoyance at people staring at him on the street, which he was gradually getting used to; of his desire to purchase a French automobile; his pleasure playing the piano and mandolin; his reasons for not riding on Sundays; his attraction to the number 13 because it brought him good luck; and of his respect and admiration for his biggest rival, Edmond Jacquelin.The latter, he thought, was the best rider in France and he was waiting impatiently for the big race. He had never as yet encountered a rider with a better, quicker, more powerful jump than his own, but if Jacquelin was that man and beat him fairly, he said, then he would shake his hand sincerely.

The eleven photographs, accompanied by glowing captions, showed Taylor's house in Worcester, his legs – "a very pretty pair of ankles!" – his splendidly muscled body – "like a bronze statue!" – Taylor playing the mandolin, and so on. The centerpiece of the article was a large photo of Taylor riding in an open automobile with the ex-sprint champion of France, Henri Fournier.

The article gives a remarkable insight into the role the media were playing in popularizing and publicizing him. Taylor's success in France was among the earliest examples of the elevation of an athletic star to the status of a popular hero. Bicycle racing was an emerging mass spectator sport of a new kind, in need of stars and heroes, and the fact that he was exotic and had charisma and mystique made Taylor perfect star material – a superb performer, disciplined, down-to-earth, good-humored, and intelligent, an underdog who had triumphed over adversity. Yet, at the same time, he was unique and somehow untouchable and incomprehensible, like a visitor from another planet.

R EPORTS OF Taylor's fame in Europe began to arrive in the United States. People in Worcester were especially interested to hear of his progress and successes. "Taylor is creating a furor in Paris," reported the *Worcester Telegram* at the beginning of April.

> He is the best advertized sporting man in Europe at the present time. … Notices taking up columns are the general rule and there is no question but that Coquelle and Breyer should make a pot of money with Taylor. … The races in which he competes will mark an epoch in the history of cycle racing in France, judging by the intense interest taken in him now. Taylor's refusal to compete on Sunday will compel Frenchmen to attend weekday racing if they want to see him ride.[18]

A month later, the newspaper rated Taylor's status in Europe even more highly. KING OF PARIS. MAJOR TAYLOR IMMENSELY POPULAR WITH EVERYBODY THERE, read one headline. Americans in Paris wrote home saying that nothing was too good for Taylor since he had begun to win races. "Splendid equipages are placed at Taylor's disposal even for the shortest trips, large crowds follow him about the streets and await his appearance at his hotel each morning…. When Major Taylor returns to this country, he will undoubtedly be the biggest drawing card ever known in the cycling world, a bigger card, in fact, than was Zimmerman when he was in the zenith of his popularity."[19]

One French journalist wrote to a friend in Chicago that he had not believed all the claims made for Taylor, but that he was utterly convinced after witnessing his startling performances. "Among the many riders who have visited us during the last five years," said the journalist,

> ... not one may be compared with him in the matter of politeness and good behavior. We were literally amazed to find him better educated than the average foreigner who comes over and possessed of far better manners than our own riders. When we think of some of the harsh treatment to which this man has been subjected on account of his color, we cannot refrain from uttering the strongest words of disapprobation of such acts, nor from thinking that some parts of your country must be in a state of savagery.[20]

Some Americans who watched from a distance what was happening to Taylor on the other side of the Atlantic were more skeptical however. They did not want to recognize the sensation he was creating. The writer of an article in *Bicycling World*, unwilling to give Taylor credit for the adulation he was receiving, argued that all the attention paid to him was merely "to create a sensation among the public and make them flock once more to the tracks. ... Major Taylor is a modest fellow, and he will need all his modesty to stand the flattery of those who are making use of him to create another boom in cycle racing."[21]

The tone of such comments was part of a consistent effort to deny and denigrate Taylor's athletic status. People who disliked him in America were in fact glad to have him out of the way and were hardly likely to recognize that he was in the process of becoming a much more important star in Europe than he had ever been allowed to be in the United States.

E DMOND JACQUELIN, who in 1900 had won a triple crown – world champion, champion of France, and the Grand Prix of Paris – was three years older than Taylor and just as experienced a bicycle racer. He had been champion of France as long ago as 1896 and had competed against all the greatest sprinters of the time, including the Americans Arthur Zimmerman and Tom Cooper. He was an exceptionally strong and muscular athlete, with a tremendous jump.

EUROPE, 1901

Brash and often vulgar, Jacquelin was wildly popular with the crowd for his temperamental personality and expressive gestures on the track, as well as his habit of arguing compulsively with judges after a close finish. Jacquelin was also an unreliable and inconsistent performer. When he was in form, he was unbeatable, but a few days after a striking victory, he might be beaten by a lesser athlete. This inconsistency was seen as his greatest weakness when pitted against Taylor's dependability.

There was a renewed frenzy of analysis and prediction in the press as May 16, the day of their first match race, approached. The two men had equally impressive records – Jacquelin was the reigning French and world champion, Taylor the reigning American champion and world champion of 1899. They were the two fastest sprinters in the world.

Yet it was impossible to imagine two more dissimilar athletes, with such completely contrasting personalities, styles, and backgrounds. Whereas Taylor was lithe, supple, and finely muscled and spun the pedals extremely smoothly, with a deceptive ease and his upper body practically motionless, Jacquelin was a jerky, heavily muscled rider, who unleashed his strength with a rough and wild show of force, who lunged and kicked his bicycle ferociously towards the finishing line.

Over and above these differences in physique, style and personality was, inevitably, the question of their race. Which race, black or white, would prove superior in the forthcoming battle? It was the first time this question had ever been tested in a cycling championship in France. It was commonly believed at the time, in France as in America, that the black man lacked intellectual ability, but compensated for this deficiency with an overabundance of physical energy and power. A writer in *Le Vélo*, praising Taylor's perfect and beautiful physique, suggested that this was a predetermined advantage. "Negroes in general," he claimed, "have a remarkable gift for physical exertion. This is a well-known fact. Because the black man is not much disposed to intellectual activity, he compensates for it with his physical strength." [22]

Yet the writer was unable to explain why Taylor had a much finer, more graceful body than Jacquelin. Other journalists were less patronizing, expressing admiration for his personality and physique. They agreed that the main reason for the intense interest in the race between Taylor and Jacquelin was that the competition was so wide open, the result so difficult to predict.

WHO WILL BE KING? demanded *L'Auto-Vélo* on the morning of the great race, "the black man or the white, the Champion of Old Europe or the star of the New World?"[23] It was the unofficial championship of the world that was at stake. All the newspaper accounts agreed that there had never been a bicycle race that had aroused such a frenzy of interest in France, perhaps in the whole world. They spoke of it as one of the most significant sporting events that had ever taken place. People traveled from all over France, from all over Europe, on special excursion trains to be there. Those who had never before shown any interest in bicycle racing were desperate to get tickets. Enormous sums of money were being wagered on the two riders.

The day before the race, when Taylor came to the Parc des Princes to do his final training for the crucial match, there were twelve hundred spectators in the stands, including many from the American colony in Paris. Taylor did not exert himself too strenuously in this final limbering up, but the crowd was intensely fascinated. After waving to the fans in the stands, he went quickly back to his cabin, annoyed by the press photographers badgering him to pose in front of their large wooden cameras on heavy tripods.

In spite of gray skies and unpleasant cold weather, 20,000 people crowded into the Parc des Princes velodrome in Paris on the afternoon of May 16, 1901, a national holiday. It was a day that would long be remembered by those who were there. The unofficial world sprint crown was at stake. The unreserved seats were completely sold out, and a noisy crowd clamored outside the velodrome, unable to gain admission. The event was news even in America. MAJOR TAYLOR AND JACQUELIN TO STAKE THEIR ALL TODAY, said the *New York Sun,* "To both men the result means everything. It will be as if they were gambling their last dollar. For the winner will be worldwide renown, for the loser the reputation of being a defeated champion." [24]

It was the biggest crowd ever seen at a bicycle race, perhaps at any sporting event. Attracted by the uniqueness of the contest between a great French champion and popular idol and the charismatic black American champion, the spectators were treated to some moments of rare athletic emotion. Despite the awful weather, everyone agreed that the occasion would be remembered as one of the most memorable days in the history of bicycle racing. Victor Breyer reported in *Le Vélo*

EUROPE, 1901

that he saw people turning pale with anxiety, biting their lips and clutching themselves with excitement and tension during the climaxes of the racing.[25] Packed into the Parc des Princes were humble workers, princes and dukes, sporting people, artists and industrialists, society ladies and actresses, pickpockets and souvenir sellers, and just about everyone who was anyone in the bicycle and automobile world. All the Parisian newspapers had sent reporters, and there were dozens of foreign correspondents. Behind the scenes and out on the track, press photographers, including the well-known sports photographer Jules Beau, worked feverishly to capture the drama and excitement of the event.

The crowd cheered wildly as the two champions emerged from the training quarters. Jacquelin, superstitious, did not want to be the first onto the track and allowed Taylor to walk in front of him. Jacquelin wore the jersey of the champion of France; Taylor was wrapped in a long, hooded, African cloak to protect himself against the cold wind. Jacquelin's bicycle was carried by his younger brother, Taylor's by his trainer, Buckner. Shedding his warm coat, Taylor mounted his bicycle and rubbed his arms and legs, grimacing at the cold.

"At the time of the match, I was in excellent physical condition for the big fuss and desired only a warm day for the race," he recollected in his autobiography. "I was doomed for disappointment, however, because the day was cold and raw and despite the fact that I wore an extra heavy sweater, I shivered as I took my warm-up trips over the track."

As they strapped their feet to the pedals and waited for the shot of the starting pistol, an anxious, expectant hush settled over the spectators, who all stood up to get a better view. The races were run in the typical French style of 'loafing' and 'jockeying,' Taylor and Jacquelin watching and waiting for the other to make a move, trying to position themselves favorably before they jumped into the final mad dash for the finishing line.

In the first heat, after the pistol was fired, the two riders stood still, balancing on the spot, neither wanting to take the lead. But Jacquelin lost his balance and fell, and the heat had to be restarted. Jacquelin took the lead this time and rode high up on the banking, gradually increasing his speed, keeping a watchful eye on Taylor who was glued to his rear wheel. About 200 yards from the finishing line, Jacquelin jumped. Taylor responded immediately, and as they entered the finish-

ing straight, he attacked with such speed that he drew level with Jacquelin. Elbow to elbow, the two fastest sprinters in the world fought
for the finishing line. Jacquelin jumped once again right on the line
and won the heat by the length of a wheel. Deafening, rapturous pan-
demonium from the crowd!

In the second heat Taylor led, again high up on the banking,
gradually accelerating. Jacquelin jumped, Taylor responded and
pulled easily ahead of him. But Jacquelin fought back with all his
strength and overtook Taylor 50 yards from the finishing line, beating him by two lengths. A victory for France!

Jacquelin had surprised those who had predicted that his chances
against Taylor were slim by beating him in two straight heats. The
crowd erupted into an orgy of wild and prolonged cheering. Jacquelin
was still the champion of the world, still the popular idol.

In a demonstration which Victor Breyer thought was in extremely
bad taste, Jacquelin rode around the track in front of the thousands
of ecstatic fans repeatedly thumbing his nose. It was exactly the kind
of gauche behavior he was famous for. He was much criticized in the
press for this unsporting gesture, and he apologized later. He said he
had been carried away in the excitement of the moment, that his rude
gesture had not been directed at Major Taylor, whom he liked and
admired, but at those who had insisted that he did not stand a chance
against him.

The crowd leaped over the fence and invaded the infield. Elegant-
ly dressed barons in silk ties and top hats elbowed common working
men in grimy clothes, all trying to reach their idol. They lifted Jacquelin high in the air and carried him in triumph back to his cabin
while the band played the 'Marseillaise.'

Taylor was distraught. He was not accustomed to losing big races.
He shouted in French, "Fini! Fini! Plus champion, moi!" Some reporters
even described him crying in his cabin while Buckner, stony-faced,
dismantled his bicycles. "Yes, I was beaten, well beaten, I have no excuses to make," he said to the press, "Jacquelin is as strong an opponent as Tom Cooper said he is and he was faster than me today."
He had been affected by the wind, he said, and even more by the
cold, which he hated so much. But his eyes lit up when the possibility
of a revenge match was mentioned, and he had no hesitation about
agreeing to meet Jacquelin again.[26]

EUROPE, 1901

Soon the news was all over Paris. The evening papers carried the results. "Read all about it, read all about it! The result of the Taylor—Jacquelin match," the newsboys shouted in the streets, "The flying negro beaten!"

Reporter Maurice Martin was especially disgusted by Jacquelin's rude thumbing of his nose, whether it was directed at his critics, or at Taylor. There was not a more interesting and likable athlete than Taylor, he said, and he did not deserve that kind of treatment.[27]

"Listen carefully," Taylor told Coquelle, the day after his defeat, pointing toward the sky with his finger. "Jacquelin thumbed his nose at me and he will be punished up there for it. I will be very surprised if I don't beat him the next time we meet."[28] The nose-thumbing incident was indeed a humiliating experience for Taylor. It would have been unthinkable for him to behave in such a way. "I was hurt to the quick by his unsportsmanlike conduct," he wrote, "and resolved then and there that I would not return home until I had wiped out his insult."

That a revenge match would take place was inevitable. Both pride and profit demanded it. Jacquelin's response to Taylor's challenge was typically swaggering. "I thought I had beaten Major Taylor so convincingly that there would be no question of a revenge match," he told the press, "but if he wants one, then I am at his disposition whenever and wherever he wishes."[29] Both Jacquelin and Henri Desgranges, director of the Parc des Princes, insisted that the race not be held on a weekday, but once again Taylor was able to dictate his terms, and the second round of the famous Taylor—Jacquelin battle was announced for Monday, May 27, once again at the Parc des Princes.

The crowd was even bigger than before. The enthusiasm was again intense. Delancey Ward, an American artist living in Paris, donated a magnificent silver cup to be presented to the winner. The day was sunny and hot, without a breath of wind, and Taylor wore a thin blue and black silk jersey with an American flag tied around his waist. The papers reported that he was like a different person. In place of the unhappy, shivering star of May 16 was a confident and smiling athlete.

As the starter called the riders to the line for the first heat, Taylor shouted, "Just a minute, please!" Amid general amusement, he stood in front of Jacquelin with his Kodak in his hands. "Don't move, please,"

EUROPE, 1901

he said, as he snapped the shutter, before handing the camera to his trainer and climbing onto his bicycle. Taylor wrote later that Jacquelin had an arrogant smile on his face when the race began.

> As we rode slowly from the tape in the first heat, there was great cheering. After some maneuvering, Jacquelin and I tried to force each other into the lead. In so doing both of us came to a dead stop. We were practically side by side, Jacquelin being slightly ahead. Balancing a few moments, I backed slowly half a revolution of my crank until I brought myself directly behind Jacquelin. That's just where I wanted to be. The grandstands were now in a frenzy. Realizing I had out-maneuvered him on this score, Jacquelin laughed outright and moved off in the lead prepared for business.

Taylor beat Jacquelin by four lengths in the first heat. As they waited for the pistol shot for the start of the second heat, he reached out and offered his hand to his rival, suggesting that it would be the final heat. It was another aspect of the psychological warfare between the two men. "My motive was to impress on Jacquelin that I was so positive that I could defeat him again that this was going to be the last heat. ... As the French idol gathered the full significance of my gesture, he mumbled something, shrugged his shoulders, and set his jaw. His sneering smile disappeared and a frown encompassed his face."

Taylor's riding was especially stunning at the finish of the second heat, when he came from behind his opponent and gained several lengths on him in the space of a few yards, leaving him behind with effortless ease. Taylor untied the American flag from his waist and rode a lap of honor, waving it to the crowds. It was his response to Jacquelin's insulting nose-thumbing. Wild applause greeted him, and the band struck up 'The Star-Spangled Banner' as he rode his lap of honor with a huge bouquet of roses on his shoulder. Hundreds of Americans poured onto the track. That was his greatest triumph in Paris.

The two champions were now on terms of equality, with one victory apiece. Some people in the crowd thought the riders and promoters were trying to create the occasion for yet another match to decide who was the superior athlete. There were cries of "It was fixed!" from those who could not believe that Jacquelin could be so convincingly beaten.

A deluge of press coverage followed the next day, when *Le Vélo* sold 150,000 copies in Paris alone. In the five-day period before, during, and after the match, 625,000 copies of the sporting newspapers were sold. The analysis went on and on. Who was the world champion now? Who was the better man, the black man or the white man? How could such inconsistencies of form be explained? Would there be a third match?

After the revenge match, Taylor and Jacquelin went to celebrate at the Chalets du Cycle, the traditional meeting place for cyclists in the Bois de Boulogne, where there was a large outdoor café. They each went in their own cars, Taylor driving the new car he had just bought, which he intended to take back to America with him. The champions were escorted by a crowd of admirers.

"Do me the honor of sharing a drink with me," said Jacquelin.

"With pleasure," replied Major Taylor, "but you know very well that I only drink water."

"Oh! for once, have a little champagne!" exclaimed Jacquelin, offering him a glass. Taylor put the glass carefully to his lips and took a tiny sip. No sooner had he swallowed the few drops of champagne then he grimaced, exclaiming "Awful! Horrible!" and pushed the glass firmly away.[30]

ANOTHER MONTH of European racing followed. Taylor continued his grandiose, triumphant tour. He appeared in Berlin, Copenhagen, Antwerp, Hannover, Leipzig, Geneva, Lyon, Toulouse, Agen, and again in Bordeaux. Against the best sprinters that Europe offered, he was everywhere unbeaten, except in Copenhagen where the Danish champion Thorwald Ellegaard scored a victory in his own city because Taylor punctured a tire in the final heat of the confrontation.

In a grueling schedule of traveling, Taylor, Buckner, and Coquelle spent many nights in first-class sleeping compartments speeding across Europe from capital to capital. Because Taylor was resolute in his determination not to race on Sundays, Coquelle and Breyer were obliged to schedule the races on national holidays in France, Germany, Belgium, and Italy. In a period of ten days, from June 1 to June 10, Taylor raced in Antwerp, Berlin, Copenhagen, Leipzig, Hannover, and again in Antwerp.

In every European city he visited, he was greeted with the same rapturous enthusiasm. Huge posters advertising his races were plastered everywhere on walls, and in Leipzig a car drove around the

EUROPE, 1901

city displaying a huge portrait of 'der schwarze Weltmeisterfahrer.'
Taylor was met at the railway station, given a guided tour of the city
in a chauffeured car, and introduced to local civic and sporting dignitaries. After wildly cheering him on in his inevitable victories, his
fans and supporters escorted him back to the train.

At the beginning of June, Coquelle and Breyer tried to persuade
Taylor to extend his European visit. There was a flurry of trans-Atlantic cables between the promoters in Paris and A. G. Batchelder, chairman of the Racing Board of the National Cycling Association in New
York. No, said Batchelder, Taylor could not stay in Europe. He had
signed a contract to appear on American tracks beginning in July, and
he was obligated to honor it. If he did not return, he would be heavily fined and probably suspended.

Professional bicycle racing in America needed the drama that
Taylor's presence created, and the bureaucracy that had often tried to
exclude him in the past was now, ironically, forced to admit that it
relied on him to pull in the crowds. It was well known in America
that Taylor's name on the bill for a race doubled the size of the crowd
and the profits at the box office.

A ND SO, Major Taylor left Paris on June 28, 1901, his first European
tour widely acclaimed as one of the most remarkable performances in the history of bicycle racing. In twenty years of the sport, such
mastery and dominance had rarely been seen. There was only one
other American cyclist to compare with him, and that was the great
Zimmerman, and most journalists who attempted the difficult task of
evaluating the achievements of two such dissimilar careers agreed that
Taylor's successes eclipsed Zimmerman's. The sport had developed
a great deal in the 1890s and standards had improved. By 1901, it was
a much more competitive and international sport.

In four hectic, dramatic months, Taylor had ridden in nearly every
important European capital and had beaten all the European champions, the best riders in the world. He had met Jacquelin, world champion and champion of France in two successful match races, which
were widely hailed as the most sensational bicycle races in the history of the sport. He had beaten Ellegaard, champion of Denmark;
Arend, champion of Germany; Grogna, champion of Belgium;
Gascoyne, champion of England, Momo, champion of Italy, and Van
den Born, champion of Belgium, in addition to most of the other lead-

ing professionals of the day. In a total of 24 races, he had taken 18 first places, 4 second places, and 2 third places. He had lost only two match races against individual opponents – Jacquelin and Ellegaard – and he had subsequently avenged those defeats with convincing victories. Spectators in each European country had flocked to see him and were thrilled by his performances.

The European tour had been a tremendous commercial success too, and Taylor had more than repaid Coquelle's and Breyer's confidence in him. Everybody, it seemed, had benefited from his crossing the Atlantic. He had brought success and profit to the promoters and good sport and goodwill to his fans. He had fulfilled all of the obligations of his star status.

Major Taylor had impressed people in Europe not only with his cycling performances, but with the strength and style of his personality, the cultured self-assurance of his demeanor, and the thoroughness and discipline of his athletic method and training. He was well-spoken, extremely polite, and not at all proud or boastful. He also had a gay side to him and a sense of humor, but at heart he was a serious and thoughtful person, committed to his religious and moral beliefs, not at all like the popular image of the tough, loud-mouthed, uncouth, professional athlete of the day.

In Paris, Taylor had been welcomed into the social life of the sport in a way that had been almost totally denied him in America. The pervasive racism against which he had always had to struggle at home was replaced in France by curiosity and tolerance. Though there was ignorance of black culture and some condescension in the attitude of the French press, there was no hostility, and in all of his European races in 1901, not a single instance of overt racism was reported.

Taylor played the part of visiting champion to perfection. He was fascinated and thrilled by all the interest in him. He gave interviews to the press, was constantly photographed, and coped patiently and tolerantly with the crowds who followed him. He was chauffeured around Paris to the houses of the rich and famous of Parisian sporting society, and his presence was urgently requested at lunches and dinners where everyone wanted to shake the celebrity's hand. Through all the adulation, Taylor remained warm and unruffled.

And as the first black American athlete to make such a big impact in Europe, he was a representative of his race and people, the black American ambassador to Europe that summer. He was very aware of

EUROPE, 1901

this revolutionary role, which had been thrust upon him. It made him all the more determined to uphold the high moral standards he had always espoused. His tour was a pioneering athletic and social achievement of great and lasting significance.

It is not surprising that he thoroughly enjoyed the experience of being in the limelight. For the first time in his life, Taylor emerged from the shadow of racial inferiority he had lived with since childhood. It is true that as 'the flying Negro' and 'the black Zimmerman,' as well as in numerous accounts in the press where his color was constantly referred to, the fact that he was black was never forgotten. It was inevitable that his color would be discussed since it was one of the reasons for his unique attraction in Europe. But to a large extent, these labels were promotional gimmicks created to give him a strong and easily recognizable identity, rather than a comment on his social standing or a judgment upon him.

Major Taylor had a proud and confident identity in Europe and was not a crushed or threatened black man. It was an honorable status he enjoyed there, as America's champion bicycle racer. For the first time in his life, it was an advantage for him to be black.

The night before his fans saw Taylor off at the Gare St. Lazare, en route for Cherbourg and the trans-Atlantic liner the *Deutschland*, his racing colleagues, supporters, and the entire staffs of *Le Vélo* and *L'Auto-Vélo* gave him a splendid farewell banquet at the Chalets du Cycle. In a mixture of English and French, Taylor thanked them for the unforgettable hospitality they had shown him in Paris. At the station, the next day, bouquets of flowers were thrust into his arms, and three cheers of congratulations rang out as the train pulled out, with Taylor leaning from the window, waving to his friends. "Taylor departed with a heavy heart at having left behind a country where he had grown accustomed to being welcomed warmly everywhere," wrote François Mercier, a correspondent for *L'Auto-Vélo*. "I would not be at all surprised if he did not shed a tear or two thinking about the hostility which he would again encounter when he arrived home."[31]

Mercier's feelings would prove to be prophetic. In America, a renewed frenzy of jealousy and racial animosity was directed at Taylor by his white rivals, who were more determined than ever to defeat him, to crush and devalue his new-found European stardom.

10

World Traveler and International Celebrity

MAJOR TAYLOR was warmly welcomed back to the United States. Upon his arrival in New York on July 4, he went directly from the docks to the track at Manhattan Beach, where a race meet was in progress. To honor his presence, the band played 'Down in Dixie,' and the crowd gave him a standing ovation for several minutes, while Taylor doffed his straw hat repeatedly. Despite six days on the ship and with very little exercise, he rode an exhibition mile, paced by a motorcycle, only 3 seconds slower than the track record.

In Worcester, a civic reception was held in his honor, and a few articles appeared not only in the local press but also in New York newspapers in recognition of his successful European tour. But little credit was given to him for the most impressive performances ever by a black American athlete abroad. The fame he had won in Paris was never fully appreciated or publicly acknowledged here. There would be no opportunity to bask in the glory of his accomplishments.

Instead of enjoying respect and honor, Taylor was almost immediately embroiled in a new round of bureaucratic squabbling with the National Cycling Association. Exhausted from the exertions of his constant traveling in Europe, he retired to his house in Worcester to recuperate. His trainer, Buckner, went to New York to deliver a letter from his doctor to the chairman of the Racing Board of the NCA, but was not well received. Taylor's contract with the NCA required that he appear at races on the national circuit, and chairman Batchelder was determined to hold him to it. The public was anxious to see him race, the promoters were advertising him in every town where he was scheduled to appear, and box office receipts would be severely affected by his absence.

USA, EUROPE, AUSTRALIA, 1902—1905

"Sick or well, you must ride at each National Circuit meet," was Batchelder's response to the doctor's letter, and he proceeded to fine him $100 for each occasion on which he failed to appear, the money to be awarded to the promoters for box office losses. Batchelder claimed that Taylor had stayed in Europe too long and had not returned in time to prepare himself for his races in America. "A champion being under greater obligation to promoter and public than any other rider," he said, "is always expected to keep faith and appear when advertised unless prevented by the most urgent reasons, which the board did not find in this instance."[1]

Taylor was incensed. He said he would quit racing altogether unless Batchelder relented. Even the white riders thought Batchelder had been over hasty. But, unwilling to engage in a dispute that might result in another suspension, Taylor swallowed his pride and paid the fines. If he had not been under contract to the NCA, he told a friend, he would have turned around and gone back to France immediately.

The writer of an editorial in *Cycle Age* reminded his readers that when Zimmerman had returned to America from Europe several years before, "There was nothing in the country good enough for him. He had nobly represented the United States in Europe. He had demonstrated that the Yankee cyclist led the world in the matter of speed. And he was rewarded as he deserved." And now came Taylor. He had done as well as Zimmerman, but he was rewarded with insulting fines.

"Who would have dared to treat the mighty Zimmerman as the N.C.A. has treated Taylor?" the writer asked. "The wrath of the whole cycling world would have fallen on the head of any one who had dared suggest such a thing. Where are we to look for an explanation? Zimmerman was a white man – in fact and in action. Taylor is a negro. Is that at the bottom of the trouble? Negro as he is, he is, without exception, the cleanest man who ever went over from this side since cycling became a sport. His principles are of the finest and they are maintained to the letter. ... And his reward is that he must submit to the modern slavery inaugurated by the N.C.A. Oh, well, he's only a negro."[2]

For the remainder of the 1901 season, Taylor battled Kramer, Lawson, MacFarland, Cooper, and Kimble for the championship of America. As the reigning American champion and the man who had beaten every big name in Europe that year, he was the object of fierce animosity. All his rivals were determined to dethrone him from the prestigious heights of his European fame. More than ever before, they collaborated tactically to prevent him from winning. They pocketed him, fouled him, and worked together in every possible way to defeat him. It was a return to the same athletic and racial hostility he had always encountered in America. It was Major Taylor against the rest. Only in two-man match races could he be guaranteed a race without a combination working against him. Nonetheless, with his expert tactical sense and his extraordinary agility and speed, he continued to win. The supercharged atmosphere of the racing that season made it all the more exciting for the spectators, of course, based as it was on such genuine and evident bad feeling between Taylor and his white opponents.

Taylor wrote that Floyd MacFarland, the lanky rider from San Jose, California, "was the ringleader of the gang of riders who had sworn among themselves to bring about my dethronement as champion of America at all costs." MacFarland's hostility was overtly racist; he never hesitated to call Taylor 'nigger.'

> At every race in which MacFarland's name and mine appeared on the program, he made it a point to stir up a conspiracy against me. Even when he was not scheduled to compete in a heat with me he would get busy among the other riders in my heat and organize combinations which aimed to prevent me from winning. ... I shall always remember Floyd MacFarland as the instigator and leading perpetrator of practically all the underhanded scheming that brought about my failure to win the championship laurels that year. ... Knowing of this diabolical scheme on the part of my opponents, I took great delight in outgeneraling and outcycling them and breezing across the tape ahead of such combinations. To me this was the sweetest revenge a man could enjoy.

MacFarland even hurled abuse at other white riders who were defeated by Taylor, insulting them for having been "beaten by a nigger." There were ugly, aggressive scenes in the training quarters and changing rooms, with the loud- and foul-mouthed MacFarland usually at the center of hostilities. The abuse directed at Taylor was coarse and unrelenting. It would undoubtedly have resulted in brawling and fighting had Taylor not been a determined pacifist.

O N ONE OCCASION, a reporter from the *New York Sun*, who was in the changing rooms at Madison Square Garden after a race, was talking with Taylor while he was packing his belongings. The reporter noticed that, "beside his racing suit, some linaments and bandages, extra wheel parts and sundries, there was stowed a copy of the New Testament. Others were standing about and one began to 'guy' Taylor a bit about his piety. The Major promptly reached for his Testament and began to quote from it, or as the racing men put it, 'to hand out Scripture.' Taylor said, 'It's alright, you think me a fool, but you are those that's wrong and ah'm right.'"[3] In order to escape from this unpleasantness, Taylor often rented a room in a neighboring hotel to gain some privacy. In the changing rooms or on a train, he often read the New Testament, which he always carried with him. Sometimes he retired to his cabin between two races to read it. At the start of a race, his lips could often be seen moving in a silent prayer.

Finding a hotel room while touring was not always easy, in spite of Taylor's prestige. In Syracuse, he had an abrupt and insulting encounter with the color line in an incident that reminded him most forcefully of the different treatment he had received in France. He went into the Vanderbilt House and, without waiting to register, sat down at a table in the lobby and began to write an urgent letter. CLERK SAYS 'GET OUT'! HURTS THE FEELINGS OF MAJOR TAYLOR...., said the *Worcester Telegram.*

> He had scarcely taken his seat when a bellboy came up to him and told him that he would have to leave the premises. Taylor paid no attention to him, and a clerk soon appeared.
>
> "What are you doing there at that desk. Get out of here!" the clerk said.
>
> "I guess you don't know who I am," said Taylor, "I've stopped here several times, and if you will let me explain, perhaps you will be more friendly."
>
> "Get out of here," said the clerk, "or you'll be kicked out." And with that he started to pull away the chair on which Taylor was sitting. Without more argument, Taylor left the hotel."[4]

Taylor was also refused a room at the Yates House in Syracuse, before finding accommodation at the St. Cloud Hotel. In all his travels in America and Europe he had never been hurt more personally than by this treatment in Syracuse. Coming so soon after he had been idolized in Europe, such treatment was especially shocking and jarring to his sophisticated, expanded awareness. Even his white opponents, in spite of their own ambivalent feelings towards him, were indignant that such an incident could occur. Taylor announced to the press that he was going to sue the hotel proprietors for $10,000 damages, but there is no record of his actually having pursued the suit.

By the end of the 1901 season, the rising young star Frank Kramer, against whom Taylor had fought a long series of bitter, dramatic duels, became champion of America by an extremely narrow margin. Kramer scored 72 points to Taylor's 64 on the national circuit. Kramer had already won thirty points by the time Taylor returned from France and began his championship drive late in the season. Taylor believed that it was MacFarland who was behind Kramer's victories, managing him, working with him, sharing his prize money, and, above all, scheming with him. But there was also no doubt that the young, golden-haired Kramer was in his own right an extraordinary rider, who would subsequently dominate American sprinting in a way that only Zimmerman and Taylor had done before him.

FOR SOME TIME, the press had been speculating about Major Taylor's love life. One newspaper claimed that he had "a dusky bride" whose identity he was anxious to conceal. Rumors circulated, and Taylor himself did nothing to discourage them. When he was breaking records in Chicago in 1898, he even fooled his manager, Harry Sager, into thinking he was married by wiring a telegram, in his presence, to a nonexistent wife.

In fact, there is no indication of any romantic attachment in Taylor's life until the fall of 1900, when, at the height of his fame, he met the young woman who would become his wife. Shortly after winning the championship of America, on Thursday, October 11, 1900, he wrote two words – "Daisy Morris" – in the small diary which he used mostly for jotting down notes about his racing and traveling expenses. We can only speculate whether he met Daisy for the first time that day or whether it was then he decided she mattered to him. What can be said for certain is that this is the first definite evidence of her having come into his life.

Taylor was an extremely eligible young man in 1900, and Daisy Victoria Morris a strikingly beautiful young woman, tall and slim, with light-colored skin, distinguished poise, and a refined manner. The daughter of a black mother and a white father, she was born in Hudson, New York on January 28, 1876, and was thus nearly three years older than Taylor. She was raised alone by her mother, receiving an

USA, EUROPE, AUSTRALIA, 1902—1905

excellent education at the Hudson Academy, a private school. Her mother died when she was only nineteen and she went to Hartford to live with a relative, the Reverend Louis Taylor, a minister of the African Methodist Episcopal Zion Church.

In Hartford, Daisy Morris moved in a cultured and educated world. She was prominent in social circles and an ardent worker in the black Amphion Social Club, which was composed of Hartford's best young people. It also put on dramas and concerts, in which she performed.[5]

In 1897, Rev. Taylor was transferred with his wife and Daisy to Worcester, where, at a social function connected either with the Methodist Church or with Taylor's own church, the John Street Baptist Church, the couple first met.

Although Taylor's status as a professional athlete and his Indiana farm background may have been suspect in the eyes of some of the society people in the privileged black circles in which Daisy Morris moved, those who knew him well did not for a moment question his respectability, his moral character, or his suitability as a partner for a young woman with class and good social standing. In fact, Taylor enjoyed a fine reputation in the black community in New England, Pittsburg, Chicago, Indianapolis, and New York, all places where he had raced and been entertained as the guest of honor at social functions. He had money and a fine house in Worcester and was one of the best-known black men in the United States – a hero to many black people. To Daisy Morris, he appeared as a dashing, exciting person, leading a dramatic, adventurous life. Add to this gentlemanly correctness, and we can imagine that he impressed her as a very exceptional person.

Their relationship blossomed. By the time Taylor left in 1901 for his trip to France, they were engaged, and Daisy received his postcards from all over Europe that summer. When he returned, the courtship resumed, and they were married on March 21, 1902, in Ansonia, Connecticut, with Daisy's uncle, who had by then moved to Ansonia, officiating at the ceremony. After a very brief honeymoon, the couple returned to Taylor's house in Worcester where he had been living with his father since the death of his sister Gertrude two years before. Taylor was preoccupied with preparations for his second European tour, which Daisy thought of as a business trip. She accompanied him to Grand Central Station, then returned to Ansonia to stay with her aunt and uncle until her husband's return. It was a strange and formal way to begin their married life together.

USA, EUROPE, AUSTRALIA, 1902—1905

31 and 32. The elegant Daisy Morris, who became Taylor's wife in March 1902

Lower right: 33. Major Taylor around the time of his marriage

Facing page: 34. Melbourne, Australia, with Theodore Robl and R. McCullagh, 1903

Above: 35. In Sydney, Australia, 1903

Above: 36. At an Australian race

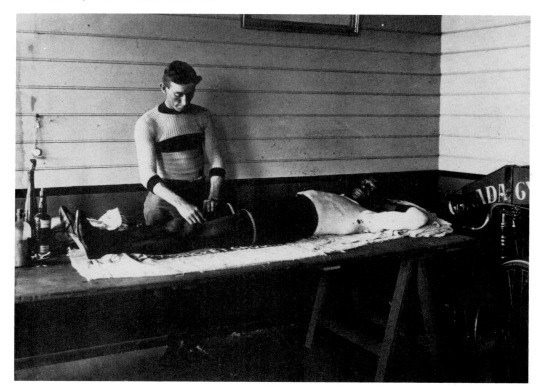

Facing page bottom: 37. Massaged by Australian trainer Sid Melville

Above: 38. With his friend, the Australian champion Don Walker, 1903

Below: 39. The scratch group at the start of a race in Australia, 1904

10° Année ≠ N° 451   50 centimes   11 Mai 1907 ≠ Tous les Samedis

LA VIE AU

GRAND AIR

Publications Pierre Lafitte & C°
Av. des Champs-Élysées ≠ Paris

Dans ce numéro
un hors-texte
Le Jockey
Alec Carter

Major Taylor, qui vient de faire jeudi sa rentrée en piste

Top left: 40. 1907 comeback, announced in a big way in the French sports press

Below: 41. Behind motor pacing machine in Paris, 1908

Above: 42. With threeyearold daughter Sydney, Paris, 1907

Below: 43. Surrounded by friends and admirers upon his return to the European race tracks in 1907

Above: 44. Taking a spill, Paris 1907
Below: 45. Motoring in Paris with daughter Sydney, 1907

Above: 46. Back in form, Paris 1907
Below: 47. Leading Poulain, Ellegaard and Friol in Paris, 1908

Left: 48. Paris, 1909. Overweight and lonely, Taylor waits for mail from home

Below: 49. On previous trips, wife Daisy and daughter Sydney, photographed here by Taylor himself, had accompanied him on his travels in Europe

50. With Friol and Dupré at the Buffalo velodrome in Paris, June 1909

Top left and bottom right: 51 and 52. At the end of the 1907 season, Taylor announced his retirement, prompting this analysis in the French press.

Top right: 53. He changed his mind and returned to Paris in 1909 for his final season in Europe.

La Vie au Grand Air

ABONNEMENTS :
Paris et Départements————24 fr.
Etranger————28 fr.
Changement d'adresse : o fr. 75

30 Mai 1908 № 506
PUBLICATIONS PIERRE LAFITTE & Cie
90, avenue des Champs-Élysées, PARIS · Téléph. 528-64, 528-66, 528-68
Publicité : HUGUET-MINART & Cie, 11, boulev. des Italiens

PUBLICITÉ :
Pages d'Annonces, la ligne————2 fr.
La page————600 fr.
Encartage————750 fr.

LA RENTRÉE DE MAJOR TAYLOR

Le fameux nègre Major Taylor vient d'arriver à Paris. Lorsque ce numéro paraîtra, il aura déjà fait ses débuts. Le Major Taylor de cette année est beaucoup plus prêt que celui de 1907 et, si la température veut bien devenir clémente, nul doute qu'il ne se place, dès ses premières exhibitions, en tête des sprinters. Nous le représentons, conduisant un petit tonneau, sur lequel a pris place Darragon.

54. Once more in 1908, Taylor made front page news in the French sports press

Left: 55. Family portrait, taken 1906 or 1907

Below: 56. With Hedspath and Jacquelin, 1908

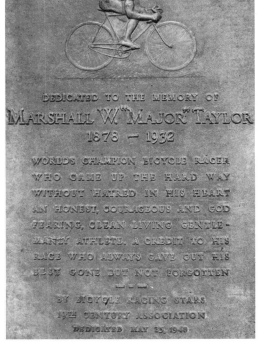

Above: 57. At the
Buffalo velodrome in
Paris, 1908

Upper right: 58. One of
the last photographs,
published 1926

Lower right: 59.
Gravestone at the
Mount Glenwood
Cemetery on the outskirts
of Chicago

Champion Bike Rider Dies

MARSHALL W. "MAJOR" TAYLOR
World champion bicycle rider, who died in the county hospital here
Tuesday, June 21, of heart disease after three months illness.

Upper left: 60. *Chicago Defender* obituary, 1932

Lower right: 61. Recent photo of Major Taylor's daughter, Mrs. Sydney Taylor Brown

FROM MARCH 1902, when he left New York to undertake his second tour of Europe, under contract again to Robert Coquelle and Victor Breyer, until the spring of 1904, Major Taylor raced almost continuously in France, Belgium, Holland, Germany, Denmark, Italy, Austria, England, Australia, New Zealand, and the United States. Except for the 1902 European tour, his wife accompanied him on the international circuit. During those two years, Taylor engaged in a practically uninterrupted epic journey as the most celebrated, best-paid sprinter in the hotly contested, hugely popular sport of international bicycle racing. Paris was his adopted European home, and he was one of the brightest stars of the flood-lit races regularly promoted by Breyer and Coquelle on weekday evenings at Paris's famous Buffalo velodrome.

He spent brief periods at home in Worcester to rest and recuperate, but for much of the time he lived in luxury hotels and fine boarding houses in Paris and the other cities he visited. He slept frequently in first-class accommodations on trains and boats, raced wherever his promoters scheduled him, and performed in a grueling succession of top-class races against all the world's best sprinters.

His color, which stood in his way in America, was the foundation of his appeal and attraction all over the world, and his speed and style continued to thrill spectators in every country he visited. During these two years, Taylor was probably the world's most sought-after athlete and almost certainly the most traveled sportsman in the world. He was, without a doubt, the world's most illustrious black athlete.

In those two brief years, Taylor went twice around the globe. In 1902, he crossed alone to Europe and returned to the East Coast in the summer to compete for the American championship on the national circuit, the last time he would participate in these championships. Then in early December 1902, he crossed the United States to San Francisco by train and boarded the *Ventura* to sail the Pacific Ocean for his first tour of Australia. He spent the winter racing in Australia and then sailed to Europe across the Indian ocean and through the Suez Canal to begin his third season based in Paris. In September 1903, he returned to Worcester, had a short rest, and then left again in November for a second tour of Australia and a second winter in the sun. In May 1904, the Taylors returned once more to Worcester via San Francisco.

USA, EUROPE, AUSTRALIA, 1902—1905

Wherever Taylor traveled, he was treated as an international celebrity. As he was leaving New York on March 25, 1902, he was visited by a delegation of black students headed by Booker T. Washington, who came to wish him well on behalf of black Americans. On board the *Kaiser Wilhelm der Grosse* on that trip, he kept company with Henri Fournier, the famous French racing driver, and Albert Clément, the automobile pioneer. His fame as a racing cyclist preceded him, and there were always crowds to welcome him and cheer him on. Everywhere he visited, civic dignitaries gave him the red-carpet treatment.

U PON HIS FIRST ARRIVAL in Sydney, Australia, on December 22, 1902, a flotilla of small boats greeted the *Ventura* as it entered the harbor, including one boat carrying a reception committee from the Summer Nights Amusement Committee, headed by Hugh Mcintosh, the flamboyant 28-year-old entrepreneur who had negotiated the contract with Taylor.

"I could not restrain my tears," Taylor remembered later, "as I looked over the side of the liner and saw hundreds of boats ... decked out with American flags, with their whistles tooting and men and women aboard them with megaphones greeting me with this salutation, 'Taylor, Taylor! Welcome Major Taylor!'" When the Taylors stepped ashore, they were welcomed by thousands of cheering people. The mayor of Sydney praised him at a press reception as "the Champion Cyclist of the World, who has met and defeated the foremost men in Europe and America and who now comes to Australia to gain fresh victories."[6]

Fearful at first that they would be restricted by the rigid color bar in Australia, perhaps even denied entry into the country upon arrival, Taylor and his wife were surprised and elated to be greeted like visiting royalty and deluged with social invitations, many of which he could not accept because of the pressure of his training and racing. If non-white people were legislated against and regarded as social outcasts by many Australians, Taylor was the unique exception who was able to break through the color bar. That fact in itself made this tour a pioneering achievement. In Australia in 1902, even more than in Europe, a black person was an extreme rarity, and many people among the thousands who paid to see Taylor's cycling feats were also catching their first glimpse of that exotic creature, a Negro.

USA, EUROPE, AUSTRALIA, 1902—1905

Bicycle racing was going through a huge surge of popularity in Australia at the turn of the century, and Taylor was widely credited with having given the sport an immense boost there. He brought American class and European finesse to the Australian tracks. His arrival, said the newspapers, was the most exciting thing that had happened in Australian cycling since Zimmerman had toured in 1895. Indeed, Major Taylor was probably the greatest athletic sensation Australian crowds had ever witnessed. He was also one of the best paid athletes in the world at that moment. The syndicate that sponsored his visit had lured him to Australia with an offer of £1,500 appearance money for three months of racing, plus whatever he could win in prizes – at a time when an average Australian worker earned about £100 a year. His superstar status was spectacularly reinforced by such astonishing earning power.

A flood of press coverage greeted his arrival in Sydney. Sports news was for once promoted on to the front page of newspapers. A GREAT WHEEL MAN, a profile of him in the *Sydney Herald* headlined.

> In appearance, Taylor is a cleanly built, neatly packed parcel of humanity. He is short in stature, with good body and hip development and slender legs, with ankles which a fashionable ballet dancer might envy. No comparison for his build would be fitter perhaps than that of the racehorse. ...
>
> His skin shines like satin, and his face smiles pleasantly under his centre-parted, close-cropped curly hair, as he walks to the starting point, but the smile does not last long. When he mounts, it gives way to an expression of thoughtfulness. ... Taylor tests his seat till he finds his position right, and sees to it that his feet are properly strapped to the pedals. ... When satisfied, he surveys the field ahead of him, and getting a grip on the handlebars, he waits for the pistol."[7]

Taylor was frequently interviewed by Australian newspapermen. Journalists sought his opinions on local rivals and on the sporting scene in Europe and the United States. They were fascinated by his character and personality, especially his intense religious convictions, which were widely publicized. One long interview which he gave to the *New South Wales Baptist* gives a fascinating insight into his personality and is a more complete statement of his religious beliefs than can be found in all the hundreds of articles written about him in American newspapers.

USA, EUROPE, AUSTRALIA, 1902—1905

THIRTY THOUSAND DOLLARS FOR CONSCIENCE SAKE, the article was headlined, referring to the amount of money Taylor estimated he had lost by refusing to race on Sundays. "For years this man of deep and strong convictions has been preaching to the sporting world a silent but eloquent sermon of example. ... He is a most unassuming man, and so modest that almost every word has to be coaxed from him."[8]

As well as giving earnest interviews about his religious convictions, Taylor was also invited to speak from the pulpits of various churches, where he welcomed the opportunity to carry his message of clean living, good sportsmanship and Sabbath observance to Australian congregations. There was no Sunday bicycle racing in Australia, however.

The racing during this first Australian tour was a spectacular athletic and commercial success. As in Europe, even Taylor's training sessions were attended by fans avid for a chance to see the champion at work. Crowds of twenty thousand people crammed into tracks in Sydney, Melbourne and Adelaide to greet 'the Worcester Whirlwind' with rapturous applause. He was the idol, the hero of the moment, as he took on the leading Australian champions, Walker, Lewis, Corbett, Gudgeon and Mutton. Spectators paid a shilling each for the privilege of seeing him race. To most observers it was obvious that, in a straight sprint, unhampered by unfair opposition and teaming, Taylor simply outclassed his rivals. Everywhere in Australia, people who met him were impressed by his gentlemanly behavior. The three month visit earned him a total of almost £4,000 - equivalent to what an average Australian worker would make during his entire 40-year working lifetime.

IN FRANCE, too, in 1902 and 1903, Taylor was still enormously popular. Though not the object of the same intense curiosity as on his first visit in 1901, he was still a preeminent personality in the Parisian sports world. Fans still paid just to see him train, and his match races against Harry Meyers (Holland), Louis Grogna (Belgium), Willy Arend and Walter Rutt (Germany), Thorwald Ellegaard (Denmark), Van den Born (Belgium) and his old rival, the French champion Jacquelin, were certain to bring a sellout crowd to the European tracks.

On top of the world at this period, Taylor was not unbeatable, but he dominated the field, beaten into second place only by the most outstanding among his contemporaries, men like Meyers, Jacquelin, and Ellegaard.

Taylor did not contest the world championship in either 1902 in Rome, or 1903 in Copenhagen, both of which were won by Ellegaard, the Danish champion. His determination not to ride on Sundays kept him from competing and from the chance to win the world's highest honors again. In 1902, however, Taylor issued a challenge to the winner even before the championships took place, and a week after Ellegaard took the title in Rome, Taylor beat him in Paris in two straight heats. *L'Auto-Vélo* said that Taylor was in "dazzling form" and "literally annihilated" the world champion. Of course, such challenges did not add to his list of championship titles, but they did add to his mystique and made the racing season lively and dramatic. Even though Taylor would not compromise his principles, he was determined to prove that he would have won at the championship had it not been held on a Sunday.

L IFE IN THE United States continued to be extremely difficult for the international star. The more famous he became abroad, the more determined his rivals became to crush him at home. Taylor had not signed up for the 1902 American championship season before he left for France in March because of his bitter experiences the year before. But his sponsor, Fred Johnson, wanted him to return to compete for the championship. So, on his return from France, he went late into the national circuit races against Kramer, Lawson, and Mac-Farland. There, he encountered a new flurry of hostility and combinations. The NCA had changed its rules to allow as many as four riders in championship races, a change Taylor alleged was directed specifically against him, for now there was a greater possibility than ever before to pocket him. In a four-man race, two of the riders could obstruct him, leaving the fourth free to win unopposed. His three rivals could then divide the prize money between themselves.

"Throughout this season, Major Taylor has been harassed to a point of desperation by these cheap fellows who seem determined that he shall not win the Championship of America again," one New York newspaper commented. "In every race a combination seems always in order to defeat Taylor by unfair tricks, even if they themselves fail to score. ... With anything like a fair show, or an equal chance and the honest observation of the rules of bicycle racing, Major Taylor would be Champion of America again."[9]

The hostility between Taylor and Kramer, Lawson, and MacFarland reached a peak that year. Once, after he had beaten the three of them through his skillful tactical maneuvering, Taylor was forced to retreat to his dressing room because MacFarland verbally and physically threatened him. Taylor made up his mind to defend himself if necessary. "This is the first time in my racing career that I ever lost my head to the extent of planning to fight for my rights at all costs," he wrote later.

> As they came into my room, I was waiting for them with a length of two-by-four which I had picked up from a lumber pile near the grandstand. Before they had a chance to lay a hand on me I made one vicious, healthy swing at MacFarland, but he dodged the blow. Then the entire outfit tried to close in on me, but I was too fast for them even on foot. I dropped my club and made for the dressing room where my trainer and I were obliged to take refuge until the police interferred. Fortunately, there was no bloodshed.

This intensified hostility explains why Taylor was more than ever anxious to make the most of his possibilities to race abroad and why his participation in American racing became more and more spasmodic from then on. To a journalist who asked him when he visited London in August 1903 what his future plans were, he responded that they were not yet decided, "but I won't race in America again! No, never!" The ever-present difficulty of securing a hotel room and the right kind of food when and where he needed it also continued to be a big problem in the States. Even in places as familiar to him as New Haven and Newark, he still had to endure personal rejection and insult.

A revealing article in the *Worcester Telegram* in August 1902 penetrated to the core of his dilemma. NO LINE IN AUSTRALIA! it was headlined, MAJOR TAYLOR TALKS OF HEADING THAT WAY. MAY SHAKE THE N.C.A. FOR KEEPS. SHABBY TREATMENT DRIVES HIM TO IT.[10] Taylor told the *Telegram* that he was thinking of giving up his pursuit of the championship after the problems he had had finding a hotel for himself, his wife, and his trainer, Bert Hazard, in New Haven. "The Worcester rider visited several hotels, but at each he was refused admission," the article explained. "Finally quarters were secured for the night, but in the morning when Major went downstairs for breakfast, he was refused service. He visited several restaurants with no success, and then it was that he packed his trunks. ... All this shabby treatment, the Major declares, has taken the heart out of him. He is without doubt the best drawing card following the grand circuit game and should the Major follow out his present intention, the track meet promoters would be the biggest sufferers."

Taylor told the *Telegram* reporter that his chances were very poor that year because of the hostility directed against him. "Man to man," he said, "I have Kramer and all the other cyclists beat to a certainty. I know it and so do they. But I realize that I have little chance the way things are running. Not only do I suffer in the races, but I am unable to get proper food in many of the cities in which I train. With an even break, and I say it without boasting, there is no rider in the world who can defeat me in a match race."

TAYLOR MADE a lot of money in those two years. Determined to keep racing, to push himself to his physical and psychological limits, he was driven by the realization that his athletic prime would not last forever, by the urge to make as much of his career as possible while he was still at the height of his powers. In fact, he was already talking of retirement at the end of the 1902 American season when the invitation came to go to Australia for the first time. The price he was paying for his success was immense; even though public acclaim buoyed him up, the fatigue was sometimes overpowering.

He talked again of retirement on his return from the third trip to Europe in September 1903, arriving in New York with his wife and seventeen pieces of baggage, including a motorcycle and the car he had bought in Paris. This tour had also been an outstanding success. He had been joyfully welcomed in Paris and again won triumphant victories in all the European capitals, traveling frequently that year with Woody Hedspath, another black professional cyclist from Indianapolis.[11] But in spite of the acclaim, he was deeply fatigued.

On that occasion Taylor told the *Worcester Telegram* reporter that his body was letting him know that it was time to retire. "I can see that years of continued riding are telling on me, and I am satisfied that I have done enough. I shall look around now for the right sort of a position in the business world, and let the other fellows do the racing. I would probably never have gone to Australia this year, had I not wanted to see the country of which I had heard so much, and to give my wife a trip around the world before we settled down to a more quiet life."[12]

Even in Europe, he thought his appeal was diminishing: " The first time I was over, many people turned out just to see what I looked like, but one can't draw on that basis forever, and while I did well again this time, I could see that I could not expect to command big crowds next year unless I went into Sunday riding, which I do not propose to do at this late date."

He also felt that bicycle racing was on the decline in the United States: "While I feel that my constitution tells me that I must give up the game, the fact that the game is losing its hold is another considera-tion that has led me to make this decisive announcement regarding my retirement.."[13]

Many athletes go through cycles of intense ambivalence about their futures. In spite of his determination to retire at the end of 1903, Taylor was unable to resist the lucrative offers that came to him again from Australia. Promoters offered him a large sum of cash and all his ex-penses to race there, plus whatever prizes he could win and a per-centage of the gate. In fact, rival promoters competed against each other to secure his services, such was his attraction. "Major Taylor was flitting about Worcester in his imported automobile, with his poodle dog," the *Telegram* noted, "letting the Australians do the guessing until the offer came that he felt he could not refuse."[14]

ONCE AGAIN, Taylor signed a contract with Hugh D. MacIntosh, otherwise known as 'Huge Deal' MacIntosh, the ambitious businessman who later, in 1908, succeeded in pursuading Tommy Burns to meet the black champion Jack Johnson in Australia in 1908 for the world heavyweight boxing title, and made a fortune selling movies of the fight in Europe and America.

Taylor's second tour, through the Australian summer of 1903—1904, was an extremely taxing one. His hated American rivals Iver Lawson and Floyd MacFarland had also been engaged, specifically to create a climate of tense athletic excitement, since the hostility be-tween them was by then well established, and their attitude towards Taylor did not improve in the slightest outside the United States. On every occasion, they worked together against him, while Taylor – honest and sporting to the core – refused to cooperate or team with any other riders to defend his position on the tracks. Lawson, in fact,

USA, EUROPE, AUSTRALIA, 1902—1905

was suspended for a year for a foul he committed in a match race in Melbourne which caused Taylor to crash heavily and left him stunned, badly bruised and lacerated, one of the most serious crashes he had ever had. Lawson was forced to cancel his Australian trip and return to Europe, where the following summer he became world champion in London.

Even the Australian riders saw little enough reason to help Taylor increase his already huge earnings, and so the black American star was isolated, left to fend for himself, against a determined opposition. Unless he paid them, shared the prize money with them, they argued, they had no reason to work with him in a race. The climate was much less friendly than the previous year and Floyd MacFarland was responsible for stirring up much of the negative feeling against Taylor among the formerly friendly Australian riders. Commenting on his relationship with Taylor, Iver Lawson told an Australian journalist, "We never speak, and we pass in the street without noticing one another."

And on this second tour of Australia, when he was welcomed so warmly again by loyal spectators, Taylor had to endure racist decisions from some referees. The match races between Taylor and MacFarland and Lawson were exciting but inconclusive, spoiled as they were by bad judges' decisions, refusals to appear and the muddle of frequent official inquiries and the withholding of prize money. When he left Adelaide in April 1904, Taylor swore to the press that he would never return to Australia. "Some of your officials have all along entertained a disgusting prejudice against me," he told the *Adelaide Observer*. "There is no tactful sympathy about them. They have regarded me merely as a revenue-earning machine, nothing more. I could fill up your paper with incidents of how this bias has been displayed."[15]

The increased animosity shown towards him by riders and officials, however, only made Taylor more popular with the crowds, who still crammed in to the tracks to enjoy the cut-throat racing between bitter rivals, and they were deeply disappointed by the confusion and chaos that spoiled Australian bicycle racing that year and often made it impossible for Taylor to give the stunning performances for which he was noted.

MAJOR TAYLOR'S first and only child, a daughter, was born in Sydney, Australia, on May 11, 1904. She was christened Rita Sydney after the city where she was born, and was known thereafter as

Sydney. Less than a month after her birth, the Taylors set sail for San Francisco on the liner *Sierra* with the Australian champion Don Walker, a staunch Christian who had become a close friend and was on his way to compete in the world championships in England. They left Australia with what the newspapers referred to as "a small menagerie," a kangaroo, several brightly colored parrots, and a cockatoo, which had been taught to cry "Major! Major! Hallo, Boy!"

A rousing farewell in Australia was followed by an icy reception in San Francisco. There, wrote Taylor, "we encountered a new epidemic of Colorphobia. ... We found it impossible to dine in the restaurants because the management drew the color line, and the same conditions confronted us at the hotels. We made the rounds of the city, only to be refused shelter and in many cases to be actually insulted." Major Taylor, a household name in France and Australia, was a nobody in California.

In the end, at Taylor's suggestion, they resorted to a ruse to be able to eat lunch. Walker went into a restaurant where they had already been refused service and ordered lunch for three, saying that his companions would be coming shortly. When the food was served, he paid the bill and then brought the Taylors in. They were not thrown out. They had planned to rest for a few days in San Francisco, but they were so disgusted with their treatment, they instead left for the East on the midnight sleeper. Such was the respect paid to a great American champion in California.

Don Walker was flabbergasted. "So this is America about which you have been boasting in Australia," Taylor remembered him saying. "From what I have seen of it in the past few days, I cannot understand why you were in such a hurry to get back home here. Do you prefer to live in a country where you are treated like this than to live in my country where you are so well thought of, and where you are treated like a white man, and where many inducements were made you to return to live? I cannot understand this kind of thing." Taylor tried to explain conditions to Walker, he wrote, "but the more I tried to smooth matters over, the more incensed he became."

According to Taylor's daughter Sydney, her parents' experiences in San Francisco were more severe than merely being refused service at hotels and restaurants. She says that a man on the street, mistaking her mother for a white woman, made insulting comments about her being with a black man. She says that Taylor told his wife and Don

Walker to go down the street a little further and then turned and confronted the man. A fight broke out, and Taylor, an expert boxer, deftly flattened him.

Taylor arrived in Worcester in June 1904 with his wife, his newborn daughter Sydney, and his animals, in a state of exhaustion, not just from the second Australian tour, where he had ridden close to 100 races, but from the cumulative effect of years of racing, training, and traveling. "I don't know whether I'll ever race again," he told the reporter from the *Worcester Telegram*. "During the last six months I raced three or four times a week. The racing was the toughest I ever experienced. In fact, I am sure that the racing I have done in the last six months was harder than all the rest of the racing I ever did." To the reporter he appeared to be in perfect health, but the stress and strain had taken its toll. Taylor himself said that he "suffered a collapse and narrowly averted a nervous breakdown." He canceled his plans to travel on to London and Paris for the rest of the summer season. "You see," he told the *Telegram*, "I can't ask my wife to go around the country and abroad with me like I could before the little girl came, and I won't go away alone. If I could find something congenial to do, I think I'd stay home for awhile."[16]

The complete rest he took in Worcester for the remainder of 1904 was the first summer break he had had since the beginning of his professional racing career in 1896. He was only twenty-five years old when the curtain fell on the first and most extraordinary phase of his life. Marriage and a child brought a new sense of responsibility. By 1904, he had accomplished the greatest feats of his life and had essentially completed his athletic contribution.

IN JUNE 1904, Robert Coquelle, Taylor's European manager, and the cycling journalist Paul Hamelle published a short, colorfully written, and, for the most past, accurate evocation of Taylor's life. Coquelle had been familiar with Taylor's racing activities from the beginnings of his professional career and perhaps closer to him since 1900 than any of his European friends. He had seen at first hand how Taylor had pushed himself to his limits, the most extraordinary thing about him.

"If anyone ever had the right to be tired," they wrote, "isn't it Major Taylor? Since he left America, he has done hardly anything else except race. ... Make no mistake about it, this athlete is also a businessman who understands very well that the saying 'time is money' applies to a racing cyclist whose speedy legs will not last forever." Coquelle and Hamelle hesitated about giving Taylor recognition as the greatest sprinter of all time, but they did say that they thought he was "the most extraordinary, the most versatile, the most colorful, the most popular cyclist, the champion around whom more legends had gathered than any other and whose life story most resembled a fairy-tale."[17]

Although he was in retirement, the sport still needed Major Taylor. Coquelle was in New York for the six-day race in December 1904, and, as always, was looking for stars to promote. He wanted a match in Paris between Taylor and Frank Kramer, champion of America for three years running. Taylor went to New York, and after a three-hour discussion at the Bartholdi Hotel under the watchful eye of NCA chairman Batchelder, they signed a contract for the following year. But as soon as Coquelle returned to Paris, Taylor began telling the American press he wasn't sure he wanted to return to racing, that he was thinking of taking up motor racing and breaking some records. Coquelle was surprised to receive copies of articles from New York newspapers reporting these doubts. He had the contract in hand, he told the readers of *L'Auto*, for which he was now working, and he expected Taylor to keep to his word.

Kramer arrived in Paris in March 1905, but Taylor hesitated, and rumors began to spread that he was afraid of Kramer, who was in splendid form that year. Taylor himself said he was ill and sent Coquelle a doctor's letter which advised him to give up racing for health reasons. Coquelle thought the illness was a fake. Nonetheless, Taylor broke his contract with Coquelle and stayed in Worcester through 1905 and 1906, resting, recovering, driving his car, watching Sydney grow, and gaining a lot of weight. Coquelle sued him, and the NCA suspended and fined him for breach of contract. The old cycle of disputes and arguments resumed. Taylor did not care. He had lost his appetite for bicycle racing. The extremes of adulation and hostility to which he was continually exposed as a public figure had drained and depressed him. He desperately needed some breathing space, some privacy, a return to the security of his home and a normal life. He needed a shelter from the storm.

USA, EUROPE, AUSTRALIA, 1902—1905

11
COMEBACK AND DECLINE

THROUGHOUT 1905 and 1906, Major Taylor remained at home in Worcester, enjoying the chance to relax with his family and friends. A celebrated local personality, he was always conspicuous driving around Worcester in his French automobile, since ownership of any automobile was highly unusual at that time. In April 1905, he was stopped twice for driving on Main Street considerably faster than the ten-mile-an-hour speed limit. On the second occasion, a policeman testified in court that Taylor appeared to have been racing with another driver and he was fined $35.

After so many years in the limelight, it was not easy for him to adjust to a provincial existence. He had, after all, been in the public eye from a very young age, and a retreat into obscurity in his late twenties would be difficult for any former champion. He still hungered for competition, and the possibility of a comeback was always on his mind. The lawsuit for $10,000, brought against him for breach of contract by Coquelle, hung over his head, and he had been suspended for life by the National Cycling Association. If he could resolve these difficulties, he might think about returning to the track. The NCA, ambivalent as ever towards Taylor, wanted him back in the sport to challenge the almost effortless superiority of Frank Kramer.

There was also an economic incentive for Taylor to return to bicycle racing. He had made a lot of money between 1901 and 1904, and he had handled it well. He owned property in Worcester, and he maintained himself and his family luxuriously, though not ostentatiously. Few black people in the United States lived as well, but he was living on his savings. In 1906 he was twenty-eight years old. Bicycle racing was his true vocation, and he still had an enormous reputation, especially in Europe. A comeback would be difficult, but not impossible.

The chance for Taylor to resolve his professional difficulties came at the end of 1906, when Coquelle, in New York as usual for the six-day race, visited his old friend in Worcester, anxious to settle the dispute between them. Taylor told him that he would race once again in Paris if the lawsuit and the suspension could be settled. He was not thinking about making a lot of money, he told Coquelle, but he needed something to occupy him. Idleness was weighing heavily on him.

Coquelle negotiated with the NCA in New York and secured backers in Paris. He smoothed over the troubles and drew up a new contract, showing his renewed faith in Taylor. THE RESURRECTION OF THE NEGRO announced *L'Auto* on March 7, 1907.[1] The Peugeot bicycle company reported that 'le nègre volant' would be riding their bicycles for his comeback in 1907, and the Dunlop tire company agreed to supply him with tires.

Soon the sensational news was all over the Parisian cycling world. Sprinters were all rubbing their hands with glee, thinking about the great racing there would be, knowing that Taylor's name on the billboards was always good for box office receipts. Unfortunately, there was not the same excitement in the United States.

Within a month, Taylor and his family arrived at Le Havre on the liner *La Touraine*. Fifty cyclists welcomed him onto French soil with a rousing cheer. Taylor was the first passenger to cross the gangplank, bounding forward with his usual energy. "You look as if you've put on a bit of weight, Major," said Coquelle, as they settled into their seats on the train for Paris.

"Oh, absolutely," replied Taylor. "Two months ago, I was 26 pounds over my normal weight. But from lots of boxing sessions, I've already taken off about 14 pounds. The weather has been too bad in Massachusetts to do any serious riding, but I've been working in the gymnasium and doing a lot of walking."

Was it true that she had been opposed to her husband's comeback, Coquelle asked Daisy Taylor. "Oh, no, not at all," she replied. "I advised him to do it. He was very undecided after your last visit to Worcester. But I urged him to take up cycling again because I don't think it's good for a man of his age to be idle. He's too young to retire. Since nature has endowed him with such an exceptional talent, he should make the most of it."[2]

The French press again went into ecstasies over Taylor's arrival. *La Vie au Grand Air* announced his return with a full-page front-cover portrait and a two-page spread with photographs of Taylor with his wife and daughter. "Major Taylor is with us once more," wrote the editor of the magazine. "Every sports lover will be overjoyed to hear the news. Stars are rare in the cycling world and the reappearance here of such a celebrity ... should bring a new surge of enthusiasm to those who hunger for new excitement in our bicycle races."[3]

A song called 'Le Nègre volant' was sung all over Paris, and Coquelle and Hamelle brought out a second edition of their book about Taylor. Once again, he was being promoted and marketed in a modern way. He was interviewed in depth about his decision to resume his racing career and the chances of a successful comeback. The press made a fuss over his daughter and wife, and a photograph of the family as they arrived at the Gare St. Lazare was published in *L'Auto*.[4]

WHEN TAYLOR first arrived in Paris, a bizarre instance of racism occurred. Welcomed like a prince at the Hotel Sydney on the Rue des Mathurins – he was better than a prince, said a newspaper reporter, because princes sometimes forgot to pay their bills and Taylor always paid his promptly – he was politely but forcefully asked to leave by the manager. The many Americans at the hotel threatened to move out if Taylor was allowed to remain, he said. They would not sleep under the same roof as a Negro. Taylor did not resist and found himself a beautiful, large apartment in Neuilly, close to the Buffalo velodrome. This newsworthy incident was reported in many of the Parisian daily papers, all of which criticized the manager's hasty and ill-considered decision.

L'Auto complained bitterly about the disgraceful episode, the first time such a thing had happened in Paris. Taylor told the reporter he was absolutely stunned. "In America, I wouldn't have been at all surprised," he said, "but in a country which has had a revolution and proclaimed the Rights of Man, it's astounding. What surprised me most of all was that the hotel manager was persuaded to change his mind so easily. But it doesn't matter. It won't make me hate the French people or stop me from working hard to regain the prestige I had three years ago."[5]

Taylor retraced his former haunts and reclaimed his cabin number 13 at the Buffalo velodrome. Everywhere he was greeted by old friends, anxious to see his little daughter Sydney for the first time and inquiring about his physical condition. One unpleasant surprise was finding MacFarland in Paris, also training for the season. They greeted each other icily at the track. A reporter asked MacFarland what he thought of Taylor's chances of recovering his former speed. "Oh, sure, the damned nigger can get back to where he was before," said Mac-

Farland. "As an American, he really disgusts me," he added, "but as a bicycle racer, I couldn't be happier. Make no mistake about it, he's the best advertisement for bicycle races. Everybody will profit from him being here."[6] Fortunately, MacFarland was unable to secure a contract and returned to the United States.

It is not hard to understand why Taylor was drawn back to Paris, into the whirl and excitement of the cycling world. He was still a celebrity there, with star status. Bicycle racing was his life and his only means of earning a good living. Retirement into obscurity was always a pale option as long as he could still delight and thrill the European crowds with his speed.

A THLETICALLY, TAYLOR'S comeback was not easy. Older, heavier, and out of competition for nearly three years, he set to work in his typically determined way, subjecting himself to his usual rigorous training program as he struggled to lose weight and regain his form. With the racing fans, he had lost little of his mystique and star attraction. Once again hundreds of enthusiasts – including many blacks – watched him train on the Buffalo track. Taylor's fight to regain his old spark became not only a private but a public affair as well. Some of his old rivals, for example, Ellegaard, Jacquelin, Meyers, and Van den Born, were still active on the European tracks, but a new generation of dynamic young sprinters had come up since 1904. Two new French riders – Gabriel Poulain, French champion, world champion in 1905 and second in the world championships in 1906; and Emil Friol, champion of France in 1906 – were ambitious to take on and beat an old star like Major Taylor.

Some of the critics were scathing about Taylor's performance when he was soundly beaten by Poulain, Friol, and Jacquelin in early season races. On one occasion, Taylor fell several times in one heat, and they mocked him, even suggesting that perhaps he had forgotten how to ride his bicycle. However, through disciplined training and intense racing, Taylor's form gradually returned. He did not contest the world championship, which was won that year in Paris by Emil Friol, because he still refused to race on Sundays, but by late July he was in fine form and beat Ellegaard in Marseilles and Poulain in Paris. On August 8, Taylor's old mentor, Birdie Munger, was in Paris on business. He had the pleasure of seeing him beat Friol, just crowned world champion in Paris, in two straight heats at the Buffalo track.

USA—EUROPE, 1905—1910

By the end of the season, having traveled all over Europe, Taylor proved in convincing fashion that he had returned to the highest levels of bicycle racing. By August, reporters noted that he had recovered all his old confidence and suppleness, that he was his old magical self, that 'le nègre volant' had finally found his wings again.

That he was still an extremely marketable asset was demonstrated when Australian promoters again approached Taylor with lucrative offers to spend the winter months racing in Australia. But he turned them all down. Instead, he announced his retirement and told the press he wanted to return to his home and family, that this time it was definitely good-bye to bicycle racing. He had wanted to prove he could come back and beat the world's best, and he had. In a two-page article published under his signature in *La Vie au Grand Air*, Taylor confessed his annoyance with journalists who had called him fat and heavy at the beginning of the season, mocking his efforts at a comeback. He was so happy to have proved them wrong, he wrote.[7]

Huge crowds turned out for his final races in Paris. A "Soirée des Adieux" was held for him at the Buffalo track. Retirement from the sport was definitely good for business. Taylor beat Poulain magnificently that evening; Coquelle reported that it was one of the best races of his entire career. His speed was still untouchable when he was in top form. He returned to the United States with the satisfaction of having completed his career by beating all the world's best sprinters.

But, hungry for competition, uncertain of what his other options were in life, still entranced by the Parisian sports world, Taylor returned once again to Paris with his family in the spring of 1908 for another strenuous season, which lasted until mid-September. He had raced during the winter in the United States, and was in much better form than the previous year. Again, he raced against Ellegaard, Jacquelin, Friol, Poulain, Dupré, Rutt, Hourlier, and Verri, the leading European sprinters, in Paris, Brussels, Milan, Antwerp, and many other cities. He continued the familiar cycle of the peripatetic athlete, constant overnight traveling, living out of a suitcase, training, massage, meeting the press, and the tension and rewards of the actual races. Sometimes his wife went with him, sometimes she stayed in Paris.

In Bordeaux, he had one of the worst crashes of his entire career, which gouged and burned the entire left side of his body. His thigh, elbow, and hand were skinned raw, and he was forced to spend more than two weeks in bed. It was difficult to recover form after such a long enforced recovery. Taylor's own remedy for these wounds was to expose them to the heat of a wood fire in his lodgings in Paris.

At the end of his successful 1908 season, Taylor did not talk about retiring. Just as he was leaving for home, he told *L'Auto* that he would be back. "I am welcomed so warmly in France, and the public is so sympathetic towards me and supports me so well, that as long as I decide to go on racing, I'll be coming back to France. After all, it's here that I've won many of my most memorable victories. ... Thank everyone for me. Please tell the spectators that I'll always have the most pleasant memories of them."[8]

On September 22, 1908, two days after Taylor left France for the United States, Wilbur Wright flew for an hour and a half at Le Mans, breaking all the world records for altitude and flight duration established by his brother Orville, who had almost been killed in a crash three days earlier. Almost a year later, on July 25, 1909, Louis Bleriot made aviation history when he was the first person to fly across the English Channel, in just thirty-seven minutes. It was against such a background of revolutionary technological advances, especially in transportation, that Taylor's final years as a world-class bicycle racer unfolded.

ENCOURAGED BY his strong showing in 1908 and determined to continue racing for another season, Taylor returned to Paris in the spring of 1909 for what was to be his sixth and last European tour. He decided to go alone that year, without his wife and daughter, a decision he subsequently regretted.

Accompanying Taylor on the liner *Dampfers* as it left New York early in May was his trainer of many seasons, Bert Hazard. As he sat down on board ship to write to his wife, the first of dozens of long letters he sent to her that year from Europe, Taylor put on a bold face with a lively description of his journey, but he also expressed the profound anxiety that would be characteristic of the whole trip. For, in addition to leaving his family behind, he had finally succumbed and agreed to race on Sundays.

Taylor really had no choice at this point in his career, for his star was on the decline. Coquelle told him he was no longer sensational enough to pull in the crowds he once had on holidays and weekdays. Thus, he no longer had the leverage he once had over his promoters.

That was the practical reality of his situation. Since he wanted to continue racing, and needed to make money, he was forced to make this enormous compromise with his religious convictions. With Coquelle presenting the ultimatum – either race on Sundays, or no contract to compete in Europe – Taylor had no choice but to capitulate.

"Be sure to pray for me all the time, dearie," Taylor wrote to his wife, "and think of me every minute, because you know how I feel that I need your prayers and sympathy just now more than ever before and of course you know why. I feel very strange and queer about this thing and you know the reason. I am very anxious about the outcome of it all and, well, I am just trusting that it may all end well. So don't forget each night, dear, to remember your boy. You be the same good girl that you have always been and take good care of things and don't take any foolish chances or run any risks, and I guess we will get out of this alright."[9]

Taylor wrote his letters from his lodging house in Paris or from hotel rooms in other cities where he was racing. Some fifty long letters in his daughter's possession provide revealing insights into Taylor's state of mind during this trying time since he is reticent about his feelings in his autobiography. He fretted constantly about not hearing from her often enough. "Daisy, My Darling Wife, I found a letter awaiting me upon my return to Berlin yesterday and I was very pleased too as it was almost three weeks since I had a letter from home. Just think of it, now that is too much, and this morning to my surprise came another. But for goodness sake please do not keep me waiting like that any more. ... I had begun to grow very impatient."[10]

In these letters, Taylor reveals his love and concern for his family's health and safety and is overflowing with affection for Sydney. "I have been wondering how my girls have been getting along and what they are doing. And what did my poor little girl say the next morning when she woke up and Dad gone sure enough. Tell me all about what she did and what she said and how she is at present. ... Now kiss poor little Sydney over and over again for me and tell her to kiss you as many times for Dad."[11] The closeness of the family is touching and Taylor feels their absence painfully.

The letters also give a glimpse of the vulnerable, emotional side of this intensely competitive man. Taylor's personal voice was a reflection of the quiet Christian modesty which was always behind the man of action. In 1909, in his thirty-first year, Taylor was becoming a sometime world champion athlete, severely challenged by younger and stronger men. In the most intimate passages, where he most exposes himself, the letters reveal a lonely, homesick champion. He suffers from sleepless nights, worries about his forthcoming races, and frets over his defeats. And he grapples with the inevitability of his athletic decline. No matter how hard he trains, the once unbeatable champion, once the fastest sprinter in the world, cannot recover his former authority. On June 14, he writes:

> Daisy, my darling wife, only a few lines to say that I did not do as well as I expected to in the Grand Prix of Neuilly. Rutt beat me in my semi-final, and he won the final also from Dupré. ... Friol, Poulain and I were all shut out in our heats. I was awfully disappointed at not having made a better showing, because I was feeling fine, never felt better, but I was not there with the kick.[12]

In addition to his races, Taylor describes his opponents, his training methods and diet, his cabin at the Buffalo track, and the black American boxers who were in Paris that year. He describes his dealings with the Alcyon bicycle company, whose bicycle he was riding, and Coquelle's encouragement when he wins a race and his disappointment when he loses. On June 29, he writes:

> I had a bit of luck yesterday at Rouen in the match with Hourlier and Devoisseau, as you will see by the clipping. They teamed against me and used me very bad in the second heat. So when we came out to ride in the final I just said to the judges ... you just go over to those other two riders and caution them about their rough riding and foul tactics and if they ride fair I will show you the best race you ever saw here. ... So ... they ... said to them, we saw you used Taylor in that second heat, and we expected him to protest, and if he had done so we would have disqualified Hourlier. Now we warn you to ride fair this time or we will disqualify you both. I won, but in spite of the warning, they rode me just as bad as in the other heat, but I beat them, so they could not be disqualified anyway, as I won on points.[13]

And on August 1, from Dusseldorf:

> I failed again in the Grand Prix of Buffalo last Thursday night, failed to even get into the final. And why? Try as hard as I may, I simply cannot ride as well as I did last year, and I have already had to make several sacrifices and concessions in my contract, which means several hundred dollars, all because I cannot win often enough. But I am trying to use the best possible judgement in every way, to get all out of this season's

riding I can, because in all probability this is my wind-up, unless I can make good in the championship. So far I have only seven hundred dollars to show for all my hard work and tiresome sleepless nights, and the season is more than half gone.[14]

Taylor's concern about money is a frequent theme throughout his letters, especially his desire to provide a better life for his "darling wife" and "my dear little baby":

Now, dearie, about coming home. It is true I am not winning as I expected to, but I am still getting paid for getting up, and as badly and as anxious as I am to see you and dear little Sydney and to be home with you once more, don't you think I had better stay a while longer and get as much money as I can before leaving, because dearie, this will surely be my finish this season owing to the poor showing I have been making so far, so for that reason I rather thought I had better make as much as possible while the sun shines.[15]

And a little later, on the same theme, he writes:

I am so pleased that you are a homeloving girl, and that you appreciate your little home and keep it up so well, it makes me long to see you in a still nicer one, or in a beautiful little farm. You know how pleased I would be to give you all those nice things if I could, don't you, dearie. But what I have given you was the best I could afford, and if the time ever comes that I can afford better, you will have still a nicer house. [16]

In August, Taylor sent home some of the poems he wrote clandestinely in his room:

I am sending you a few verses that I have written for you, you will find them enclosed in a separate envelope and you must not let anyone see it, dearie, as I do not want it to become generally known that I am poetically inclined. I know that you will say that I am only wasting valuable time riding a bicycle when you read these verses, and I know it too, and I am thinking seriously of taking up this work where poor Paul Lawrence Dunbar had to leave off. You remember everybody who knew us both down in Washington said we resembled each other enough to pass for twins, and ever since then I have been more or less anxious to try my ability along this line. I am sure I have the makings of a great poet. I am something of a composer as you already know, so I am going to send you the music for these verses just as soon as I have finished it.[17]

Above all, however, the letters express his despondency over his failing career and his homesickness. On the point of leaving to compete
in the world championships in Copenhagen, his confidence was at a
low ebb.

> I rode yesterday against Poulain, Meyers and Arend, and what do you
> think, I actually finished last in every heat. Meyers won, Poulain second.
> Well, I cannot possibly do any better, I have tried and tried, and have
> done everything possible to get going faster, but nothing I have tried
> seems to be of any use, so there. I am really discouraged for once in
> my life, and I am starting for Copenhagen at eight o'clock. It is now six
> a.m., and I would much rather be starting for home, dearie. However,
> I am going to be brave and try to make the best of it, but it surely makes
> me feel bad to think that I am well and strong but cannot beat these
> fellows. Well, I hope it will be over with soon. It came near being over
> with yesterday, as I had another fine of a hundred francs to pay and it
> was most unjust at that. But say, sweetheart, when a man is married
> and has a good wife as I have, and a nice little baby girl, he will *take
> a good deal*, and stand for many things that he would not, were he *not*
> married. So ... I just paid my fine like a little soldier, but it *did hurt* me
> so. I stand for many things now that I never thought I could put up
> with, and for which I never would stand up before I married. ...
>
> Now love and kisses and God's blessings to both of my sweethearts
> from your poor, weary, homesick, lonesome, tired and most worn out,
> discouraged, fat, disgusted, but *game and true* husband, and that does
> not begin to express how I feel.[18]

A few days before he left for home, he wrote:

> Well, dearie, I had a talk with Coquelle about next season, and it is all
> off. He did not tell me outright that he could not engage me, but told
> me openly that he could not give me what I asked for and of course, I
> could not come over for what he offered me, so I may try riding on the
> other side next year, though I should hate to get mixed up with those
> dirty sand-baggers any more. You see, dearie, Coquelle has no money
> himself, and he cannot guarantee me a dollar. ...
>
> Now after the terrible experience of this season, I am not at all grieved
> because I am not coming over again next year, but quite to the con-
> trary, I am indeed pleased. As I told you several times before, dearie, I
> am full up with this business, and have been for a long time, and this
> season's work just put the finishing touches on it. I regret very much
> now that I ever came back again, because if I had finished last year,

you see how nice it would have been for you and little Sydney to have been with me on my last successful racing season, and we could have finished by trimming them all, and on top. One thing that I am pleased for dearie, and that is that you and Sydney were not here to see everybody trimming me this year, so perhaps it is just as well that you did not come.

Well, at any rate, I can say that I had a good, honest, faithful try, and did the very best I could every time, and the fault was surely not mine. … Oh, well, if I can finish up these last two races without a fall and get home safely, I will be most thankful indeed. …

Say, dearie, how anxiously I am counting every minute of the time that remains, just as I imagine someone in jail or prison must feel after doing about five years hard labor. Each month that I have put in over here seems like a year to me, but thank God it will soon be over with, and then I can return to you, dearie, well and strong, just as I left you, please God.[19]

Taylor's letters during his 1909 tour in Europe are poignant evidence of the courageous fight he waged against his physical decline and his emotional difficulties. They have about them a poetic, autumnal quality, a reflection of the sensitive man behind the public personality of Major Taylor, champion cyclist.

TAYLOR'S DESPONDENCY at the end of his final European season did not prevent him from showing his class and his tactical experience in one final, telling victory. He had been unsuccessful in the world championship races held in Copenhagen, the first time he had competed since he had won the title in Montreal in 1899. But on October 10, a few days before he left Europe for good, he beat the reigning world champion and champion of France, Victor Dupré, in his hometown, Roanne, near Lyon. Taylor's hard work and persistence through an extremely difficult and taxing five-month season finally brought him a consolation prize, a satisfying reminder of his world-class stature. The promoters presented him with a gold broach for his daughter, and the Alcyon bicycle company took one last opportunity to publicize the fact that the famous 'nègre volant' had been riding their bicycle.

In spite of this last minute victory, Taylor's season had been very disheartening for a man unaccustomed to defeat. In his letters to his wife, he recognized with pain and regret that his European career was drawing to a close. Nevertheless, he told his French journalist friends on leaving Paris that he would be back. He did not announce his retirement, as he had done many times before. He had made a big mistake coming without his family, he told the press, and he would definitely bring them in 1910. He boasted of his longevity in the sport. "Don't forget," he said at the Gare St. Lazare, as he was about to board the train for Cherbourg, "that I am the most senior sprinter in the world now. My first race was in 1893."[20]

But both Coquelle, who was at the station to bid him farewell, and Taylor himself knew that he was tired, dispirited, and sick of bicycle racing. As the train pulled out of the station, he was leaving the scene of his greatest triumphs behind him forever, to return to an uncertain future in the United States. Ironically, in his autobiography, Taylor dismissed his last season in Europe in a peremptory way: "In the spring of 1909, I returned to Paris," he wrote, "and was even more successful on this occasion than I was the year before. ... To enumerate my successes would be a matter of repetition."

Taylor's hometown newspaper, the *Worcester Telegram*, which had followed and reported his career with care and affection over the years, interviewed him as soon as he arrived home at the end of October. FAMOUS RIDER TOO OLD FOR RACING. FINDS IT HARD TO GET IN CONDITION, it said.

> It is his farewell to Europe. Advancing years have put on him the handicap which nothing can beat out. Everybody predicted two years ago when he went across to Europe to race that he couldn't do anything after three years absence from the game. Taylor astonished the racing world by showing practically the same speed that made him a marvel of the racing game several years ago. Last year he was able to repeat, and he thought he could this year. But he couldn't and he is satisfied himself now that never again will he be able to show his old time speed on the bicycle. The wonderful Worcester rider has had a longer period of supremacy than almost any other bicycle rider ever had, due to his good living and conscientious training.

"I expected to do better work on the wheel this year than I did last," Taylor told the *Telegram*, "but I didn't. I rode very well, but I didn't have any luck. If I had had a little, I would have made an excellent showing. ... I couldn't get quite right."[21]

The end of his career was in sight. He raced during the summer of 1910 in Salt Lake City, at which time he was still described in the *Salt*

Lake Tribune as "the highest priced bicycle rider in the world." He competed for the $800 purse and was still tactically superb, but the spark had gone out of his jumps and sprints, and he was consistently beaten by Iver Lawson and Jackie Clarke. Taylor was deeply tired, and he lacked the motivation so natural to him as a young man, the drive that had catapulted him to his greatest victories.

W HEN TAYLOR RETIRED in 1910, he was thirty-two and had been racing bicycles more or less continuously since he was fifteen, except for that brief period of retirement in 1905 and 1906. It was more than half his lifetime. During those years, he had competed all over the world and traveled hundreds of thousands of miles throughout the United States, Europe, and Australia. The world of professional bicycle racing, like any other competitive sport, was a grueling one. Training, racing, continual traveling, the inevitable crashes, the same repetitive cycle of preparations, the demanding psychological and physical battles with opponents – all these stresses had taken their toll.

Zimmerman had once discussed his own retirement with Taylor, after he had conquered the whole world, and Taylor recalled Zimmerman's warning. "My boy," he had said,

> ... when you have reached your zenith and have defeated every rider in the world, as I did, and when you have achieved all the success the racing game has to offer, then your enthusiasm will begin to wane and your star will begin to set. When you begin to dislike the game, and your enthusiasm for everything connected with it fades, then you will know that your racing career is just about finished. One thing I would advise you, when you succeed in winning the world's championship and other honors, do not stay in the game so long that you become a second or third rater. ... Nothing is more pathetic than to see the once brilliant athlete or world's champion walloped repeatedly by inferior riders.[22]

When Taylor finally quit racing, he was perilously close to the situation Zimmerman described. He had hung on in the sport because that was the only thing he was superbly good at. As long as his name had a drawing power at the box office, as long as promoters were willing to engage him, Taylor was willing to ride. But by 1910, he could no longer deny that his career was over.

USA—EUROPE, 1905—1910

When people asked him why he quit racing so early and criticized him for not remaining in the sport as long as possible, he emphasized to them the stress he had endured:

> Little did they realize the great physical strain I labored under while I was competing in those sixteen years of trying campaigns. Nor did they seem to realize the great mental strain that beset me in those races, and the utter exhaustion which I felt on the many occasions after I had battled under bitter odds against the monster prejudice, both on and off the track. In most of my races I not only struggled for victory, but also for my very life and limb. Only my dauntless courage and the indomitable fighting spirit I possessed allowed me to carry on in the face of tremendous odds. My trying experience on the tracks had exacted their toll on me, and I was certain the day had come for me to step out of the sporting limelight. Father Time was gaining on me.

Looking back, Taylor thought not only of his victories and the glory, but also of the danger. "I cannot help but recall the many narrow escapes I had in my races, and shudder as I think of the many brave and outstanding riders who were killed or maimed for life in the pursuit of success on the track. I am grateful for having escaped serious injury in my races, and that I was able to leave the track in perfect physical condition."

Taylor had indeed been lucky in this respect, for he had escaped serious accidents. There had been many crashes, of course, and nasty abrasions and burns from the cement surfaces of the tracks, and several times he had been laid up in bed in order to recover. But none of the accidents had been life-threatening. The finely tuned sense of balance and control that he had taught himself back in his trick-cycling days on the sidewalk outside Hay and Willits bicycle shop in Indianapolis had enabled him to avoid many dangerous situations.

"I felt I had had my day," he wrote in his autobiography *The Fastest Bicycle Rider in the World,* "and a wonderful day it was too. As I think back over those old days, I have no retrospective regrets. Many of my good friends ask me if I would like to live the old days again. My answer in each case is, positively no."

USA—EUROPE, 1905—1910

12
DIFFICULT
ADJUSTMENT

A TRIBUTE TO MY SILENT STEED

I now hand up my silent steed
That served my purpose well indeed
Just like a true and faithful friend
It stuck right by me to the end. ...

Now as a reward for faithfulness
My trusty bike has earned its rest
But not in the attic all covered with dust
Nor in the cellar to get all rust

But in my den on a pedestal tall
Or better still upon the wall
Where I can see it every day
And it will keep the blues away

We rode to win in every race
Fairly we played in every case
If life grows dull and things break bad
Just think of the wonderful days we've had.

THESE FOUR STANZAS from a longer poem, one of the many in
Major Taylor's autobiography, attest more to the difficult adjust-
ment he was facing than to his literary skill. Sadly, the sentiments he
expresses are typical of those every outstanding athlete faces when
he retires from the sport in which he has excelled. As a professional
athlete, Taylor's life had been minutely organized according to a strict
routine. Everything he did was secondary to his concentration on plan-

WORCESTER, 1910—1917

ning, training, and competing. The purpose of his life was to win, and the strain and anxiety of preparation was rewarded with the satisfaction of victory.

Retirement brought Taylor a measure of relief from the stress of competition, but it also left a vacuum. No longer the fastest bicycle rider in the world, he faced the difficult questions of what to do with the rest of his life and how to earn a living to support his family. He was certainly not in immediate need, but his savings would not last forever.

It is difficult to say exactly how much money Taylor had saved from his career in bicycle racing when he retired from the sport in 1910. One account says that he had accumulated as much as $75,000 in cash; others mention a figure of about $35,000. Certainly he was a wealthy man when he retired, the wealthiest black man in Worcester and among the wealthiest in the United States. In addition to this substantial amount of cash, which should be multiplied by at least ten times to approximate present-day values, he also had valuable assets – a fine house in Worcester, an automobile (still a rare possession in those days), and a houseful of possessions collected during his travels abroad. He also owned other property in Worcester, three of the typical Massachusetts triple-deckers, which he rented out, and some plots of land.

Taylor's wealth and fame as a black athlete set him apart from other people in Worcester, where he was recognized as an important local personality by both blacks and whites. He straddled the black and white worlds in a unique way, with a foot in each, yet belonging completely to neither. He had succeeded in the white world, traveled extensively in Europe and Australia, was sophisticated and at ease with influential people, and lived in an extremely comfortable fashion befitting his star status. On the other hand, he was devoted to the John Street Baptist Church and remained close to the black community in Worcester. Blacks respected him for having earned his reputation and money by hard work. He was an example to them of a black person who had been able to succeed in life through his talent, tenacity, and moral uprightness.

Following the example of many of his bicycle racing colleagues, Taylor decided to look to the rapidly expanding automobile industry for future business possibilities. He had extensive experience in the bicycle industry and was an expert machinist. He had been one of the first people in Worcester to own cars and motorcycles, and had always been interested in the latest developments in automobile technology. Birdie Munger, his friend and adviser, had become a successful manufacturer of automobile tires ten years before and was the "inventor of a demountable automobile rim."[1] Although there is no record of contact between Taylor and Munger at this time, it seems highly likely that Munger advised him and had some strong ideas about how Taylor should invest his money after his retirement.

Soon after he had hung up his racing wheels for good, Taylor decided he needed more training in engineering and applied for admission to the Worcester Polytechnic Institute. The official reason given for his rejection was the lack of a high school diploma. "My feeling is that they could have waived the requirement in his situation," said his daughter, Sydney Taylor Brown, "but they chose not to because he was black. No matter how well he was thought of, there were certain things that blacks just could not do."[2] Negroes simply did not go to white colleges in 1910.

His failure to gain admission was a huge disappointment. It meant that he could not hope to gain professional recognition in the field of engineering. He might speculate, of course, or go into business, but there were still insuperable social barriers which his fame and status were powerless to overcome. Undaunted, Taylor pressed on with his project to design and build a sprung automobile wheel.

In the background of Taylor's business activities in the years immediately after his retirement is the huge expansion of the automobile industry. Since the turn of the century, men with engineering and technical expertise, including many ex-bicycle racers, had tended to move from the manufacture of bicycles into the industry. It was a natural progression, and the basis for many fortunes was laid during those years.

"It is difficult for an outsider to fully appreciate the wonderful development of every branch of this industry," said J. M. Gilbert, the general manager of the U.S. Tire Company to a newspaperman at the end of 1911. "Even we, who are connected with it … fail occasionally to understand the remarkable growth in popularity of the automobile. It has come to be such a widely recognized private and public utility that there appears to be no limit to the possibilities. And from the standpoint of the tire manufacturer, constant activity is necessary to keep pace with this marvelous development." Four million pneumatic tires, he said, would be required "to shoe the automobiles running in America" during the year 1912.[3]

There were disadvantages, however, to the pneumatic tires then in use on cars. They punctured easily, they blew out, they were cut by the rims, they wore out fast, and they were expensive. Inventors interested in challenging the monopoly enjoyed by the rubber tire companies saw great opportunities in the exploration of alternatives to the rubber tire.

Taylor had his eye on a piece of the prize. Like Munger, he understood the importance of efficient cushioning in automobile wheels, and he invented a wheel divided into a number of independently sprung sections. An internal spring mechanism in each section was intended to absorb both the weight and the shock as the wheel traveled over a rough surface. Taylor machined and assembled a prototype at the Worcester workshop of his friend B. Austin Coates, who owned a manufacturing company that made horse and sheep clippers.

Taylor was not alone with his idea of breaking into the marketplace with a new product that would prove cheaper and more durable than the unreliable and expensive rubber tires. There was an energetic search going on. An avid reader of popular technical magazines, he clipped articles from *Scientific American, Popular Mechanics, Motor Age,* and the *Automobile Trade Journal* on the sprung wheel and pasted them into a small scrapbook. Discussion of the sprung wheel idea centered around how to combine durability, reliability, and resiliency in a correct design. Taylor's personal solution was just one among dozens of suggestions put forward by ambitious, ingenious inventors during the second decade of the new century. Surrounded by people capable of giving him expert feedback, he pressed forward with his invention confidently, determined to see it through to completion.

Taylor's activities soon attracted the attention of the Worcester newspapers: MAJOR TAYLOR INVENTS A PRESSED STEEL TIRE FOR AUTOS WHICH WILL GREATLY REDUCE MAINTENANCE COSTS, read one headline. "Major Taylor has solved the high cost of living for automobile owners, and next to aviators, there's no class that has to settle for higher prices than the owners of the buzz wagons," the article continued.

WORCESTER, 1910—1917

> Taylor has a new tire to take the place of the costly rubber tire. He
> thinks it will show all the good qualities of the rubber tire, and will last,
> which rubber tires do not. He's not the only one who thinks so. His
> new tire was tested yesterday and the men who rode with him are more
> confident of its success than Taylor himself.
>
> The former bicycle speed merchant has been working on his invention
> several months and has it perfected. ... Those who recall Taylor's days
> of bicycle racing are sure he's got the goods.[4]

By the beginning of 1912, Taylor was looking for a company to test
his sprung wheel and to put his invention into production. His attorney wrote to Charles H. Metz in Waltham to discuss the terms under
which his company would carry out a testing procedure. The letter
suggested a three-month testing period, during which Taylor would
be paid a small salary and expenses while traveling between Worcester and Waltham. The attorney underscored the cash outlay Taylor
had already made and guaranteed that Metz would receive an equal
amount of stock for his mechanical expertise during the test and for
his ability to personally secure capital for the new company.[5]

A similar testing venture was proposed to the famous Pierce-Arrow
automobile company in Buffalo, but for all the careful negotiating and
testing, Taylor was unable to reach an agreement with either company. He finally came to an agreement with his old friend Fred
Johnson, of the Iver Johnson Company in Fitchburg, who had sponsored him during his victorious 1900 American season and his first,
triumphant European tour. They agreed to develop the tire together,
raise capital, and find shareholders.

By the beginning of 1914, the Major Taylor Manufacturing Company, makers of the 'Metal Taylor Tire,' was formed. Taylor and
Johnson, the president, agreed to invest an equal amount of capital,
$15,000 each. The other members of the enterprise were white Wor-
cester businessmen, who were either co-investors or allocated shares
in the company on the basis of in-kind assistance given to Taylor
during the developmental phase. He worked hard at pushing the
project forward, also seeking black investors in Worcester, so confident was he of the success of the venture.

A search for further information about the fate of the Major Taylor
Manufacturing Company has proved unsuccessful. The company
failed. It never launched the new tire despite the optimistic predic-

tions. The operation was not financially viable, and production never began. The details of what happened remain a mystery.

Probably Taylor miscalculated seriously in his timing, or he received bad advice. The leaders of the pneumatic tire industry were at that very moment working on new and better cord casings for rubber tires, which successfully overcame the same problems the advocates of sprung wheels were trying to resolve. The sprung wheel idea was a technological blind alley, soon outmoded by other, superior ideas.

Some have suggested that Taylor was cheated out of his money by his partners in the enterprise, but this explanation cannot be confirmed. Fred Johnson, a wealthy man, the head of a company that mass-produced firearms and bicycles, easily survived the loss of his $15,000 stake. But for Taylor, the loss was more serious, representing a sizable proportion of his savings, banked from years of strenuous exertions on the bicycle racing tracks of the world.

The failure of the company was a bitter blow as well as a severe financial loss. It also represented a loss of credibility and reputation. One successful business enterprise might have led to others and to a strengthening of his financial stability. But this failure in his first ambitious business undertaking limited his opportunities in the future. Whatever the reason for the collapse of the company, Taylor had lost a large amount of money through poor investment. His wife criticized him for having shown too much confidence in his white partners, who she thought took advantage of him, and the whole affair became a source of tension between them.

Taylor now undertook a succession of five or six different business enterprises, all connected either with the automobile industry or with metal manufacturing, which appear to have been modestly successful. From the ambitious but ill-fated sprung wheel idea, he turned to automobile oils. He started an oil manufacturing and distribution company called the Excello Manufacturing Company, "makers of 'Excello' Automobile Oils and 'Triple-Wear' Lubricants." "Buying cheap oil to save a dime is like stopping the clock to save time," declared a Christmas card, which he presented to his customers. The company operated in Worcester between 1913 and 1915, after which it went out of business.[6]

The years that followed these ventures were financially difficult ones, and Taylor tried his hand at various occupations. In 1917 he worked as a "salesman," according to the Worcester city directory, and in 1918, his draft registration card describes him as a "machinist," working for the Persons Arter Company in Worcester. He was exempted from military service during World War I because by then he was almost forty years old.

By 1919, Taylor had changed his employment again, the Worcester directory listing him as a partner in a firm called Taylor and Quick. Between 1922 and 1924, he was the proprietor of "Major's Tire Shop" in Worcester, a description which indicates that he had been forced to give up any ambitious ideas of manufacturing or distribution and was engaged in the mundane business of replacing and repairing car tires. The last listing in the Worcester directories that gives an occupation for Taylor is in 1926, when he is described simply as "auto repairer."[7]

The search for more information about Taylor's business activities during these years has not been successful, but the brief, dispassionate listings in the city directories tell an unambiguous story. Taylor's fortunes continued to decline in the years following his retirement from bicycle racing. There were no opportunities to capitalize on his fame as an athletic star after his retirement in 1910 – no positions as a sports commentator, no lucrative television commercials. There were no longer professional bicycle racing teams, which might have employed his valuable services as a trainer or director. Taylor was confronted by the same problems of discrimination in retirement he had faced during his career. Society had hardly changed, and opportunities for a black person were still extremely limited. His status as a retired star might open certain local doors for him, but others remained as tightly closed as ever. The magical days of his stardom were over.

TAYLOR'S CAREER as the only outstanding black professional cycling champion was radically political as a statement of black pride and achievement during the fifteen years he was winning races all over the world. There could have been no more practically and powerfully political life than Taylor's as he struggled against white opposition in the United States and carried out his triumphant, ambassadorial tours in Europe and Australia.

But his personality and activities during these efforts to maintain his former dignified existence after his retirement from racing do not always present a flattering picture, especially in the light of today's black awareness and activism. It would have been logical, after his retirement from bicycle racing, for Taylor to have used his influence and fame to become involved in the political reform movements growing in the United States to alleviate the enormous social problems that black people faced. For example, in 1906, the Niagara Movement, led by W. E. B. DuBois, had met at Harper's Ferry and drawn up an aggressive program of political demands on behalf of black Americans. The Niagara Movement led to the establishment of the National Association for the Advancement of Colored People in 1910, an organization that campaigned for the end of forced segregation, for equality of education for black and white children, and for the complete enfranchisement of the Negro.

But politically, Major Taylor was conservative. According to his daughter, he had some contact with famous black American leaders, including W. E. B. DuBois, Booker T. Washington, and Marcus Garvey, as well as other well-known black personalities and friends from his bicycle racing days, who often visited him in Worcester, talking and laughing with him for hours. He subscribed regularly to *Crisis*, the NAACP's radical publication, and other black newspapers. But amid all this growing reformist agitation, Taylor was never politically engaged, never attended political meetings, belonged to no political organizations and espoused no political causes.

Although he may have sympathized with the progressive ideas of his black friends, it appears that he was unwilling to get involved in their causes. And he did not agree at all, says his daughter, with Garvey's "back to Africa" radicalism. "My father never saw that as a solution, for all blacks who were mistreated, to go back to Africa."

Taylor's essentially modest personality may have prevented him from seeing himself as someone who could have an impact on political life. Though he had a wide experience of the world and talked intelligently and articulately to the press, he was always described as a timid man. He was not an intellectual, and he may have lacked the confidence to launch himself into a life of public speaking and political agitation. In retirement, he did not seek the limelight or crave publicity, and the role of a leader was evidently one which he did not seek to create for himself. He did not go out ambitiously into the world any more, but preferred to deal with the issues that were close at hand, his family and his community.

Religion had always given Taylor firm guidelines for his personal behavior and defined how he thought others should behave. As a black person and an athlete, he always felt an especially strong need to prove his respectability, to show that his behavior was impeccable. "His determination not to ride on Sundays was one of the things he insisted on because he wanted to prove that he was respectable even though he was an athlete," says Sydney Taylor Brown, "He had a great need to prove that he was a respectable person, to continue to prove it to himself and me. If he had been a doctor or a lawyer, he wouldn't have had to make such an effort to prove this. The people my mother associated with before they married were all the Negroes in that part of the world who were university people and Ministers, and Major Taylor was not."

Throughout the second part of his life, in retirement, Taylor was deeply committed to the John Street Baptist Church in Worcester.

"My father maintained his black identity in Worcester through his church," says Mrs. Brown. He had more experience of the world than the majority of black people, and he was seen as a knowledgeable figurehead in the black community. People looked up to him and came to him with their problems when they needed advice. He devoted a sizable proportion of his income to the church and helped church members financially for as long as he still had money himself. "He not only gave money to the church," says Mrs. Brown, "but any project that they had, he was the main one. 'Oh, Mr. Taylor's going to take care of that,' they said." In addition, he refused to collect rent from tenants of his, church members in need, and this concern for others contributed to his financial problems, as well as leading to tension between him and his wife.

In spite of his charitable deeds, Taylor did not have an intimate relationship with the people he helped. He did not invite them to his house socially, for most of them were servants, janitors, chauffeurs, and doormen. Without any black peers in Worcester and isolated because of his fame, he sought out his few white friends for stimulation and companionship. But he was a local personality, one of the few famous people in Worcester, and was recognized wherever he went. People would stop him in the street, shake his hand, and pass the time of day. He was a 'greeter' for the city, one of the people who were invited to city hall to welcome visiting dignitaries. Proud of Worcester, he took visitors on sight-seeing tours in his splendid car.

When he was not working, Taylor frequented a local drugstore opposite city hall, where he socialized with his acquaintances and was often seen, impeccably dressed in a hard straw hat and carrying a cane. "It was a great big drugstore, with round tables and men sitting with chocolate sodas and candy and cigarettes and cigars," says Mrs. Brown.

> Every day I can remember my father would eventually end up at the drugstore. Everybody in Worcester, all his buddies, all the men, would pass by. They didn't go to beer taverns, there was no beer there. ... You could always see him either out on the corner, or inside. It was a kind of club. I've met him in there many a time, because my mother asked me to go downtown and get him. No, I don't seem to remember him as being the kingpin, but he was very popular with these people, and their wives knew him, and their kids knew him and they'd always say, "Hi, Mr. Taylor," that kind of thing. And of course, he was nice to kids, *he liked to be liked* and he in turn always bought children sodas and things like that.

AT HOME, Taylor kept a neat workshop, filled with tools and lathes, where his daughter remembers watching him work and where as a small girl she worked on her own bicycle. "He used to make me clean the bicycle," she says, "and not just wipe off the shiny parts. I had to take an oil cloth and wipe those gears and the chain so that it wouldn't dirty my stockings and dress." Upstairs, he had a full-size billiard table where he played for hours with his friends, and his collection of clocks was spread throughout the house. Taylor loved animals and had a succession of dogs and birds, some of which he had brought back from his travels. His Australian cockatoo, trained to call "Hallo Boy!" to him used to sit on his shoulder and peck his ear.

Taylor's wife always maintained a spotless and orderly house and garden. She was also meticulous in her own dress and appearance. "She was the kind of person who never came out of her bedroom until she had combed her hair," says their daughter. "She would sit on the side of her bed, she had long, long hair, and she'd comb and she'd comb and she'd braid and she'd braid, and when she came out of her bedroom, she didn't even have bedroom slippers on. She had her shoes and her stockings on when she came out of her room, and she was *dressed*."

Taylor himself was meticulous about health matters, insisting on regular examinations and dental appointments for himself and his family and laxatives at the end of the week. He believed in wholesome

food and regular meals at fixed hours. He still rode his bicycle on occasion on the long bicycle path called the Speedway in Worcester, but
when he went downtown, it was always in his car.

Taylor applied the same disciplined habits and correct behavior for
himself and his family after his retirement that he maintained during
his rigorous athletic training. He insisted on having things done the
way he wanted them done, says Sydney Taylor Brown, and this was
a source of friction in the family. He tended to be an exuberant man
outside the house, but was frequently severe, moody, and introverted
with his own family. His daughter resented the fact that he was
humorous and jolly with her friends, but was much less relaxed with
her when they were at home together.

Though outwardly Taylor doted on Sydney, and praised her ex-
travagantly to his friends, he was actually ambivalent in his feelings
towards her. He desperately wanted a son, Mrs. Brown says, to be his
athletic heir and successor, and he was immensely disappointed when
Daisy had a miscarriage when she was pregnant with their second
child and was unable to conceive again. Sydney became increasingly estranged from her father who, she felt, considered her his wife's
child.

Her father was self-conscious about color, Mrs. Brown recollects,
calling him a man who was "color struck" – preoccupied with color
and shades of color. He had been attracted to his wife's fairer com-
plexion and was unhappy that his daughter took after him. "Even
though he loved his country and he loved his race, I don't think he
was proud to be a Negro. I always resented the fact that he didn't
want me to be dark." During the summer months when she was a
child, Taylor would tell her constantly to pull her hat down over her
face to protect her skin from the hot sun, she says.

Taylor was also ashamed of his rural background, hating everything
connected with farming all his life. The differences in class and social
expectations between Taylor and Daisy became more marked as they
grew older. "I don't think she felt that he wasn't good enough for her,"
Mrs. Brown suggests, "but I think he was very keenly aware of the
fact that she wasn't the same kind of person that he was."

Next to the confident, socially sophisticated Daisy, Taylor felt – now
that he could no longer prove himself athletically – socially inferior.
As he began to lose money, it became harder and harder for him to
maintain a pretense of equality. Such emotional complexities were at

the root of the developing tension and alienation between husband and wife. Outwardly, they kept up appearances, but inwardly their relationship grew increasingly bitter.

Gradually, Taylor became more withdrawn and uncommunicative. He socialized lightheartedly with his friends and their children, but sometimes he would hardly speak at the dinner table. He felt boredom, regret, and anger at his situation, and he became increasingly stern and rigid in his domestic life, the only place over which he still had some semblance of control.

When Sydney wanted to enroll at the Sargent School of Physical Education in Cambridge to train as a physical education teacher, Taylor, knowing and disliking the fact that she would have to go to the South upon graduation to teach at a black school, insisted that she go instead to the Massachusetts College of Pharmacy. Somewhat perversely, he did not think it appropriate for his own daughter to pursue an athletic career. Daisy supported Sydney in her choice, and Taylor was forced to acquiesce. But he refused to pay her fees, which prompted Daisy to make the difficult decision to go to work as a seamstress in a drapery store in Worcester. She was determined that Sydney be able to pursue the career of her own choice. More and more, Taylor retired to his study, shutting himself off from his family, perhaps lost in reflection about the excitement of the life he had left behind him and the fame he had once enjoyed on the bicycle tracks of the world.

IN SEPTEMBER 1917, Major Taylor came back into the public eye in a familiar role for one last race. The occasion was an old-timers race held at the Newark velodrome, one of the few East Coast tracks still offering a regular program of bicycle racing. The *Newark Evening News* announced the race as the RHEUMATIC STAKES FOR AGED BIKERS, and quipped that "there will not be a great amount of speed on tap in this event, but there will be some very stylish cases of gout on view. The most prominent of the octogenarian pedalers is Major Taylor, the famous colored rider who won the championship in 1900. Taylor accepted the invitation to ride by wire last night. Having just returned from a hunting trip, the Worcester man stated that he is in great form and would be there with 'both feet.'"[8]

Bicycle racing was still able on occasion to attract the crowds that it had in Taylor's prime, and more than 10,000 spectators were on hand to watch the professional meet before the old-timers race. The extraordinary Frank Kramer, himself a thirty-eight-year-old veteran, beat the reigning national sprint champion, Arthur Spencer, in two straight heats. After the race, in a typical gesture of good sportsmanship, Taylor shook Kramer's hand and said, "Frank, your riding in those two heats was the most perfect bit of match racing I ever witnessed!"

With the main events concluded and a chilly evening wind gusting around the track, "Either sentiment or curiosity" held the crowd in their seats to watch the old-timers race. "The fan folks were bent on seeing what a denatured vintage of the far distant past could do," joked a reporter, "and the scramble of the old boys furnished a satisfying demi-tasse as a topper to a heavy, but palatable, meal of racing."[9] Nat Butler, once a teammate of Taylor's and one of his keenest rivals in the national circuit championship races between 1897 and 1900, was there, and so too was 'Mile-a-Minute' Murphy, now a New York policeman, who fired the starting pistol.

Amid the overcharged atmosphere of sporting nostalgia, the most poignant note of the evening was the presence of Birdie Munger at Taylor's side. Munger, whose status as an old-timer reached back to the earliest days of the sport on the high-wheel and who had been a rival of Zimmerman in the late 1880s and early 1890s, "motored from New England to see the ancients." He smashed one car, borrowed another, and after a day and a night, with stops only for meals and repairs, reached the velodrome in time to start Taylor in the contest. "When Munger was a big man in cycling," the *Newark Evening News* reminisced,

> Major Taylor was his valet. When the little colored boy was not pressing clothes and shining the master's shoes, he was riding one of the master's bikes. One day, with Munger away, Taylor started in a 100-mile road race, winning first place. ... Learning of the little darkey's triumph, Munger furnished him with light racing equipment and started him in a track race, and Taylor won again. Informing Taylor, who was then sixteen years of age, that some day he would be the fastest bicycle rider in the world, Munger became Taylor's manager and handled the colored boy until he won the American championship in 1900.

> Yesterday was the first time Taylor ever rode in a race on Sunday in America. During his racing career he could have had thousands of dol-

lars in prizes and bonuses had he consented to race on the Sabbath, but religious scruples could not be overcome by cash.[10]

As Munger crouched to push Taylor from the starting line, Taylor "turned to his former mentor and remarked, 'Well, Birdie, you started me in my first race and you're starting me in my last race.'" Munger's presence at the race was a telling reminder of the affection and attachment that still existed between the two men.

Taylor won the race ahead of Arthur Ross, John Chapman, and Howard Freeman. A photograph published in the *Evening News* shows Taylor on the wide banking of the track in a tactically strong second position, preparing for his final sprint.

"From a racing standpoint the event for the aged exceeded the expectations of all who gave the race a thought," the evening newspaper reported.

> The relics themselves were astonished at their show of agility and the speed that had lain dormant in their systems.

> There's a saying in the bike game that class will always tell. Twenty years ago, Major Taylor was the class of the field ... and he was the class of the same field yesterday, despite the triple roll of fat that curved over his collar and a layer of adipose tissue around the belt-line that is thicker than the armor plate on a battleship. The dusky demon won and won as he pleased with yards to spare, making a show of his Caucasian brethren. Some in the beaten eleven were as fat as the Major while others were lithe, slender and, in appearance, quite youthful from the neck down, but class overcame the handicap of fat and weight.[11]

WORCESTER, 1910—1917

13
AUTOBIOGRAPHY
AND ILLNESS

A S HIS DRAMATIC bicycle racing career receded into the past and he saw his fame gradually forgotten, Major Taylor thought more and more about putting his memories in writing, and he finally decided to work on an autobiography. The project proved to be a huge and ambitious undertaking, which occupied him much longer than he had anticipated. From its very inception, Taylor was motivated not only by the need to reassure himself that his achievements would not be forgotten but also by a desire to use the story of his life as an example to other blacks in their struggle to achieve equality in a racist society.

"The primary object of this narrative," he wrote in the Foreword to *The Fastest Bicycle Rider in the World*, published in 1929, "is not for any personal glory or self-praise, but rather to perpetuate my achievements on the bicycle tracks of the world, for the benefit of all youths aspiring to an athletic career and especially boys of my own group as they strive for fame and glory in the athletic world.... I am writing my memoirs ... in the spirit calculated to solicit simple justice, equal rights and a square deal for the posterity of my down-trodden but brave people, not only in athletic games and sports, but in every honorable game of human endeavor."

Sydney Taylor Brown believes that her father was motivated by these considerations, as well as by the possibility of earning some money from the sale of the book. "I feel that his ego was such that he wanted everything he had done down in black and white, to put it on the record," she says.

And I do know that he really did want to inspire black kids. ... About the time I came along, there weren't too many black kids who were even in college, it was all they could do to get through high school; their fathers couldn't afford it. Major Taylor wanted young black kids to know that whatever they wanted to do, if they *really* wanted to do it, to get in there and *try*. And while trying to do it right, not to gamble and cheat and to have a lot of self-respect. This was what he said over and over again."[1]

At the beginning of March 1923, Taylor wrote to Robert Coquelle, asking for information and photographs to help him with the autobiography. "Dear Bob," he wrote, "No doubt you will be surprised to have a letter from me after such a long time, and you will be further surprised to learn that I am racing again, not on a bicycle, but on paper, as I am writing my autobiography, the part of my life that I devoted to racing. I am more than half through it at present and it promises to be very interesting. It is the biggest job I ever tackled."[2] He asked Coquelle for information and photographs to include in his book and said he hoped it would soon be finished.

But the task of organizing and writing the book was a formidable one. During his career, Taylor had conscientiously clipped hundreds of articles about his races from American, French, and Australian newspapers, reaching back to the very beginning of his professional life, and he pasted them into several large scrapbooks. A good number of the clippings were in French, which he did not read well, and he had no editorial assistance, despite the fact that he had no expertise as a writer, especially of such an extended project. Nonetheless, he set to work, incorporating all these documents into a chronological, historical narrative of his bicycle racing career.

The only help and advice he had came from his friend Harry Worcester Smith, a wealthy Englishman. Taylor also employed the services of a stenographer and typist, who came to his house on a regular basis to work with him. If it was true when he wrote to Coquelle at the beginning of 1923 that the book was already half-finished, his progress after that was extremely slow.

Taylor continued to work on the autobiography despite other pressures that were building in his life. The writing would be interrupted by periods of hospitalization, worsening finances, and increasingly strained relations with his wife. As he struggled through 1924 and 1925, Daisy wondered whether the project, which he had obviously underestimated, would ever be completed. Sydney Taylor Brown, who was then at college in Cambridge, remembers coming home one weekend and finding her mother exhausted from the strain under which she was living because of the book. "Her whole regime was upset because the dining room was full of papers and the typist, a white woman, was there all day," she says. "Her whole house was in disarray, and she would say, 'We'll never get through!' I don't think her heart was really in it. I just think she thought, 'Well, it's one of those things your father wants to do.' But she didn't say to me, 'It couldn't be a success' or 'It's a waste of time.' She just didn't seem to be enthusiastic the way he was."

In spite of a modest success in his tire repair business between 1922 and 1924, Taylor was not able to earn enough money to continue to support himself and his family in the comfortable lifestyle to which they were all accustomed. The brutal truth was that he had for years been living beyond his means and dipping into his savings, and by the early 1920s, his capital was rapidly diminishing, forcing him to begin to liquidate many of his assets to pay his expenses.

One by one, his various properties were sold, and in February 1924, he took out a loan on his house on Hobson Avenue. Mrs. Taylor Brown remembers her mother crying because Taylor had been forced to sell off yet another piece of the fine jewelry he had bought her during his affluent years. One necklace, she says, was so valuable that they had had a replica made and kept the original in the bank. Taylor went to the bank and withdrew his wife's jewelry from a safe deposit box piece by piece and converted it into cash. Even the $10 gold coins, which he had given his daughter as birthday presents over the years, were taken out of the bank and sold.

Just when his problems were building into a crescendo of misfortune, Taylor became seriously ill, and it may have been the necessity of paying expensive hospital bills which precipitated the financial crisis that forced him into the drastic step of selling the Hobson Avenue house. The splendid house in an upscale, white, neighborhood, the purchase of which had created such an uproar in 1900 at the height of his success, was finally sold in January 1925. The loss of his home, a powerful symbol of Taylor's worldly success, was a terrible blow, a crushing indication of the decline of his fortunes. He had lived there for twenty-five years, and it had been his sanctuary from the exhaustion of his hectic racing tours.

Taylor used the proceeds from the sale of the house to settle unpaid loans and other debts. There was not enough money left over even to buy a smaller house, and the Taylors moved into a modest rented apartment on Blossom Street in Worcester.

WORCESTER—NEW YORK, 1920—1930

"They rented from a Mr. Dean, who was a barber with a huge bar-
bershop downtown that catered specifically to whites," says Sydney
Taylor Brown; "Mr. Dean owned the Blossom Street house, a triple-
decker not far from the Worcester downtown, and they lived on the
first floor and rented one of the other floors to my mother and father.
Mr. Dean was an old friend of theirs. ... It's possible the Deans did
not collect rents regularly from them in their difficult financial situation. It may even have been the mounting debt of the rents that was
partly responsible for the final move away from that house in 1930."

The illness that required Taylor's hospitalization for varying periods
of time was shingles, a debilitating nervous disorder that intensified
under the psychological stress to which he was being subjected.
During his periods of hospitalization, Sydney reports, Daisy visited
him in the hospital, "to sit with him and be with him, bring him straw-
berries and things like that. There were times when he would go
home, but then he would become ill again and have to go back."

Taylor's illness was one more burden, besides the autobiography
and financial worries, on his already strained marriage. Like many
couples, they had maintained their marriage for the sake of their
daughter and also because of their religious and moral principles. Although they continued to live together, "there was a rift that caused
them to have separate beds, separate bedrooms," Mrs. Brown confided. "I don't know exactly when it occurred. You know, back in
those days, everybody had to sleep together in a big, double bed. But
my mother actually moved into the guest room, and she never came
back. Of course, they didn't tell me why."

With Daisy working as a seamstress, at first to pay Sydney's college
fees, then Taylor's mounting hospital bills, it was not surprising that
she cried a lot. "She certainly had come down in the world with a
bang," a longtime friend said. "I'm sure that was a great source of
humiliation to him," says Mrs. Brown, "and to her too, but she was
determined that I was going to go to school, wherever I wanted to
go." Accustomed to accompanying her famous husband around the
world first class and being entertained in the houses of the wealthy
in Europe and Australia, Daisy was increasingly despondent, but she
was also a resilient and resourceful woman. It was Major Taylor's
pride, in the end, that took the more severe beating. He was forced
to confront the bitter truth that he was no longer able to support his
wife, a loving obligation he had always conscientiously fulfilled.

WORCESTER—NEW YORK, 1920—1930

B Y THE END OF 1926, Taylor's fortunes had declined to such an extent that Harry Worcester Smith was alarmed. An internationally famous gentleman jockey and steeplechase winner, with whom Taylor shared a passion for cars and engineering problems, he often invited Taylor to his large estate, Lordvale, at North Grafton, near Worcester. Smith was close enough to the Taylors to appreciate the full impact of their difficulties, and he persuaded the editor of the *Worcester Evening Gazette* to publish an article that he wrote about Taylor's troubles and to appeal for help.

A CHAMPION LAID LOW, AN APPEAL ISSUED ON BEHALF OF MAJOR TAYLOR, VETERAN SPORTSMAN, WHOSE FAME WAS WORLDWIDE JUST A FEW YEARS AGO, read the front-page headline of the newspaper on December 17, 1926. Wrote Smith: "No citizen who has ever lived in Worcester has made the worldwide name enjoyed by Major Taylor. The Major, a black boy, not only won every bicycle championship in America, but achieved the highest honors in France, Austria, Belgium, Denmark, Switzerland, Holland, England, Australia, New Zealand and Canada. ... The black man, racing against white for large purses, fighting combinations of race against race all over the world, wrote his name in flaming letters high in the sky of sportsmanship. None ever shone brighter." Smith then summarized Taylor's failed business endeavors, his loss of property to repay his debts, and, at the age of forty-seven, the "insidious grippe that laid hold of the fame that no human was able to conquer, and today those bronze legs, which were sculptured in Paris and pictured all over the world ... are hardly able to carry their master." Smith concluded his appeal by saying that Taylor, "deserves the appreciation of all, especially since he is a man whose habits have been clean and to whom none can point the finger of scorn," and he asked for checks to be sent to him at Lordvale.[3]

The *Worcester Telegram* picked up the story of the appeal the following day and printed another account of Taylor's misfortunes. FRIENDS OF MAJOR TAYLOR, WORCESTER'S WORLD CHAMPION, RALLY TO HIS RELIEF. APPEAL MADE ON BEHALF OF FAMED BICYCLIST, NOW AMONG THE NEEDY, said the headline to a rather melodramatic account of Taylor's life and present troubles:

> A colored man walked down Mechanic Street yesterday. His legs were none too steady and made him smile reflectively. They were the legs that won for him the sobriquet of 'The Colored Whirlwind,' legs which had blazoned his name on the sports pages of the United States and

seven European countries. ... The man was Major Taylor and now his legs are tired. Tired from a long siege of illness that has taken a heavy toll of his finances.[4]

The photograph published with this story shows Taylor, besieged by difficulties, looking intently and sternly, almost shamefully, past the photographer. But he is smartly, even finely, dressed in a bowler hat, a shirt with a detachable collar and neatly knotted tie, and a heavy, expensive-looking overcoat. Tenaciously, he clung to his pride and self-respect.

The response to the appeal was immediate. Within a week, nearly $1,200 had been collected. Some people sent a dollar; others sent as much as $100. Many contributors asked to remain anonymous. Donations arrived from the New England area, Canada, and even Australia. George Tuohey, a retired Boston sports promoter, who had known Taylor early in his career, sent a check and a letter of admiration, which was printed in the *Telegram* :

> I have known the Major for upwards of 30 years. ... I agree 100 percent with your estimate of him. Like Gunga Din, he "was white, clear white, inside," generous at all times, especially to the unfortunate of his own race, but generous and free-handed to all.
>
> His clean manhood has never been questioned, nor was his sportsmanship, even by those who resorted to every trick to defeat him. In spite of great provocations at times, Major Taylor rode cleanly. He helped establish bicycle racing and put it on the solid foundation that has held it in public estimation wherever he appeared. He brought honors to Worcester. For that Worcester should not forget him in his need.[5]

Perhaps the most interesting of the letters in response to the appeal came from James Wilson, who remembered Taylor when he first arrived in Worcester from Indianapolis.

> In the late eighties and early nineties, when I held the Championship of Worcester County on the high-wheel bicycle and the safety, I attended many bicycle race meets in Worcester and other cities and I well remember a young colored boy who had come from Indianapolis to live in Worcester. He was infatuated with the exciting sport and could always be found in the training quarters, admiringly looking over the rubbing down of the athletes.

WORCESTER—NEW YORK, 1920—1930

Of the hundreds of racing men, some of whom afterwards became famous on the track, none could have guessed that the agile, wiry, little colored boy with the broad shoulders and the tapering waist would one day become the fastest bicycle rider in the world. During all these 30 odd years, I have watched the career of Major Taylor, with a great deal of interest when he was in the zenith of his power and fame, and with a good deal of sympathy and pity as I have seen him in recent years on the downward road financially and physically.

There was no cleaner sport, nor fairer contestant ever threw his leg over a saddle. At the various race meets I attended, it was always the talk of the racing men that Major Taylor was the cleanest boy of them all, that he never drank, smoked or swore, that he never played a dirty trick on the track, that he never retaliated against the many foul tricks that were put over on him because of his color.[6]

Smith was delighted with the response to his appeal. "Christmas has been brightened a great deal for the man who at one time was Worcester's champion bicycle rider," he said.[7] Taylor stayed in the background while the appeal was progressing. It was a humbled man who spoke with the reporter from the *Telegram* who interviewed him. "Thank all the friends who have helped," he said. "Wish them all a Merry Christmas. I feel all right, but I am badly in need of rest and must be quiet at all times. It is a wonderful thing to have friends come to your support in a time of need and I cannot say enough to thank them."[8]

Undoubtedly, he appreciated the money, but for a man who had proudly supported himself from a very young age and become one of the world's best-paid athletes, such a public advertising of his plight must have been profoundly humiliating, a devastating blow to his pride. His successes and problems had always been played out in the glare of publicity, but this personal tragedy was certainly one event in his life he would have preferred not to have seen spread all over the Worcester newspapers.

The *Worcester Telegram* article appealing for help mentioned that Taylor's autobiography was "finished and in the process of editing," but it was still not ready to be published, and he continued working on it during 1927 and 1928. At the same time, he tried to solicit money to publish the book, a very expensive proposition. Where the money came from in the end is not clear. Perhaps either Harry Worcester Smith or Mr. Dean, Taylor's friend and landlord, made him a sizable loan or gift, or perhaps he paid some final visits to the safe deposit box to cash in Daisy's remaining jewelry. But he did succeed in raising the money.

Early in 1929, Taylor went to New York to consult with Birdie Munger about material to go into the book. The reunion was an emotional one because, "so affected was Munger in recalling fond memories of days gone by that he broke down and wept." It was also a final reunion, because Munger died in New York a few months later, before the memoir was published.[9]

Munger's death was a sad event for Taylor, already weighed down by so much misfortune. He had been a decisive, indispensable presence in Taylor's life since, as a teenager, he had been his valet in the famous batchelor quarters in Indianapolis. He had been his patron and supporter as he made his start in professional cycling and been amazed as he watched him prove himself in the frantic racist turmoil of his first two seasons on the track. He had been Taylor's teacher and guide, his technical director and business adviser, his road manager and friend. He had risked his own reputation to stand by a black athlete at a time when it was considered socially reprehensible to do so. He had harnessed Taylor's youthful infatuation with the bicycle, stood by him emotionally, and shared his disappointments. Munger had adopted Taylor as his own son, become to all intents and purposes, his second, his *white*, father.

Even though the copyright date in the autobiography is given as 1928, it was not published until 1929, more than six years after Taylor began it. He called it *The Fastest Bicycle Rider in the World: The Story of a Colored Boy's Indomitable Courage and Success Against Great Odds*. Self-published under the imprint of the Wormley Publishing Company, at 14 Blossom Street, Taylor's own address, it represented a kind of foolish grandeur. For, unable to interest a commercial publishing house in the project, he had published the book himself, a brave but foolhardy business venture.

To acknowledge the deep gratitude he felt towards the man who had made his cycling career possible, Taylor dedicated the book

TO MY TRUE FRIEND AND ADVISOR, LOUIS D. 'BIRDIE' MUNGER,

whose confidence in me made possible my youthful opportunities for riding. Mr. Munger prophesied that one day he would make me the

'Fastest Bicycle Rider in the World' and lived to see his prophecy come true.

The dust jacket shows Major Taylor literally astride a globe on his bicycle, and on the back of the jacket there is a revealing summary of his essentially puritanical moral philosophy, the ideal of the gentleman athlete.

> Perseverance and Fair Play as Essentials to Success. That these factors go a long way towards helping everyone in the attainment of their goal is clearly portrayed in this unusual story of Major Taylor. His career from the very beginning was characterized by clean living, fair play and cheerfulness always.

> Beginning at the bottom, he slowly worked his way to the top, achieving finally the crown for which every bicycle racer yearns, that of World Champion. His indomitable spirit and fairness won favorable recognition in all parts of the world. Although repeatedly hampered by unfair racing tactics on the part of his opponents because of his color, the Major's superior skill and untiring power inevitably brought him to the tape a victor.

> His friendship with foremost bicycle racers the world over is a tribute to his fine character and friendly disposition. His example is one that may well be followed by athletes and others everywhere.

Although Taylor's whole life was lived in opposition to racism, he does not make frequent, explicit reference to the subject in the autobiography itself. Only in selective paragraphs throughout the book do we find his thoughts on race and the position of black people in American society. Instead, he relies on the history of his racing achievements to tell his life story. But in the Foreword, he does make very clear the motivating force behind the book.

> These reminiscences, covering the most colorful chapter in all the history of bicycle racing, bring out very clearly many of the outstanding qualities characteristic of my race, such as perseverance, courage, and that marvelous spirit of forgiveness.

> It also proves to the world ... that there are positively no mental, physical, moral or other attainments too lofty for a Negro to accomplish if granted a fair and equal opportunity. The records and success that I achieved in my chosen line of athletic sports ... and the brilliant performances of other colored athletes ... will verify this somewhat emphatic assertion. ...

WORCESTER—NEW YORK, 1920—1930

A perusal of the following autobiography ... will reveal many of the secrets of my great success, notwithstanding the tremendous odds and almost tragic hardships that I was forced to do extra battle against owing to color prejudice and jealousy of the bitterest form. With the aid of the press, however, the strict application to the rules of training, and the help of God, I was able to overcome that bitter intensity of feeling to some extent, or sufficiently at least to accomplish my life's greatest objective, namely, to become 'the Fastest Bicycle Rider in the World.'

Judging by the manner in which colored athletes have repeatedly demonstrated their skill and prowess in the athletic world, it is quite obvious what might well be accomplished on a whole as a race in other pursuits of life if granted a square deal and a fair field. We ask no special favor or advantage over other groups in the great game of life; we only ask for an even break.

I am writing my memoir, however, in the spirit calculated to solicit simple justice, equal rights, and a square deal for the posterity of my down-trodden but brave people, not only in athletic games and sports, but in every honorable game of human endeavor.

TAYLOR SET OUT to sell his memoir with determination, traveling locally at first, around New England and New York, and then looking further afield when he had exhausted nearby possibilities. "I really don't think that he wrote it just because of the money, but I do think he did *need* the money," says his daughter. "He really went out and sold those books. He put those books in his car and went to Springfield and he'd actually go to see the people he knew and then he'd go to the next town. He even came over to Pittsburgh."

In September 1929, Taylor went to New York, still the business center of professional bicycle racing, knocking on doors, on a self-promotion tour. *The New York World* considered him still of sufficient interest to review the book.

Major Taylor, famous Negro cyclist of 20 years ago ... is visiting New York. His hair is graying. his muscles are no longer supple as once upon a time, but Major Taylor vividly recounts when he was known throughout the civilized world as the 'King of Cyclists,' the 'Worcester Whirlwind,' and the 'Flying Negro,' as if it were yesterday. For a number of years Taylor was the most talked of wheelman in America and Europe. Thousands acclaimed him in sensational races at Madison Square Garden. So great was his popularity that he was booked as a strong attraction in vaudeville. When seen at the 135th Street branch of the YMCA, Taylor talked enthusiastically about his new book.[10]

Taylor's determination to sell his book personally was the dominating motive of his final years. The task of distributing it was an arduous one, and he undertook it single-handedly with the same tenacity and discipline that he applied to his training and racing earlier. By marketing and distributing his own book, he was in effect saying, "Respect me, remember me, honor me for who I once was and for what I achieved."

His decision to leave Worcester on prolonged promotional trips precipitated his separation from his wife. Even if he discussed the idea of her accompanying him, she was not willing to leave home to travel to strange cities with him. Tired and dispirited, Daisy saw only the money that had already been expended on the book and was more and more reluctant to dwell on thoughts of her husband's past greatness.

But for Taylor, there was no other alternative but to move forward with his project. Unsuccessful at adjusting to life away from the sport that had made him rich and famous, he turned to the memories of his past glory. Tragically, his pursuit of recognition for his former greatness drew him to Chicago and to his final defeat.

WHAT KIND of a book is *The Fastest Bicycle Rider in the World?* How successful is Taylor's autobiography as the story of his life? Working from his voluminous scrapbooks covering the years 1896 to 1904 and from memory, and quoting frequently and at length from the extensive newspaper coverage of his racing career, Taylor struggled to build a detailed, persuasive story of his unique experiences as a pioneer black athlete. He puts himself firmly in the center of his chronological account and fills the narrative with descriptions of the many races that dominated his life for so many years.

He does not shy away from describing the racist opposition he had to confront and overcome on a daily basis as he asserted his right to participate in professional bicycle racing on terms of equality with white riders. He makes very clear that the hostility directed at him was extremely personal. "Floyd MacFarland's attitude towards me, both on and off the track, was one of genuine hatred and bitter prejudice," he writes. And, "Kimble felt that in order to uphold those inherited ideals of his forefathers, he was obligated to hate me with a genuine bitterness."

He succeeds in creating a compelling picture of the intensity of feeling directed at him by individual white riders and by the bureaucracy of the sport in the United States, at the same time recognizing those who, like Birdie Munger, stood by him and supported him.

And Taylor describes, without boasting or conceit, his satisfaction with his many victories. "On more than one occasion during my career it was my good fortune to enjoy many rare thrills, such as I imagine comparatively few people have ever been privileged to enjoy," he writes, going on to describe the pleasure of

> ... the climax that followed a bitterly fought out victory over a vast field of competitors, who with their managers and trainers had concentrated both their mental and physical forces in figuring out and practicing certain tricks ... in order to trim the 'nigger.'

> With this victory, came the sublime thrill that was beyond the power of words to express, and the fact of having defeated single-handed the whole crooked outfit, the riders, their trainers and managers, made it a victory fit for the kings.

Victory for Taylor was always a victory of black over white. "It was not always the mere excitement of out-generaling, and outracing my opponents ... that gave me the greatest thrill, but the real climax was the glory of vindication and the joy of retribution following each success." He did not dislike white people in general, Taylor emphasized several times in the book, but he was very aware that many of them disliked *him* intensely. That made his victories over them all the more sweet. There was always an element of revenge in his victories, especially in the United States.

However, Taylor rarely allows these emotions to surface, and the reader who perseveres in this 431-page work is rewarded with the many facts of his life rather than an insightful exploration of his psychological and emotional journey. He writes of his boyhood at the Southards, his youth in Indianapolis, how he was inspired by the example of Arthur Zimmerman, his rapid rise in the professional cycling world, his championship victories and world records, and the constant battles he had with Eddie Bald, Tom Butler, Frank Kramer, Iver Lawson, Floyd MacFarland, and Owen Kimble. He discusses his racing and training methods and the tactics used against him by his opponents and how he overcame them. He discusses the continual bureaucratic problems he had with the LAW and the NCA. He writes about his European races and his travels in Australia.

Taylor has to be given enormous credit for the courage that led him to write the autobiography and for the persistence with which he saw the project through to completion. But *The Fastest Bicycle Rider in the World*, a long, dense, unwieldy book, has many problems and is difficult to digest. It is not easy reading, weighed down as it is with detailed information about individual races, rather than portraits of personalities or the social background of his racing activities. Lacking a formal education or an introspective temperament, he produced a labored, ponderous memoir.

Taylor badly needed professional editorial advice as he planned and wrote his book, especially to help him decide what to include and what to exclude. While he is justified in writing at length about his American career, he gives far too little space to his sensational arrival on the European cycling scene in 1901, and one longs for an extended, personal account of his experiences during those vibrant Parisian seasons. He gives far too much space to his two successful tours of Australia, while his final three seasons in Europe are hardly mentioned, probably because they represent his declining years.

Concentrating on his victories and triumphs, Taylor omits his failures, his disappointments, and the loneliness he suffered during the season of 1909, when he was in Paris without his wife and daughter. It is only in his soul-searching letters to his wife at the end of the 1909 season that we get a glimpse of his emotional state, but these are not included in the autobiography.

While Taylor reminds his reader of the severity of his external difficulties as a black pioneer in a racist society, he is unwilling or unable to write about his personal problems, to reveal his inner self, his doubts and fears. He does not include his retirement years, his difficulty adjusting to life outside bicycle racing, nor his problems with his wife and daughter.

It is not surprising that Taylor did not reveal his most intimate thoughts and feelings in public. He had spent his whole life learning to suppress and hide his anger and frustration at the white world. He had perfected a modest, gentlemanly, formal persona, which he presented to the world to protect himself and prove his respectability. That self-control protected him from exposing his emotions in public,

WORCESTER—NEW YORK, 1920—1930

and also from the increased hostility that would have accompanied such expression. His undeserved reputation as an 'uppity nigger' would certainly have increased otherwise. During the height of his racing exploits, he proved himself with his victories, not with words. Even with his own family, he was unable to cast off the protective mask he had cultivated all his life.

Although it is a disappointing autobiography, *The Fastest Bicycle Rider in the World* was Major Taylor's final act of defiance, and takes its place in the history of black American literature as one of the most important early autobiographies by a black athlete. In it, he relived his triumphs of the past and once again asserted his strength and authority. He wanted the story of his career to be a story of courage and determination, a conscious assertion of the possibility of success against overwhelming odds, rather than a story of doubt and fear and the inevitability of final defeat. As a black American, the ever-present problem of racial prejudice required that he put on a bold face as he confronted a basically hostile world.

WORCESTER—NEW YORK, 1920—1930

14
CHICAGO TRAGEDY

THE STORY of Major Taylor's final years is difficult to reconstruct in detail. As hard as I searched in Chicago, attempting to track down people who might be able to throw some light on his two years there, and the circumstances of his death, frustrating gaps still remain for that period, which may never be satisfactorily filled. Just about everyone who might have provided information about Taylor before his death in 1932 is now dead.

By 1930, Taylor had become just another anonymous black American struggling for survival in those harsh and difficult times. He did not keep in touch with his estranged wife, who had moved to New York, nor with his daughter, now married and living in New Orleans, and therefore even she knows very little about his final two years.

Yet, amid intriguing question marks, the main outlines of these years can be glimpsed. Sometime in 1930, a final rift occurred between Taylor and Daisy, and she left Worcester for New York. They gave up their modest apartment and sold their furniture or put it into storage.

Sydney Taylor Brown believes it was her mother who had struggled to hold the marriage together. "She tried to keep up appearances," she says, "right up to the very end. But she was the one who took the initiative to leave him. My mother tried for a long time to pretend that things weren't as bad as they were."

The end of his twenty-eight-year-old marriage, following his earlier financial collapse, was a crushing blow to Taylor. He felt that Daisy had abandoned him, and he could no longer live as a failure in the city where he had so long enjoyed the limelight.

Taylor was fifty-one years old in 1930 when he decided to leave the city that had been his adopted home for thirty-five years and for which he had always had the greatest affection. He loaded the many unsold copies of *The Fastest Bicycle Rider in the World* into his car and drove to Chicago, probably stopping in Pittsburgh and Indianapolis, where he had friends, to try to sell the book. It is not clear whether he intended to leave Worcester permanently or whether he was planning initially just to spend some time on the road and then perhaps to return later to Massachusetts. Perhaps he himself did not know.

Chicago was a logical choice as his destination because he had spent a lot of time racing there in his younger days and knew the city well. He thought he might keep the wolf from the door by selling his autobiography, and he hoped to make a new start in Chicago, where his fame might still count for something.

Taylor was not a strong or healthy man, however, when he set out on the road, and although he still owned a car, his resources were evidently minimal. His brother William and his sisters lived in Chicago, but it is unlikely that he sought their help. For apart from infrequent gifts of money and railroad tickets for them to visit him on occasion, Taylor had never been very close to his siblings. His daughter says he had a difficult relationship with them. "I do know that his family, his brothers and sisters, whenever they were in trouble, somebody died or somebody got themselves into difficulty, they would always wire my father for money. It was always illness and death, all through his life. And he would send this money, but I think he would later find that he had been taken, that they had taken advantage of him. My mother always said they took advantage of him." It would have been out of character for Taylor to appeal to his family at this critical juncture of his life, after he had been famous and independent for so many years.

Instead, on arriving in Chicago, Taylor went to the South Wabash Avenue branch of the YMCA, the first YMCA founded specifically to cater to a black community in the North.[1] It was a natural place for Taylor to go for support in his straitened circumstances, for he had a special relationship with the YMCA. It was the YMCA that had so often provided him with accommodation when other hotels were closed to him. In Indianapolis, as the young champion of Dan Southard, he had been excluded from the YMCA gymnasium because of his color, a rejection which had made a profound impression on him. Later, in Worcester, he had been overjoyed to discover that he would be allowed to become a member. The training he did there helped to lay the foundations of his meteoric rise in professional bicycle racing in 1897. In New York and Boston he had often stayed at the YMCA, and even in Australia, he had been a guest speaker for the organization.

But Chicago had changed a great deal since Taylor had gone there from Indianapolis in the early 1890s to race and since he had established his world records. The golden days of bicycle racing on the road in Chicago, when thousands of cyclists poured out to the edges of the city on Saturday afternoons to watch the time trials, were a distant memory.

Migration from the South had accelerated throughout the twenty years between 1910 and 1930. Nearly 2 million black people had uprooted themselves from rural poverty during that period to seek a better life for themselves in the northern cities, and about 200,000 had chosen Chicago as their new home.[2] The poverty, overcrowding, unemployment and homelessness Taylor found in Chicago as a result of this migration and the Great Depression had dramatically changed the character of the Wabash Avenue YMCA, whose modest rents and meals were the only ones he could afford.

The YMCA itself was in deep financial trouble, but it still managed to help members overcome their individual financial problems. Former YMCA members, like Taylor, who were unemployed, were given free membership. Loans were arranged so that members could pay rent and buy food, money which the authorities understood very well they had little chance of recovering. Meals were offered to the unemployed at a discount, and the price of a bed for the night was reduced. Many destitute men were given free accommodation or allowed to stay at the YMCA on a deferred payment plan.

THE SUFFERING and hardship Taylor experienced in Chicago was on a much larger scale than anything he had encountered in Worcester. On the South Side, he was reunited, finally, with his roots, the world of poverty that he had succeeded in leaving behind when he became a successful professional bicycle racer. In 1930, more than at any time since he was a boy, Taylor found himself again confined and restricted by the world of his birth.

From the YMCA, Taylor went out every day to try to sell *The Fastest Bicycle Rider in the World*. Not many people in the black community could spare the $3.50 he was asking for it. His best customers, he realized, were likely to be among the many retired white professional bicycle racers and people once connected with the bicycle industry in the 1890s, now working in the bicycle, automobile, and engineering industries in Chicago. These people would certainly remember him and perhaps be interested in his autobiography. Taylor knocked on doors all over Chicago, carrying a box of his books with him, and passed from contact to contact looking for new customers. It was a difficult, weary life for a sickly, proud man.

Christopher Sinsabaugh, a Chicago automobile pioneer, provides a brief but tantalizing glimpse of Taylor in Chicago in his personal memoirs, published in 1940. "Major, to my mind, was one of America's greatest riders and the only colored man to amount to anything as a racing cyclist," he writes. "The last time I heard of Major Taylor was when a wizened colored man, looking not unlike a minister and wearing glasses, called on Jim Levy, veteran Buick dealer in Chicago who used to race with Taylor. It was Taylor himself and he sold Jim one of his books."[3]

Taylor also called on James Bowler, a native Chicagoan who had been a top-ranking professional racer between 1898 and 1902 and who had appeared with Taylor in many national circuit races. Bowler had been at the Garfield Park track in Chicago in 1899 when Taylor established his 1-mile world record and steered a triplet there for Taylor to train behind. He had also raced in Montreal in 1899 when Taylor won his world championship title. Taylor and Bowler had once, in fact, dead-heated in a race in 1899 and tossed a coin to decide the winner. After retiring from cycling, Bowler went into business in Chicago, became involved in city politics, and by 1930 had a continuous record of twenty-one years as a member of the city council.

While there is no indication of a close relationship between the two men, they had shared many experiences together, and Bowler understood Taylor's predicament. He either helped him find a job or employed him himself. He is the only person who can definitely be identified as having been close to Taylor during his declining years in Chicago.[4] Although he was evidently desperately poor at the time, Taylor appears to have held firmly onto his self-respect. His job and the sales of his book evidently earned him enough money, until he fell ill again, to keep his head above water. But, in the harsh economic climate, *The Fastest Bicycle Rider* was unlikely to have made him much more than a little pocket money during the depression.

Keith Kingbay, who worked many years for the Schwinn Bicycle Company in Chicago, emphasized that the bicycle and automobile industries were both severely affected during the Depression years and that few people had much energy left over to help others at the time, so preoccupied were they in looking after themselves. "The industry was in the doldrums," said Kingbay, "and the old-time cyclists were not really old enough yet to start taking an interest in the past and what had happened to the other old-timers. The Depression was going on and many of these fellows were doing everything they could to keep body and soul together. They weren't in a position to go out and lend assistance to somebody else."

And in Major Taylor's case, said Kingbay, there was still the problem of segregation and intense racial prejudice. "Regardless of some people who still thought of Taylor as a hero, you had a dramatic bigotry towards blacks. Most people just weren't going to have anything to do with blacks. This bigotry was very much alive in the 1930's. I'm sure that they didn't think of it as bigotry, but Taylor was not one of them, a person they would gather in close and take home for dinner, as you would do today."

Chicago was a rigidly segregated city and the white world had little enough reason to be interested in the plight of a retired black bicycle racing champion who had fallen on hard times. Following his failed attempts to recapture a little of the recognition and prestige he had once enjoyed out in the white world, Taylor became immersed in the difficulties and companionship of the Wabash Avenue YMCA.

There is little hard evidence upon which to build an accurate picture of the circumstances of Taylor's life at this time. Certainly, he was in severely reduced circumstances and in a precarious position in Chicago, dependent as he was on the YMCA, without a regular source of income and in frail health. And this intimate contact with poverty and need, the semi-public nature of the eating and sleeping arrangements at the YMCA, could only have been profoundly depressing and demoralizing for him. Here was a painful reminder of the hardship he had succeeded in escaping from for most of his life. He was well acquainted with the plight of his own people, but he himself had been cushioned from poverty. He had been accustomed for many years to a gracious, private style of living, surrounded by nice things.

The gritty, harsh reality of a welfare hotel during the Depression could only have been a terrible shock to Taylor, a well-educated, sophisticated man who had always insisted on respectability, politeness, good manners and high standards of behavior. Living on Chicago's teeming, suffering South Side, he must have been constantly and forcefully reminded of the comfortable life he had left behind him and often thought of the splendid fame he had enjoyed in Europe as a young man. His financial failure, and the collapse of his marriage,

CHICAGO, 1930—1932

must inevitably have been a constant, bitter memory. The previous twenty years had been a gradual process of loss and decline. He had lost his reputation, his property, his money, his health, his wife and daughter and lastly the familiar, reassuring surroundings of his hometown, suffering a drastic and dramatic reversal of his fortunes. Probably he endured periods of prolonged depression, even despair.

But I do not see Taylor as a man who sank permanently into self-pity or became a tragic, totally crushed shadow of his former self. He had long been familiar with hardship and oppression and had always relied on his faith and moral stamina to sustain him. It was a permanent strength of Taylor's character that he saw the positive side of life and did not harbor grudges or bitterness.

There was an extraordinary, dogged determination in Major Taylor. Early in his life, he had stood up against the entire white cycling world and insisted on his right to equality in it. My feeling is that his confidence and his stoical strength equipped him well to weather the storms of his Chicago misfortune.

Although Taylor had become an emotionally severe, rigorous, disciplinarian in his dealings with his family, there is never any hint of psychological instability in him. He seems always to have been in control of himself and his emotions, however trying his circumstances, taking responsibility and working to overcome difficulties rather than being overwhelmed by them.

It does seem probable, given Taylor's intense religious belief and his tendency throughout his life to preach the Gospel, that he could have been found at the South Wabash Avenue YMCA administering to and helping men who were in much worse circumstances than he was. It would have been very much in character for him to have understood that a job needed to be done there and to have undertaken it quietly, unassumingly, without asking for a reward. There are several hints, during his life, that he thought seriously about becoming a minister, so fervent was his Christianity. At the YMCA, he may have found the beginnings of a new and fulfilling vocation for the latter part of his life.

TAYLOR'S HEALTH, which had been very delicate since his several periods of hospitalization for shingles in the mid-1920s, deteriorated suddenly in March 1932. The shingles had weakened his heart and caused other problems, and it is probable that he suffered a stroke or a heart attack. The stressful circumstances in which he had been living were almost certainly a contributing factor.

Alderman Bowler, "his white benefactor," helped him gain admission to Provident Hospital and "saw that he had one of the best surgeons in Chicago operate."[5] Provident Hospital, like the Wabash Avenue YMCA, catered specifically to the South Side black community, and was well know for its pioneering work in heart surgery because of the heart surgery unit established there by Daniel Hale Williams, a famous black surgeon. The heart operation did not alleviate Taylor's problems, however, and his condition continued to deteriorate. In April 1932, he was moved from Provident Hospital to the Cook County Hospital. Apparently, it was once again Bowler who organized the move, perhaps because he could no longer bear the financial burden of maintaining Taylor in a private hospital.

Taylor languished in Cook County Hospital for two months, gravely ill. Nothing definite is known of his final days. Bowler evidently stood by him until this point, and it seems probable that he continued to visit Taylor and help him. Probably friends from the YMCA also visited him. Although he must have understood the seriousness of his condition, Taylor made no attempt to contact his wife or daughter. The rift between them appears to have been complete and final, the possibility of reconciliation sadly absent. If he had any contact with his brother and sisters in Chicago, there is no evidence of it.

The last days of this man who had been so famous and attracted so much attention during his lifetime are now shrouded in mystery. Probably, near the end, he was so incapacitated by a stroke that he was unable to speak, and became totally helpless. It was a pitiful and tragic end for a man whose superb cycling achievements had made him, for a few brief years, the most famous athlete in the world.

MAJOR TAYLOR died at 2:30 P.M. on Tuesday, June 21, 1932, in the charity ward of the Cook County hospital. There is no information about who was with him when the end came. He was fifty-three years old, older by about ten years than the average life expectancy of a black male at the time.

The principal cause of death is given on his death certificate as "Nephrosclerosis and Hypertension," with "Chronic myocarditis" as an important contributory cause.[6] Taylor's death was therefore caused by a combination of factors. The intense training regime he had followed for years had greatly developed his heart. He had always had a tendency to put on weight quickly, and after his retirement, his more sedentary lifestyle increased the strain on his heart. Like many black males, he developed high blood pressure, which was intensified by the anxiety of his financial and matrimonial problems. The shingles he suffered from in the mid-1920s further damaged his heart and kidneys and led to an onslaught of coronary and renal problems which finally killed him.

The death certificate gives his residence as the YMCA at 3763 South Wabash Avenue. The certificate clarifies certain details about the circumstances of his death but leaves other questions unanswered. For example, the informant is listed as "Hospital Records," information most likely offered by Taylor himself, but the certificate also lists his date of birth and the name of his wife as "Unknown," indicating that Taylor was not the source or that he wanted to hide this information. On the other hand, James Bowler, who knew Taylor well as a young man, may have given information to the hospital official who filled out the certificate. Taylor's age is accurately given as "About 54," as well as his "Trade or Profession" – "Bicycle Rider" – and the "Total time spent in this occupation" – "41 years." Also accurate are his parents' names and his place of birth.

Taylor's death was reported on the front page of the *Chicago Defender*, the city's black newspaper: MAJOR TAYLOR, FAMOUS BIKE RIDER, DIES PENNILESS, read the headline. DIES HERE IN CHARITY WARD. ONCE STARTLED WORLD ON BICYCLE TRACK. The article described how Taylor had fallen ill in Chicago and been helped by Alderman Bowler before dying penniless in the Cook County Hospital. It gave a brief sketch of his bicycle racing career from his earliest days and talked about his role as a pioneering black athlete. "In the field of professional athletics Major Taylor is the only member of his Race, outside the field of boxing, who ever held a world title. He won fame and reknown throughout the world. He practically blazed and made the trail single-handed."[7]

A photograph of Taylor accompanied the obituary, the last one ever taken of him. In it, he looks frail and thin. His face appears intense, serious, and distinguished, not unlike a minister's. Despite his poverty, he is smartly dressed in a neat shirt and tie, with a white handkerchief tucked tidily into the upper pocket of his jacket. He holds a book, probably his autobiography.

CHICAGO, 1930—1932

In spite of the announcement of his death, Taylor's body lay unclaimed in the morgue of the Cook County Hospital. No one stepped forward to make funeral arrangements. Perhaps those people who were aware of his death, his friends at the YMCA, for example, expected someone else to make the arrangements, especially his wife, or they were too poor themselves to pay for a gravesite and a funeral. In the racial climate of the times, Bowler, a prominent white public official, may have considered it inappropriate or even undesirable to be intimately involved with the death and burial of a black man. Chicago was an extremely segregated city, the most segregated in the United States by the 1920s, according to many accounts. Daily social contact between blacks and whites was rare. The black and white communities lived further apart, physically and psychologically, than they ever had before.

Taylor's wife and daughter did not receive the news of his death until some time later when someone sent Sydney Taylor Brown's husband a copy of the *Chicago Defender* obituary. At first, she was afraid to tell her mother and waited a long time before doing so. Mrs. Brown was in New Orleans when she got the news, having a difficult first pregnancy, and her mother had come from New York to be with her. She had not seen her father since her graduation from the Sargent School of Physical Education in Boston in 1925. Even on that occasion her mother and father had been so alienated that they did not sit together.

After more than a week had passed without anyone claiming the body, Major Taylor was buried at public expense in a "pauper's grave," in a plain wooden box, in the welfare section of the Mount Glenwood Cemetery, a Jim Crow burial site about 30 miles south of downtown Chicago. Just a handful of people accompanied him to the grave, probably including James Bowler and friends from the YMCA.

The *Chicago Defender* was the only American newspaper to publish an obituary and even that was not a thorough appreciation of his achievements. Neither the Worcester nor the New York newspapers reported his passing, although a brief mention appeared in the *American Bicyclist*.[8] By moving to Chicago, Taylor had cut himself off from all his connections.

In Paris, however, Robert Coquelle, Taylor's European manager and old friend, received the news of his death, and soon the important French weekly sports magazine *Le Miroir des Sports* sent a writer to interview him about Taylor. In an article headlined A GLORIOUS ERA OF TRACK CYCLING COMES TO AN END WITH THE PASSING OF MAJOR TAYLOR, Coquelle's personal obituary describes his shock at hearing of the miserable circumstances in which Taylor had died, and he reminisces about Taylor's sensational arrival in Paris in 1901 and the stunning number of his victories during his first three European tours: forty-two first places in 1901, forty in 1902, thirty-one in 1903. Everybody in France remembered 'le nègre volant,' he said, a phenomenon rarely encountered in any sport.[9]

THE FINAL CHAPTER of Taylor's story took place in 1948, sixteen years after his death. In 1941, a group of ex-professional bicycle racing stars, anxious to maintain contact among themselves and aware that the memory of their youthful athletic careers was growing fainter, formed an association, the' Bicycle Racing Stars of the Nineteenth Century,' based in Chicago. They exchanged addresses and news about those bicycle racers who had played a prominent part in the momentous early days of the sport. There were nearly 200 members and they gathered for an annual reunion to reminisce and renew old friendships.

When the group learned about the circumstances of Taylor's death, Alec Kennedy, chairman of the association, approached Frank Schwinn, owner of the Schwinn Bicycle Company, the most prestigious bicycle manufacturer in the United States, with a proposal to remedy the appalling neglect of Taylor's memory. Schwinn agreed to pay for an exhumation, the transfer of Taylor's remains to a more honorable place in the cemetery, and the erection of a memorial. According to a former employee, "had Schwinn known in 1932 that Major Taylor was in a hospital, and in a county hospital like that, he would have been over there, to give some help, some assistance. He was very, very much a humanitarian, he had a tremendous empathy for everyone. Frank Schwinn would do an awful lot of those kinds of things, without ever tying his name or his company's name to them. That was his own personal money that he used to do these things."[10]

Early in 1948, Taylor's remains were exhumed from the unmarked grave and placed in a more prominent and distinguished location in the cemetery, the Memorial Garden of the Good Shepherd. A bronze plaque was prepared for a dedication service.

CHICAGO, 1930—1932

Kennedy, himself an ex-professional bicycle racer, sent out an invitation that tactfully expressed the sense of shame he felt at the manner of Taylor's death, and perhaps also for the way he had been treated during his lifetime.

> He was the first and only colored man to break into the leading world's sport of his time – pro bicycle racing – fifty years ago, coming up the hard way without any hatred in his heart, to become the greatest bicycle man in the world in his time. He defeated every National Champion in America, England, France, Germany, Belgium, Holland, Denmark, and Australia ... covering a period of ten years when bicycle racing was the world's greatest athletic event. An honest, courageous, God-fearing, clean-living, gentlemanly athlete."

The association was honoring Taylor, explained Kennedy, "with the idea that the colored youth may accept him as an ideal to help them pattern their lives after his fine character for generations to come."[11]

On Sunday, May 23, 1948, a hundred people, both black and white, gathered beside the new grave, which was spread with wreaths and garlands of flowers and decorated with the American flag, to give Taylor an honorable, if belated, second funeral. Taylor's wife Daisy and daughter Sydney were not present[12], but among those who attended were several from the growing number of black athletes who, even in 1948, were seen as pioneers because they had succeeded in breaking into white-dominated sports. The keynote address was given by the outstanding runner Ralph Metcalfe, who broke world records in 1932, competed in the 1932 Los Angeles Olympics, and shared the limelight with the great Jessie Owens at the extraordinary Berlin Olympic Games in 1936.

Also present were members of the Olde Tymers' Association of the Wabash Avenue YMCA and Tom Hay, of the Hay and Willits bicycle shop in Indianapolis, who had dangled the bewitching medal in front of the young Marshall Taylor during his very first race in Indianapolis in 1892 and thus given him the incentive to win.[13]

The small bronze plaque, which still marks Taylor's grave, has on it a striking, sculpted image of the black champion, in his prime, stripped to the waist, showing his superb muscular development. DEDICATED TO THE MEMORY OF MARSHALL W. 'MAJOR' TAYLOR, 1878—1932, it reads:

CHICAGO, 1930—1932

> World's champion bicycle racer who came up the hard way without
> hatred in his heart, an honest, courageous, and god-fearing, clean-living,
> gentlemanly athlete. A credit to his race who always gave out his best.
> Gone but not forgotten.

The hommage paid to Major Taylor in 1948 was a brief respite from
the neglect he had suffered since his death. Even after this highly unusual reburial, he was still not accorded the wider recognition he
deserved. The golden age of American bicycle racing has receded into
the past until it exists only as a faint memory. Occasionally, an article
appears in a cycling magazine or a Worcester or Indianapolis newspaper reminding readers of an outstanding black pioneer athlete
called Major Taylor, who in his day was known as the fastest bicycle
rider in the world. But many of these articles are sketchy and inaccurate. It was not until 1982, when the city of Indianapolis named a
new track after him, that his extraordinary life was given some con-
temporary recognition. Certainly, he deserves to emerge from the
shadows where he has languished for so long into the spotlight of
permanent recognition as one of the most extraordinary talents in
American sports history. In spite of the incredible hardships that he
endured as a black athlete struggling in a white world, Major Taylor
never became a bitter man and his spirit of forgiveness is one of his
noblest qualities.

"Notwithstanding the bitterness and cruel practices of the white
bicycle riders, their friends and sympathizers, against me, I hold no
animosity towards any man," he wrote near the end of his autobiography.

> This includes those who so bitterly opposed me and did everything
> possible to injure me and prevent my success. Many of them have died
> and when I am called home I shall rest easy, knowing that I always
> played the game fairly and tried my hardest, although I was not always
> given a square deal or anything like it. When I am finally run off my
> feet and flattened by that mighty champion Father Time, the last thought
> to remain in my mind will be that throughout life's great race I always
> gave the best that was in me. Life is too short for a man to hold bitter-
> ness in his heart, and that is why I have no feeling against anybody. ...
> In fact, I have never hated any rider that I ever competed against. As
> the late Booker T. Washington, the great Negro educator, so beautiful-
> ly expressed it, "I shall allow no man to narrow my soul and drag me
> down, by making me hate him."

CHICAGO, 1930—1932

AUTHOR'S POSTSCRIPT
ABOUT THE PHOTOGRAPHS
ILLUSTRATIONS, PICTURE SOURCES, AND CREDITS
NOTES AND SOURCES
GLOSSARY OF BICYCLE RACING TERMINOLOGY
BIBLIOGRAPHY
INDEX

AUTHOR'S POSTSCRIPT

I first became interested in Major Taylor's life in 1975, when I was doing research for a book about the development of bicycle technology. I read Taylor's autobiography, *The Fastest Bicycle Rider in the World*, and realized that he occupied an extraordinary niche in the sport's history. Soon after, I made contact with Taylor's only child, Sydney Taylor Brown, then in her early seventies. She graciously allowed me to photocopy the fascinating scrapbooks, full of newspaper clippings and other mementos her father had kept of his racing activities. These scrapbooks are a primary source for much of the information in this book. Mrs. Brown helped and encouraged me in many ways. She understood the pioneering importance of her father's life and gave her approval to this biography. Since meeting with her, I have continued my research over the last ten years in the United States and in France.

A great deal was written about Major Taylor during his lifetime. His dramatic career was extensively reported in newspapers and magazines in this country and in Europe. These accounts are the major source for this book. Apart from Taylor's autobiography and interviews with his daughter and the very few people still alive who knew him, there is only a patchy, inaccurate record of his life in encyclopedias. In fact, no biography of any American champion bicycle racer, even a white one,

exists, whereas in France, the life stories of the great champions have all been told several times.

Writing Major Taylor's biography has not been easy. His activities spanned three continents, his racing career was long and packed with action, and his relationship with the cycling bureaucracy complex. The more I probed into his life, the more I realized how fascinating and enthralling his story was, what an important and unique personality he had been. It continues to amaze me that his story has not been told a dozen times before.

Ultimately, it is ironic that this quintessentially American biography should have been written by a white Englishman. What this seems to say is that even today, Taylor is a prophet without honor in his own country. I hope the fact that I am neither black nor an American has not prevented me from understanding and appreciating Taylor's heroic and ultimately tragic life. That I have had a lifelong passion for bicycle racing will, I hope, count in my favor.

My most fervent wish is that this book succeeds in focusing attention on the fame and respect which Major Taylor so justly deserves. He should be elevated to his rightful place as one of America's greatest sports heroes. If the book generates a renewal of interest in the history of the sport in which he excelled so courageously, then I will be doubly thankful.

ABOUT THE PHOTOGRAPHS

Many of the photographs which illustrate this book offer a fascinating glimpse into the development of early photo-reportage, or photojournalism, on both sides of the Atlantic. Because he was an athletic star, Major Taylor's activities were extensively covered by photographers as well as by newspaper reporters.

Hundreds of photos of him were published during his career, many of them in magazines and newspapers which had only used engravings or line drawings a short while before. The rapid change in the kind of illustrations used by newspapers and periodicals came about through the growing use and acceptance of the technology of the halftone screen.

Though the halftone screen was invented by the early 1880s, it did not gain general currency in magazines until the early 1890s, or in newspapers until somewhat later because of the rougher, porous newsprint which absorbed the ink and spread out the dots of the halftone image. Otherwise, line drawings and engravings, many of which were actually copied from photographs, were used.

The Spanish-American War of 1898, in Cuba, gave a tremendous boost to American photojournalists willing to go out of their way, and into danger, to obtain photographs especially for immediate publication in mass-circulation magazines in the United States. Photographers and artists were sent to the front to compete directly with each other in covering this war. In France, sporting events, the early development of the auto-mobile and early aviation held a special fascination for the early press photographers, with their large, heavy plate cameras and slow film and shutter speeds.

This new demand for photographs to be published in the press in the centers of journalistic activity, New York, London and Paris, and the use of the rapidly improving halftone screen process, created a new profession among those photographers who saw that they could make money specializing in this kind of work, and these men were the first true photojournalists. They went out and took photographs of newsworthy events, with a specific customer in mind, saw their pictures rapidly processed and in mass-circulation within a few days. The 1890s was the first decade in which true photojournalists were working in this way.

Jules Beau, a Parisian news photographer, many of whose photographs of Taylor appear in this book, was such an early photojournalist. Like the rest of the Parisian press, he found Taylor newsworthy, and was constantly photographing him, submitting his work to the magazine *La Vie au Grand Air.* Jules Beau's coverage of the Taylor-Jacquelin race of May 1901 is a classic early coverage of a sporting event. His photographs were used in extensive spreads in *La Vie au Grand Air* and *La Vie Illustrée* in Paris, and also in *Cycling* in London. It was out of coverage of events such as these, with a strong interest in the personalities of people in the news, that the picture story, staple diet of later magazine photojournalism, grew.

In America there was no such extensive coverage of Taylor's activities, although his photograph did appear frequently. Perhaps because it would have been considered inappropriate, or not in good taste, to advertise and publicize a black sports figure in the energetic way it was done in France. The tendency was to play down, rather than to idolize, his achievements. The *National Police Gazette* of February 16, 1901, did publish a fine, large photograph of him, however, and numerous photographs of him were published in newspapers and bicycling periodicals between 1897 and 1904.

Major Taylor's career was at its height between 1896 and 1904, at exactly the time that this new profession of photojournalism was coming into existence. The photographic documentation of Taylor is a very early example of the recording and reporting, in photographs, of the career of any athlete. In fact, the photographs in this book may constitute the very earliest, thorough photojournalistic coverage of the career of any athlete.

Jules Beau, who photographed Major Taylor in Paris, was a pioneer sports photographer and photojournalist.

ABOUT THE PHOTOGRAPHS

ILLUSTRATIONS, PICTURE SOURCES, AND CREDITS

1. The sixteen-year-old Marshall Taylor's picture appeared, for the first time, in an Indianapolis newspaper when he won the road race to Matthews. (Unidentified 1895 newspaper clipping, Taylor scrapbook.)

2. The start of the *Worcester Telegram* road race in 1896. In the integrated competition, two black racers are clearly visible. Taylor is in the front row. (Reproduced from *Worcester Centennial, 1848—1948*, published in 1948.)

3. A portrait of the eighteen-year-old Taylor, which appeared in an East Coast newspaper in 1897. (Unidentified newspaper clipping, Taylor scrapbook.)

4. The young Taylor in about 1896, when he first arrived in Worcester, Massachusetts. (Unidentified newspaper clipping, Taylor scrapbook.)

5. Racist caricatures appeared in a cycling magazine as Taylor broke records and squabbled with the governing bodies of bicycle racing in 1898. (*Bearings,* 1898, Taylor scrapbook.)

6. Taylor was a member of the integrated Boston team that raced against a team from Philadelphia in July 1897 in his first season as a professional. Here he is with (left to right) Frank Butler, Burns Pierce, Nat Butler, and Eddie McDuffie. This is possibly the earliest photo of an integrated American professional sports team. (*Bearings,* July 29, 1897, Library of Congress.)

7. Taylor riding one of the chainless bicycles upon which he established world records in 1898 and 1899. (Reproduced from Hamelle and Coquelle, *Major Taylor.*)

8. Taylor on the chainless bicycle on which he won the world championship and broke world reords in 1899. (Uncredited photo, Taylor scrapbook.)

9. By the end of 1898, after he had broken the one-mile world record, Taylor was famous enough for his photograph to appear on the front page of an important French sports magazine. (*La Vie au Grand Air,* November 1, 1898, Library of Congress.)

10. Taylor at the peak of his American success; a publicity photo by E. Chickering of Boston. (*The Wheel,* July 5, 1900, Library of Congress.)

11. Taylor's house in Worcester, Massachusetts. (*La Vie au Grand Air,* May 4, 1901.)

12. Taylor's employer and mentor, Birdie Munger. Detail from a group photograph with other members of the Chicago Bicycle Club in 1891. (Abbott Bassett Scrapbook, National Museum of American History, Smithsonian Institute.)

13. The first great American cycling champion, Arthur Zimmerman at the start of a race about 1893. (Detail from a start group photograph, source unknown.)

14. Taylor caricatured by the French cartoonist O'Galop in 1901. (*La Vie*

au Grand Air, May 26, 1901, Bibliothèque Nationale, Paris.)

15. Taylor has a remarkable voice, says the caption to this photo, as he accompanied himself at the piano singing an American song, "Hallo, my Baby!" (*La Vie au Grand Air*, May 4, 1901.)

16. In Taylor's first race in Europe in April 1901, he faced German champion Willy Arend (center) and Danish champion Thorwald Ellegaard (hidden on right), at the Friedenau track in Berlin. (Uncredited photo, Taylor scrapbook.)

17. Taylor with Henri Fournier, ex-sprint champion of France and a leading race car driver, and the car with which Fournier won the Berlin-Paris race in 1901. (*La Vie au Grand Air*, May 4, 1901.)

18. The front page of France's leading sports magazine heralded Taylor's imminent arrival. (*La Vie au Grand Air*, March 10, 1901, Taylor scrapbook.)

19. Press photographers follow Taylor and Jacquelin onto the track for the first of their two sensational match races, Parc des Princes, Paris, May 16, 1901. By wearing an African cloak, Taylor defied convention and showed pride in his roots. (*La Vie Illustrée*, May 24, 1901, Bibliothèque Nationale, Paris.)

20. Taylor training for his crucial race against Jacquelin, Parc des Princes, Paris, 1901. (Jules Beau collection, Bibliothèque Nationale, Paris.)

21. Taylor and Jacquelin on the line at the start of one of the heats of their first match race, May 16, 1901. (Jules Beau collection, Bibliothèque Nationale, Paris.)

22. Taylor leaves the track after his defeat by Jacquelin. (*La Vie Illustrée*, May 24, 1901, Bibliothèque Nationale, Paris.)

23. Taylor, held up by his trainer, Buckner, shakes Jacquelin's hand at the start of the second heat of the second match race, hinting that a third heat would not be necessary, Parc des Princes, May 27, 1901. (Jules Beau collection, Bibliothèque Nationale, Paris.)

24. After a resounding victory in his second match race against Jacquelin, Taylor poses with journalist Maurice Martin (left) and painter Delancey-Ward (right), who presented the silver cup. Robert Coquelle is on the extreme right. (Jules Beau collection, Bibliothèque Nationale, Paris.)

25. The judges' stand and the huge crowd at the Taylor-Jacquelin match, Parc des Princes, May 1901. (Jules Beau collection, Bibliothèque Nationale, Paris.)

26. Taylor starting a sprint race against (left to right) Bourotte and Grogna, at Arras, France, 1902. (Jules Beau collection, Bibliothèque Nationale, Paris.)

27. Parc des Princes Velodrome, Paris, 1903. Parisian bicycle racing attracted large crowds of people. (Jules Beau collection, Bibliothèque Nationale, Paris.)

28. A rare action shot in Paris, 1903. Taylor coming from behind to contest a sprint with Meyers and Ellegaard. The difference between Taylor's extended 'modern' position

and the contracted positions of the other two champions is clearly visible here. (Jules Beau collection, Bibliothèque Nationale, Paris.)

29. The Indianapolis rider Woody Hedspath teamed up with Taylor during the 1903 European season. (*La Vie au Grand Air,* June 5, 1903. Bibliothèque Nationale, Paris.)

30. Taylor and Ellegaard start a race at one of the night meets, made possible by artificial light, promoted at the Buffalo Velodrome, Paris, from 1902 onward. (Jules Beau collection, Bibliothèque Nationale, Paris.)

31. The elegant Daisy Morris became Taylor's wife in March 1902. (Uncredited photo, Taylor collection.)

32. Daisy Taylor, about 1902. (Uncredited photo, Taylor collection.)

33. Major Taylor about the time of his Marriage. Taylor chose this photograph as the frontispiece of his autobiography *The Fastest Bicycle Rider in the World.*

34. Taylor in Melbourne, Australia, 1903, with (left to right) motor-paced rider Theodore Robl, and R. McCullagh, secretary of the Melbourne Bicycle Club. (Uncredited photo; Taylor scrapbook.)

35. The Sydney Mail described Taylor as "the finest sprinter of two continents, perhaps of a third," when it published this handsome photo of him in 1903. (Sydney Mail, January 7, 1903, Taylor scrapbook.)

36. Taylor at a race meet in Australia. Uncredited photo, Taylor scrapbook.)

37. Taylor massaged by his Australian trainer, Sid Melville. (Uncredited photo, Taylor collection.)

38. Taylor poses with the Australian champion Don Walker. (The Australasian, January 10, 1903, La Trobe Collection, State Library of Victoria, Melbourne.)

39. The start of the scratch group in an Australian race, 1904. Taylor is at the extreme left. (Uncredited photo, Taylor scrapbook.)

40. When he returned to European tracks in 1907 after a two-year retirement, Taylor was still a big enough star to appear on the front page of the leading French sports magazine. (*La Vie au Grand Air,* May 11, 1907, Bibliothèque Nationale, Paris.)

41. Taylor behind motor pace in September 1908. (*La Vie au Grand Air,* September 5, 1908, Bibliothèque Nationale, Paris.)

42. Taylor, with his three-year-old daughter, Sydney, talks with a journalist at the Buffalo Velodrome, Paris, upon his return there in 1907. (Uncredited photo, Taylor collection.)

43. Surrounded by friends and admirers, Taylor returned to the track, scene of many of his earlier triumphs, in May 1907. (*La Vie au Grand Air,* May 11, 1907, Bibliothèque Nationale, Paris.)

44. Taylor takes a fall, Paris, 1907. (Jules Beau collection, Bibliothèque Nationale, Paris.)

45. Taylor was always interested in automobiles. Here he drives in Paris with Sydney in 1907. (Uncredited photo, Taylor collection.)

46. Taylor, back in form again in 1908, the second year of his comeback, at the Buffalo Velodrome. The handlebar extension that he pioneered is clearly visible here. (Photo by Branger, Agence Roger Viollet, Paris.)

47. Taylor leads Poulain, Ellegaard, and Friol at the Buffalo Velodrome before a capacity crowd, Paris, 1908. (Jules Beau collection, Bibliothèque Nationale, Paris.)

48. An overweight Taylor, at twenty-nine, checks for letters from home, Paris, 1909. (Uncredited photo, Taylor collection.)

49. Daisy and Sydney Taylor waiting for a train in Europe. (Photo by Major Taylor, Taylor collection.)

50. Taylor in action against French champions Friol and Dupré at the Buffalo Velodrome, Paris, June 1909. (*La Vie au Grand Air,* June 5, 1909, Bibliothèque Nationale, Paris.)

51—52. At the end of his difficult 1907 comeback season, Taylor announced his retirement. But he returned to Europe once again in 1908 and 1909. (*La Vie au Grand Air,* August 24, 1907, Bibliothèque Nationale, Paris.)

53. Taylor at the beginning of his final season in France. The captionthat was printed with this photo announced that he had decided to race on Sundays and comments, "Perhaps he is telling himself here that his defeat in his first race was a just reward for the betrayal of his convic-

tions." (*La Vie au Grand Air,* May 22, 1909, Bibliothèque Nationale, Paris.)

54. Taylor's career was closely reported by the French press. "He is much better prepared this year than last," says the caption to this cover photo. (*La Vie au Grand Air,* May 30, 1908, Bibliothèque Nationale, Paris.)

55. The Taylor family about 1906 or 1907. (Uncredited photo, Taylor collection.)

56. Taylor (held up by Hedspath) with Jacquelin at the Piste Municipale, Paris, in 1908. The American boxer Sam McVea is on the right, half hidden. (Jules Beau collection, Bibliothèque Nationale, Paris.)

57. Taylor at the Buffalo Velodrome, Paris, 1908. (Photo by Branger, Agence Roger Viollet, Paris.)

58. Taylor in 1926, published when a public appeal was launched on his behalf. (*Worcester Telegram,* December 18, 1926, courtesy of *Worcester Telegram.*)

59. Taylor's grave in Mount Glenwood Cemetery, on the outskirts of Chicago. The bronze plaque was paid for by the owner of the Schwinn bicycle company. (Photo by Andrew Ritchie.)

60. The last photo of Taylor, taken in Chicago shortly before his death. (*Chicago Defender,* July 2, 1932, courtesy of the *Chicago Defender.*)

61. Taylor's daughter, Sydney Taylor Brown. (Photo by Andrew Ritchie.)

PICTURE SOURCES AND CREDITS

NOTES AND SOURCES

All quotations in Taylor's own words, unless otherwise noted, are from Marshall W. 'Major' Taylor, *The Fastest Bicycle Rider in the World* (Worcester, Mass: Wormley Publishing Co., 1928).

All quotations from Taylor's daughter, Mrs. Sydney Taylor Brown, are from the author's interviews with her, conducted in 1975 and 1987.

Many of the newspaper clippings about Taylor, which he pasted into his scrapbooks, are unidentified and undated. When quoting from these clippings, as much information as possible is given. When they are either unidentified or undated, or both, this is stated.

NOTES TO CHAPTER 2, EARLY GUIDANCE AND INSPIRATION

1. Records of black rural families at that time are few and hard to locate. Gilbert Taylor's parents, who were probably from Kentucky, are not known, nor is it known at what point they won or bought their freedom. Saphronia Kelter's parents were Robert and Sarah Kelter, both from Louisville. The origin of both branches of Taylor's family in the slave plantations of Kentucky does not seem to be in question. Birth certificates for Indianapolis were first filed in 1882, so there is no record of Taylor's birth in 1878. The most likely documentation of his birth would have been a certificate of baptism given to his parents by a minister.

2. For details about the flight of free Negroes and escaped slaves into Indiana from Kentucky before and during the Civil War, see Jacob P. Dunn, *Greater Indianapolis*, vol. 1 (Chicago: Lewis Publishing Co., 1910). Dunn writes on pp. 250—251:

> The Civil War brought a rapid change in the colored population of Indianapolis. At the census of 1850, the total of negroes in the city was 405. In 1860, it had increased only to 498. The law against the immigration of free negroes remained on the statute books, but from the beginning of the War it was a dead letter and an escaped slave was a free negro in practical construction. The "refugees" soon began coming this far north, and increased in number after the Emancipation Proclamation. In 1870, the negro population of Indianapolis had reached 2,931, and more than that had

come here, many having found employment in the adjacent country. They were not unwelcome. There was a shortage of labor, especially of agricultural and unskilled labor. Work was plentiful and wages were good. Of course, many came destitute.

3. Taylor's father fought in a black regiment of the Union army, and a careful search of military service records at the National Archives in Washington would probably yield more information about his military career. In his old age, he lived with Taylor in Worcester for some time, until he was accepted into a veterans home in Marion, Indiana, where he died in 1909. For more information about the recruitment of a black regiment into the Union army in Indianapolis, see ibid. p. 251.

4. The retail store where Taylor began working in 1892 was started by two young men, Thomas Hay and Bert Willits in the early 1890s and was located at 113 West Washington Street, Indianapolis, opposite the State House. As business outgrew these small quarters, it was moved to 70 North Pennsylvania Street, the first bicycle shop to move to that street. Others, including H. T. Hearsey and Company, Taylor's second employer, followed later to make this street into Indianapolis' 'Bicycle Row.'
Early in 1895, Hay and Willits formed their own manufacturing company to make the 'Outing' bicycle. By the end of the year, they had built and sold 1,200 bicycles. In 1896, they tripled their sales, and by 1897 5,000 'Outing' bicycles were sold and they employed 275 people. See *Hyman's Handbook of Indianapolis*, Max R. Hyman, Editor, M. R. Hyman Co., 1897, p. 378.

5. Unidentified newspaper clipping in Taylor scrapbook.

6. ibid.

7. Henry T. Hearsey's store was located at 116—118 North Pennsylvania Street, Indianapolis, between 1891 and 1899. They were the agent for Columbia and Crescent bicycles but also sold their own brand, the 'Ben Hur,' which they advertised as MADE RIGHT HERE AT HOME.

8. On Hearsey's importation of the first safety bicycles from England, see William Herschell, "Zig-Zag Cycling Club of the Gay Nineties," *Indianapolis News*, February 7, 1931.

9. On Hearsey's role in the bicycle industry in Indianapolis and the United States in general, see J. P. Dunn, *Indiana and Indianans* (American Historical Society, Chicago and New York, 1918, p. 1704).

10. For more information about the Zig-Zag Cycling Club of Indianapolis, see William Herschell, *Indianapolis News*, February 7, 1931.

11. In August 1885, Birdie Munger, then twenty-three and Captain of the Detroit Bicycle Club, made the headlines when he established a new 24-hour road record of $211^1/2$ miles on the high-wheel over the extremely difficult and variable roads about Boston. For accounts of Munger's record-breaking ride, see the *Boston Globe*, August 1, 1885, and *Bicycling World*, August 7, 1885.

12. The advertisement appeared in *The Referee*, December 22, 1893.

13. Unidentified, undated Boston newspaper clipping from Taylor scrapbook.

NOTES AND SOURCES

14. *Indianapolis Sentinel*, August 23, 1893.

15. *Indianapolis Sentinel*, August 24, 1893.

16. ibid., August 25, 1893.

17. Arthur Zimmerman, who seemed like a God to Taylor in the summer of 1893, was in fact only twenty-four years old at the time and at the peak of his meteoric bicycle racing career.

Born in Camden, New Jersey, in 1869, he had begun to race when he was twenty and had first attracted attention in 1890 when he beat the celebrated amateur champion, Willie Windle, up until then considered unbeatable, at Peoria, Illinois.

Some people speculated that Zimmerman made as much as $30,000 that year in an immensely successful European tour in England, France, Italy, Belgium, and Switzerland. He was the first American professional bicycle racer to undertake such a tour. The crowds loved him and the press pursued him. Hundreds of thousands of people paid to see his races that summer. In France he was dubbed 'le Yankee volant' (the flying Yankee). The sensation caused by Zimmer-man's arrival was referred to constantly when Taylor was in France for the first time in 1901. They called him 'le deuxième Zimmerman' (the second Zimmerman) or 'le Zimmerman noir' (the black Zimmerman).

In 1893 and 1894, Zimmerman was conceded to be the best, the most completely developed, professional bicycle racer in the world, and he had the victories to prove it. His career was a pioneering one because he elevated the sport to a new level of seriousness. He raced and trained methodically and scientifically, applying himself to racing in a thoroughly modern way.

The most significant thing about Zimmerman was that his overwhelming superiority, and his spectacular record of victories, attracted an audience hungry for speed and sensation to the bicycle racing tracks in ever-increasing numbers and carried the sport to a new level of popularity and prominence. Such a dominant figure invited and encouraged opposition, and other competitors clustered around him, vying for honors, prizes, and money. Zimmerman helped to create the vibrant, richly endowed sport that beckoned to other athletes. He laid the foundation upon which other bicycle racers, like Major Taylor, could subsequently build their international careers. See *Zimmerman on Training* (Leicester, England, 1893) and J. M. Erwin and A. A. Zimmerman, *Conseils d'entrainement et relation de son voyage en Europe* (Paris, Librarie du 'Vélo,' 1895).

NOTES TO CHAPTER 3,
BICYCLE BOOM AND JIM CROW

1. See Andrew Ritchie, *King of the Road* (London: Wildwood House and Berkeley: Ten Speed Press, 1975), for more information about the development of bicycle technology.

2. Hundreds of articles in daily newspapers and magazines in the mid-1890s discuss the bicycle boom, which was examined and commented upon from many different viewpoints. Many newspapers had a regular cycling column at the time. See *Scientific American*, July 20, 1895, which summarizes some of the social changes brought about by the growth of the bicycle. The *New York Evening Post*, June 2, 1896, said, "As a social revolutionizer, the bicycle has never had an equal. It has put the human race on wheels, and thus changed completely many of the most ordinary processes and methods of social life. It is the great leveler, for not till all Americans got on bicycles was the great American principle that every man is just as good as any other man. . . fully realized. All are on equal terms, all are happier than ever before."

3. *The Referee*, February 22, 1895.

4. Unidentified, 1897 newspaper clipping from Taylor scrapbook.

5. *Indianapolis News*, February 21, 1905, obituary of George Catterson.

6. *Indianapolis Sentinel*, June 23, 1895.

7. ibid., July 7, 1895.

8. ibid., July 1, 1895.

9. ibid., July 1, 1895.

10. ibid., July 1, 1895.

11. *Bicycling World*, June 3, 1892.

12. *Wheelmen's Gazette* (Indianapolis), March 1893.

13. ibid., May 1893.

14. For accounts of the LAW convention in Louisville, see *Bearings*, February 23, March 2, March 9, March 30, 1895; *Outing*, April, May, June, 1894; *Cycling Life*, March 29, 1894; *The Referee*, March 30, 1894 and February 8, 1895.

15. *Bearings*, February 23, 1894.

16. Quoted in Robert A. Smith, *A Social History of the Bicycle* (American Heritage Press, 1972), p. 163.

17. *Bearings*, March 9, 1894.

18. ibid., March 30, 1894.

19. ibid., March 30, 1894.

20. ibid., March 9, 1894.

21. ibid., March 2, 1894.

22. *The Referee*, March 30, 1894.

23. Bennett, Lerone. *Before the Mayflower: A History of Black America*. New York: Johnson Publishing Co., 1961. p. 259.

24. Meier, August. *Negro Thought in America, 1880—1915*. Ann Arbor: University of Michigan Press, 1963. p. 161.

25. Quoted in Hughes Langston and Milton Meltzer. *A Pictorial History of the Negro in America*. New York: Crown Publishers, 1956. p. 232.

NOTES TO CHAPTER 4,
PRECOCIOUS TEENAGER, COLORED
CHAMPION OF AMERICA

1. Indianapolis News, July 4, 1899.

2. The number of cycling clubs in Chicago, and other major American cities, in the mid-1890s was really quite astonishing. In Chicago there were certainly more than thirty, probably as many as fifty. Some were racing clubs, others, such as the Norwegian Turners' Club or the Plzen Cycling Club (all Czech members), were more socially oriented. Many institutions and workplaces had their own clubs, such as for example, the Post Office Cycling Club or the Chicago Public Library Cycling Club. A similar number of clubs existed in the Boston area. By the end of the decade, the number of clubs had declined as the most intense phase of the bicycle boom calmed into a routine practical use. See "Wheelmen say cycling is dead as organized sport," Chicago Tribune, November 19, 1899. However, though the number of amateur participants in racing declined, the number of spectators at races remained high.

3. See "Fast time made by a colored rider," Chicago Tribune, July 28, 1895; and The Referee, August 1, 1895.

4. Indianapolis Sentinel, September 3, 1895.

5. See The Fastest Bicycle Rider in the World, p. 8.

6. Washburn, Charles G. Industrial Worcester, 1917, p. 318.

7. See "More Bikes Than Ever," Worcester Telegram, October 14, 1895.

This article was apparently reprinted from a New York newspaper.

8. See "The Worcester Cycle Mfg. Co.," Bearings, January 9, 1896.

9. See ibid.

10. Worcester Telegram, June 9, 1895.

11. Worcester Spy, October 20, 1895. This article contains the first extended recognition of Taylor's racing achievements and details about his early life.

12. Unidentified, undated newspaper clipping, Taylor scrapbook.

13. Worcester Telegram, June 14, 1896.

14. Worcester Telegram, May 10, 1896. The entire front page of the paper was devoted to coverage of the race that day.

15. ibid., May 10, 1896. For a discussion of the impact and significance of 'Bloomers' in the cycling craze of the mid-1890s, see Smith, Robert A. A Social history of the Bicycle. New York: American Heritage Press, pp. 97—109.

16. Worcester Telegram, May 26, 1896.

17. Indianapolis Sentinel, July 21, 1895.

18. ibid., September 8, 1895.

19. Unidentified Indianapolis newspaper, September 4, 1896, in Taylor scrapbook.

NOTES TO CHAPTER 5,
RISING STAR

1. See Barry Hecla, "Cycle Racing as an Occupation: Some Points for Would-Be Zimmermans," *The Referee*, May 12, 1895.

2. See "New York's Big Meet," *Bearings*, December 10, 1896.

3. *Brooklyn Daily Eagle*, December 6, 1896.

4. *The Referee*, December 10, 1896.

5. Unidentified newspaper clipping in Taylor scrapbook.

6. *The Referee*, December 10, 1896.

7. *Worcester Telegram*, December 10, 1896.

8. Unidentified newspaper clipping in Taylor scrapbook.

9. ibid.

10. *Brooklyn Daily Eagle*, undated clipping in Taylor scrapbook.

11. Unidentified newspaper clipping in Taylor scrapbook.

12. ibid.

13. *Bearings*, December 24, 1896.

14. *Worcester Spy*, December 13, 1896.

15. Unidentified newspaper clipping in Taylor scrapbook.

16. *Bearings*, December 17, 1896.

17. *Le Vélo* (Paris), December 23, 1896.

18. See Duncan, H. O. *Vingt Ans de Cyclisme Pratique*. Paris: F. Juven, 1897, which has an extensive account of the six- day race on pp. 116-127.

19. *Worcester Telegram*, undated clipping from Taylor scrapbook.

20. *Spaldings Official Bicycle Guide for 1898*. New York: American Sports Publishing Co..

21. See "Intercity Race Today," *Boston Globe*, July 21, 1887.

22. *Boston Journal*, July 22, 1897.

23. *The Referee*, December 10, 1896.

24. *New York Sun*, June 26, 1897.

25. Unidentified newspaper clipping in Taylor scrapbook.

26. *Harrisburg Telegraph*, July 28, 1897.

27. *Bearings*, August 12, 1897.

28. All from unidentified newspaper clippings in Taylor scrapbook.

29. *Boston Herald*, September 16, 1897.

30. For an interesting summary of the racial climate at the turn of the century, see Lacy, Dan. *The White Use of Blacks in America*. New York: McGraw-Hill, 1972, Chapter 7, "In Which Control of the Powerless Blacks Is Perfected."

31. *Bearings*, September 16, 1897.

32. Unidentified newspaper clipping in Taylor scrapbook.

33. ibid.

34. All accounts of the Newark incident from unidentified newspaper clippings in Taylor scrapbook.

35. *New York Sun*, September 18, 1897.

36. *Worcester Telegram*, September 18, 1897.

37. *New York Journal*, undated newspaper clipping in Taylor scrapbook.

38. *Worcester Telegram*, September 20, 1897.

39. Unidentified newspaper clipping in Taylor scrapbook.

40. See article "Choked Taylor," *Boston Globe*, September 24, 1897.

41. *Bicycling World*, October 1, 1897.

42. ibid.

43. ibid.

44. See "Career of Major Taylor. How the Colored Whirlwind Forced His Way to Front Rank of Cycle Riders Despite Obstacles." Unidentified Boston newspaper, December 12, 1900, in Taylor scrapbook.

45. *Bearings*, September 30, 1897.

46. *Bearings*, September 9, 1897.

47. Unidentified 1897 newspaper clipping in Taylor scrapbook.

48. *Bearings*, October 14 and October 28, 1897.

49. Unidentified newspaper clipping in Taylor scrapbook.

50. ibid.

51. *Bearings*, October 14, 1897.

NOTES TO CHAPTER 6,
NEW HORIZONS, NEW OPPOSITION

1. Unidentified newspaper clipping in Taylor scrapbook.

2. It is not clear why Taylor was never directly sponsored by Munger's company, the Worcester Cycle Mfg. Co. Perhaps Munger was too involved with the day to day running of the company to spare the time to oversee Taylor's career, or perhaps his finances did not allow it. He is not mentioned in 1898 accounts as being actively involved in Taylor's affairs, though he must have continued to advise him.

3. *Worcester Telegram*, undated clipping in Taylor scrapbook.

4. Unidentified newspaper clipping in Taylor scrapbook.

5. ibid.

6. Most of the lynchings of blacks were for alleged murder, rape, or assaults, but some were for astonishingly trivial incidents, such as "using offensive language," "making boastful remarks," or "trying to act like a white man." In 1898, records show that 102 black people were lynched nationwide, while for the period 1882—1927 only Mississippi, with 517 black lynchings, was more violent than Georgia, with 510. In fact, the 1890s were the peak years for lynchings of blacks in the South. Lynching figures quoted are taken from A. F. Raper, *The Tragedy of Lynching*. Chapel Hill: University of North Carolina Press, 1933, and White, Walter Francis. *Rope and Faggot*. New York: A. A. Knopf, 1929.

7. Unidentified newspaper clipping in Taylor scrapbook.

8. ibid.

9. *Savannah Press*, March 19, 1898.

10. Unidentified newspaper clipping in Taylor scrapbook.

11. *Cycle Age*, April 28, 1898.

12. Unidentified newspaper clipping in Taylor scrapbook.

13. ibid.

14. ibid.

15. Unidentified newspaper clipping in Taylor scrapbook.

16. *New York Sun*, May 22, 1898.

17. Unidentified newspaper clipping in Taylor scrapbook.

18. *Boston Herald*, June 18, 1898.

19. *Worcester Spy*, July 13, 1898.

20. *New York Journal*, July 11, 1898.

21. Unidentified Philadelphia newspaper, Taylor scrapbook; *Philadelphia Press*, July 17, 1898.

22. Unidentified newspaper clipping in Taylor scrapbook.

23. *Worcester Telegram*, undated, late July article in Taylor scrapbook.

24. "Black Wheelman First to Cross the Line," *Green Bay Gazette*, August 16, 1898.

25. Unidentified newspaper clipping in Taylor scrapbook.

26. *New York Journal*, undated clipping in Taylor scrapbook; unidentified newspaper clipping from Taylor scrapbook.

27. Unidentified newspaper clipping in Taylor scrapbook.

28. ibid.

29. Unidentified Philadelphia newspaper clipping in Taylor scrapbook.

30. *Philadelphia Press*, September 27, 1898.

31. *Worcester Telegram*, September 27, 1898.

32. *Cycle Age*, November 17, 1898.

33. Unidentified Chicago newspaper clipping in Taylor scrapbook.

34. *Worcester Telegram*, October 20, 1898.

35. Taylor's sponsorship, in the fall of 1898, by the Waltham Mfg. Co. and the Sager Gear Co., was one of the very earliest commercial sponsorships of a black American athlete and probably the first use of a black athlete for advertising purposes. Such sponsorship of professional cyclists had been common since the beginning of the 1890s.

The chainless bicycle made its appearance in 1898 and 1899 and enjoyed a brief popularity before fading and disappearing. Many manufacturers came up with a chainless design at that time, hoping to woo new adherents and popularize the new idea. It never became a serious rival to the conventional chain-driven bicycle. The chainless mechanism was essentially a shaft with pinions at each end. The main advantage of the chainless was that its enclosed mechanism stayed clean and well-oiled even under the dirtiest road conditions. Its disadvantages were that the rear wheel of the bicycle was more difficult to remove and the gearing could not easily be changed.

36. *Cycle Age*, November 24, 1898.

37. *Philadelphia Press*, undated clipping in Taylor scrapbook.

38. Unidentified newspaper clippings in Taylor scrapbook.

39. The technique of maintaining a maximum speed over the mile was for Taylor to be paced by a succession of quads or quints going flat out. Each team rode a lap with Taylor tucked in behind its rear wheel. As the first team tired, he switched to a second, at a point where the speed of the two teams was equal. Such a maneuver demanded practice and careful timing. A botched change-over in one of the four or five changes necessary to ride the mile would lose crucial seconds.

The difficulties of the changing-over technique, the complication of maintaining the cumbersome multicycles and especially the enormous expense of the teams of between 15 and 20 riders needed to break records in this way meant that the search for speed had to take a new direction. Taylor's records were among the last established in this way. In November, 1898, he shouted constantly for more speed.

It became increasingly obvious that a motor-driven pacing machine was the only way to achieve smooth, consistent, uninterrupted high speed. The search for speed for racing cyclists led to the rapid development of electric, gas and petrol-driven machines which could achieve a constant speed of about 40 mph. Such machines played an important part in the development of early motorcycle and automobile technology.

40. *Worcester Spy*, undated clipping in Taylor scrapbook.

NOTES TO CHAPTER 7,
THE FASTEST BICYCLE RIDER IN
THE WORLD

1. *Indianapolis Sentinel*, January 16, 1899.

2. *Pittsburgh Press*, December 11, 1898 and February 19, 1899.

3. *Worcester Telegram*, undated clipping in Taylor scrapbook.

4. Unidentified newspaper clipping in Taylor scrapbook.

5. *Cycle Age*, February 16 and March 30, 1899. A very full account of the pros and cons of the conflict between the LAW and the NCA was published in *Cycle Age*, June 1, 1899.

6. *New York Morning Telegraph*, undated clipping in Taylor scrapbook.

7. *Syracuse Telegram*, May 27, 1899.

8. The role and importance of the motorized pacing machines, which began to appear on bicycle racing tracks in 1898, on the overall development of the motorcycle and the automobile at the turn of the century has not been much studied. Certainly the pacing machines were significant technologically in the search for a faster and more efficient motorcycle. At first there was competition between electric, steam and gasoline-powered pacing machines. Quickly, the electric and steam-driven machines lost favor and the gasoline-powered ones became the favorites.

Those mechanics and racers from the bicycle world who became involved with the pacing machines were part of a large-scale movement of skilled manpower from the bicycle industry into the rapidly expanding automobile business and into aviation. The progression was an extremely natural one for many men who saw economic opportunity in those fields. The Wright brothers were originally bicycle mechanics and Taylor himself invested unsuccessfully in the automobile industry. The huge gasoline-powered engines which were used to drive the powerful pacing machines in the heyday of motorpaced bicycle racing, from 1905—1910, were adapted for use in the first airplanes.

9. Unidentified newspaper clipping in Taylor scrapbook.

10. Unidentified Boston newspaper clipping in Taylor scrapbook.

11. *Queens County Evening News*, 1926 (month and day unknown). This newspaper published an extended account of the event, written by Murphy himself.

12. *Chicago Tribune*, July 1, 1899. Murphy's sensational ride was reported in all the daily newspapers in the U.S.

13. *Scientific American*, July 15, 1899 (which includes a photograph and diagrams). Other accounts can be found in *Cycle Age*, July 6 and July 20, 1899 and *La Vie au Grand Air* (Paris), July 9, 1899.

14. Unidentified newspaper clipping in Taylor scrapbook.

15. ibid.

16. ibid.

17. *Chicago Times-Herald*, August 4, 1899.

18. *Cycle Age*, August 10, 1899.

19. *Montreal Daily Star*, August 7, 1899.

20. *Montreal Gazette*, August 11, 1899.

21. *Boston Globe*, August 11, 1899.

22. Of the first five black world champions, among whom Major Taylor was the second chronologically, four were boxers. The first was George Dixon (1870—1909), known as 'Little Chocolate,' who won the bantamweight world title by beating his British and American rivals in a series of fights through 1890 and 1891, and defended it until 1900. "He lived a life of dissipation. After winning the title, wine, women and song were sweet music to his ears. He made a fortune and he squandered it." (Fleischer, Nathaniel. *Black Dynamite, the story of the Negro in the prize ring from 1782—1938*. New York: C. J. O'Brien, Inc., 1938). He died penniless, an alcoholic, in New York.

Joe Walcott (1872—1935) won the welterweight world title December 18, 1901, holding it until 1904. He died in a car accident. Joe Gans (1874—1910) won the lightweight title on May 12, 1902 and held it until 1908.

Jack Johnson (1878—1946) won the heavyweight world title in Sydney, Australia on December 26, 1908, defeating Tommy Burns and defended it against various "White Hopes" until 1915. Johnson also died in a car accident. See the excellent biography of Johnson: Roberts, Randy. *Papa Jack: Jack Johnson and the era of white hopes*. New York: The Free Press, 1983.

For more details of the careers of these four pioneer boxers, see Nathaniel Fleischer. *Black Dynamite*.

Major Taylor's cycling career contrasted strikingly with those of the black boxing pioneers. Firstly, cycling was not a physical contact sport. Secondly, cycling was a widely recognized, mainstream, popular sport between 1890 and 1910 and did not have the marginal, disreputable image of boxing. Interestingly, Taylor was a fine boxer himself, gave exhibition matches in Paris and always boxed as part of his training.

23. Unidentified Montreal clipping in Taylor scrapbook.

24. *Cycle Age*, August 17, 1899.

25. Unidentified newspaper clipping in Taylor scrapbook.

26. *Cycle Age*, August 17, 1899.

27. Unidentified newspaper clippings in Taylor scrapbook.

28. *Cycle Age*, November 2, 1899.

29. Unidentified newspaper clipping in Taylor scrapbook.

30. *Cycle Age*, November 23, 1899.

31. *Chicago Daily News*, November 18, 1899.

32. Various unidentified newspaper clippings in Taylor scrapbook; and *Chicago Times-Herald*, November 19, 1899.

33. *Worcester Spy*, undated clipping in Taylor scrapbook; *Worcester Telegram*, November 20, 1899.

34. *Worcester Telegram*, November 20, 1899.

35. Ibid.

36. *Worcester Spy*, undated clipping in Taylor scrapbook.

37. *Worcester Evening Gazette*, December 18, 1899.

NOTES TO CHAPTER 8,
CHAMPION OF AMERICA AT LAST

Worcester Telegram, November 30, 1899.

2. *Le Vélo*, January 6, 1900.

3. *Worcester Telegram*, December 22, 1899.

4. *Le Vélo*, January 8, 1900.

5. *La Vie au Grand Air*, January 7, 1900.

6. Unidentified newspaper clipping in Taylor scrapbook.

7. *Worcester Telegram*, January 24, 1900.

8. *Boston Post*, undated clipping in Taylor scrapbook.

9. Ibid. The house on Hobson Avennue still stands today. Initially, it had the house number 2 and has since been assigned number 4. It bears a plaque commemorating Major Taylor.

10. Unidentified Worcester newspaper clipping in Taylor scrapbook.

11. *Worcester Spy*, undated clipping in Taylor scrapbook.

12. Gertrude Taylor died at the end of April and Taylor sadly accompanied her body back to Indianapolis for burial. There, he returned to the house on Northwestern Avenue, where his father Gilbert was living, and presided with a mature sense of family responsibility over Gertrude's funeral at Simpson Chapel and her interment at the Crown Hill Cemetery, where his mother, Saphronia, had been buried only two years before.

13. *Worcester Telegram*, February 9, 1900.

14. Ibid.

15. *Cycle Age*, February 22, 1900.

16. *Worcester Spy*, undated clipping in Taylor scrapbook.

17. *Worcester Telegram*, February 21, 1900.

18. Ibid., March 13, 1900.

19. *New York World*, undated clipping in Taylor scrapbook.

20. *The Wheel*, June 7, 1900.

21. *Cycle Age*, September 27, 1900.

22. *North Conway Reporter* (New Hampshire), April 5, 1900.

23. *Worcester Telegram*, February 21, 1900.

24. Ibid., April 24, 1900.

25. *Worcester Spy*, April 29, 1900.

26. Unidentified Boston newspaper clipping in Taylor scrapbook.

27. *Worcester Telegram*, May 11, 1900.

28. Ibid., May 29, 1900.

29. *Bicycling World*, June 21, 1900.

30. *Worcester Spy*, June 24, 1900; *The Wheel,* July 5, 1900.

31. Unidentified newspaper clipping in Taylor scrapbook.

32. Unidentified newspaper clipping, August 11, 1900, in Taylor scrapbook.

33. Unidentified newspaper clipping in Taylor scrapbook; *Worcester Telegram*, August 18, 1900.

34. *Indianapolis News*, September 3, 1900.

35. Unidentified Erie newspaper clipping, September 17, 1900, in Taylor scrapbook.

36. *Cycle Age*, October 25, 1900.

37. Ibid.

38. *Worcester Telegram*, October 23, 1900.

39. *Cycle Age*, December 13, 1900.

40. *New York Journal*, December 8, 1900.

41. *Le Vélo*, January 21, 1901.

42. "La venue en France de Major Taylor," *Cyclette-Revue* (Paris), March and April, 1944.

43. *Worcester Telegram*, January 10, 1901.

44. *Le Vélo*, January 3, 1901.

NOTES TO CHAPTER 9, SUPERSTAR

1. *Worcester Telegram*, March 5, 1901; *Worcester Spy*, March 4, 1901.

2. *Le Vélo*, January 27, 1901; *La Vie au Grand Air*, March 10, 1901.

3. The daily sporting newspaper *Le Vélo*, which specialized in coverage of cycling events, was founded by Pierre Giffard and Paul Rousseau in 1891. Until 1900, it was the only daily cycling newspaper in the world. In 1900, its rival, *L'Auto-Vélo*, was started by Henri Desgranges and Victor Goddet, under the patronage of the Count de Dion, the automobile pioneer.

The two papers were not only journalistic rivals, but were involved in rival promotions at the Velodrome Buffalo (*Le Vélo*) and at the Parc des Princes (*L'Auto-Vélo*). A lawsuit between them forced *L'Auto-Vélo* to change its name to *L'Auto*, and it was editors Desgranges and Goddet who organized and promoted the first Tour de France in 1903. *L'Auto* was for many years the largest circulation daily sporting newspaper in the world, selling more than many ordinary newspapers.

4. "Le Nègre à Paris," *Le Vélo*, March 12, 1901.

5. Ibid.

6. *Le Vélo*, March 13, 1901.

7. *Cycle Age*, April 4, 1901.

8. *Le Vélo*, March 16, 1901.

9. Ibid.

10. Ibid.

11. "Le Major en Piste," *Le Vélo*, March 23, 1901.

12. Taylor was an expert machinist, and he claimed in his autobiography that he invented the adjustable extension handlebar stem which is still called the 'Major Taylor outrigger' and was a pioneer in adopting it. "Today the extension handlebars and the position I perfected for myself on my racing wheel are accepted as the standard by bicycle sprinters the world over," he wrote.

Although he does certainly appear to have been the rider who made the most consistent use of this adjustable extension stem, it cannot be said with absolute certainty that he alone invented it. Like many ideas in an emerging and changing technology, the idea for an extended stem appears to have been in fairly general currency by the turn of the century. Perhaps what can be said is that Taylor was the leading exponent of the idea. Taylor was certainly on the cutting edge of developing bicycle technology, however, and involved in 1898—1899 with the chainless bicycle and with several other leading bicycle manufacturers during his career.

13. *L'Auto-Vélo*, March 26, 1901.

14. *Le Vélo*, April 2, 1901.

15. "Le Nègre," *Le Vélo*, May 14, 1901.

16. *Le Vélo*, May 5, 1901.

17. "Ma Tournée en Europe," by Major Taylor; *La Vie au Grand Air*, May 4, 1901.

18. *Worcester Telegram*, April 8, 1901.

19. Ibid., May 8, 1901.

20. Quoted in *Cycle Age*, April 18, 1901.

21. *Bicycling World*, April 11, 1901.

22. "Le Nègre," *Le Vélo*, May 14, 1901.

23. *L'Auto-Vélo*, May 16, 1901.

24. *New York Sun*, May 16, 1901.

25. *Le Vélo*, May 17, 1901.

26. *L'Auto-Vélo*, May 17, 1901.

27. *La Vie Illustrée,* May 24, 1901.

28. *Le Vélo*, May 18, 1901.

29. Ibid.

30. *Le Vélo*, May 29, 1901.

31. *L'Auto-Vélo*, June 29, 1901.

NOTES TO CHAPTER 10
WORLD TRAVELER AND
INTERNATIONAL CELEBRITY

1. *Worcester Telegram*, July 22, 1901.

2. *Cycle Age*, July 18, 1901.

3. *New York Sun*, August 1, 1901.

4. *Worcester Telegram*, August 2, 1901.

5. See "Marshall Walter Taylor – The World Famous Bicycle Rider," *The Colored American Magazine*, September 1902. A photograph of Mrs. Major Taylor appeared on the cover.

6. Quoted in *The Fastest Bicycle Rider in the World*, p. 235.

7. *Sydney Herald*, January 26, 1903.

8. *New South Wales Baptist*, undated 1903 clipping in Taylor scrapbook. Reprinted in *Sydney Telegraph*, January 7, 1903 because of public interest in the subject.

9. Unidentified New York newspaper clipping in Taylor scrapbook.

10. *Worcester Telegram*, August 1, 1902.

11. Woody Hedspath, the only other black American racing cyclist to achieve success in bicycle racing at the time, was much better known in Europe, where he did most of his racing, than in America. He remains, nevertheless, a shadowy figure. He evidently followed closely in Taylor's footsteps and was one of several even lesser known black cyclists who, inspired by Taylor's success, sought careers in bicycle racing. Hedspath lived in Belgium for many years and married a ballet dancer. He

specialized in motor-paced racing and also raced in North Africa.

12. *Worcester Telegram,* September 24, 1903.

13. Ibid.

14. *Worcester Telegram,* November 13, 1903.

15. *Adelaide Observer,* April 23, 1904.

16. *Worcester Telegram,* July 6, 1904.

17. Hamelle, Paul and Robert Coquelle. *Major Taylor, Ses Débuts, Sa Carrière, Sa Vie, Ses Aventures.* Paris, 1904.

NOTES TO CHAPTER 11, COMEBACK AND DECLINE

1. *L'Auto,* March 7, 1907.

2. *L'Auto,* April 2, 1907.

3. *La Vie au Grand Air,* May 11, 1907.

4. *L'Auto,* April 20, 1907, together with an article by Coquelle "Major Taylor est arrivé!"

5. *L'Auto,* April 21, 1907.

6. *L'Auto,* April 23, 1907.

7. *La Vie au Grand Air,* August 24, 1907.

8. *L'Auto,* September 20, 1907.

9. Ms., letter, May 4, 1909, Taylor collection, Pittsburgh.

10. Ms., letter, August 13, 1909.

11. Ms., letter, May 4, 1909.

12. Ms., letter, June 14, 1909.

13. Ms., letter, June 29, 1909.

14. Ms., letter, August 1, 1909.

15. Ms., letter, August 13, 1909.

16. Ms., letter, no date.

17. Ms., letter, August 5, 1909.

18. Ms., letter, no date.

19. Ms., letter, October 1, 1909.

20. *L'Auto,* October 17, 1909.

21. *Worcester Telegram,* October 25, 1909.

22. Quoted in *The Fastest Bicycle Rider in the World,* p. 417.

NOTES TO CHAPTER 12, DIFFICULT ADJUSTMENT

1. Obituary of Louis de Franklin Munger, *New York Times*, July 31, 1929.

2. Interview with Sydney Taylor Brown. This and all subsequent statements by Mrs. Brown are from the author's interviews with her.

3. Unidentified newspaper clipping in Taylor scrapbook.

4. Unidentified clipping from a Worcester newspaper in Taylor scrapbook.

5. Letter to Metz, February 7, 1912, Taylor papers, Pittsburgh.

6. Worcester city directories, Worcester Public Library.

7. Ibid.

8. *Newark Evening News*, September 15, 1917.

9. Ibid.

10. ibid.

11. See article "Major Taylor is the best of ancient pedal pushers," *Newark Evening News*, September 17, 1917.

NOTES TO CHAPTER 13, AUTOBIOGRAPHY AND ILLNESS

1. Interview with Sydney Taylor Brown. This and all subsequent statements by Mrs. Brown are from the author's interviews with her.

2. Copy of a letter to Robert Coquelle, March 1923, Taylor papers, Pittsburgh.

3. *Worcester Evening Gazette*, December 17, 1926.

4. *Worcester Telegram*, December 18, 1926.

5. Ibid., December 23, 1926.

6. Ibid., December 24, 1926.

7. Ibid., December 23, 1926.

8. Ibid., December 26, 1926.

9. *New York World*, September 8, 1929; "Louis de Franklin Munger, better known to all his friends as Birdie, died suddenly of heart disease at his home, the Hotel Dauphin, in New York City, on July 30, 1929, at the age of sixty-five". Munger's obituary appeared in the *New York Times*, July 31, 1929.

10. *New York World*, September 8, 1928.

NOTES TO CHAPTER 14,
CHICAGO TRAGEDY

1. For a history of the South Wabash Avenue YMCA, see Dedmon, Emmett. *Great Enterprises: 100 Years of the YMCA of Metropolitan Chicago.* New York: Rand McNally, 1957.

2. For details of black migration north, see Bennett, Lerone. *Before the Mayflower: A History of Black America.* New York: Johnson Publishing Company, 1982, p. 344.

3. Sinsabaugh, Christopher. *Who, Me? 40 Years of Automobile History,* 1940.

4. James Bowler died in 1957 – see obituary, *Chicago Tribune,* July 19, 1957. The author was unable to obtain further information about Bowler's relationship with Taylor.

5. Invitation to 1948 memorial service sent out by the Bicycle Racing Stars of the Nineteenth Century Association, Taylor papers, Pittsburgh.

6. Death certificate, Cook County Courthouse, Chicago, Ill.

7. *Chicago Defender,* city edition, June 24, 1932 and national edition, July 2, 1932.

8. *American Bicyclist and Motorcyclist,* July 1932.

9. "Avec Major Taylor disparait une époque glorieuse du cyclisme sur piste," *Le Miroir des Sports,* July 12, 1932.

10. Interview with Keith Kingbay, April 1987.

11. See Note 5.

12. Mrs. Daisy Morris Taylor survived Major Taylor by 33 years. She died, 89 years old, on April 21, 1965 in Pittsburgh, PA.

13. *Chicago Defender,* May 22 and 29, 1948 and *American Bicyclist and Motorcyclist,* July 1948, printed accounts of the memorial service. Among the well known black athletes attending were Duke Slater, Bobby Anderson, Mel Walker, John Brooks, Claude Young and Leroy Winbush.

GLOSSARY OF BICYCLE RACING TERMINOLOGY

BANKING: the curved, sometimes steeply sloping, turns of an oval-shaped bicycle racing *track*.

BELL LAP: the last lap of a race; the bell is rung as the riders pass the finishing line before the final sprint.

BICYCLE: although there was a great deal of development in bicycle technology during the period, 1890—1910, covered by this book, the bicycles Major Taylor and his rivals rode were recognizably the close predecessors of the track bicycles of today. Track bicycles, during the 1890's, were custom-built for a rider and were extremely light and responsive, weighing as little as 16 pounds, with a single fixed gear and no brakes. Experimentation continued to perfect light, reliable and durable tires and professional riders were often supplied by tire manufacturers eager to have their latest models tested. Just as today, riders used toe clips and shoes with cleats.

CENTURY: an organized non-competitive 100 mile bicycle ride.

CHAINLESS, or SHAFT DRIVEN BICYCLE: in a brief period of experimentation in the late 1890's, chainless (shaft driven) bicycles were introduced as an alternative to the standard chain driven bicycles.

COMBINATION: two or more riders working together to defeat an opponent.

CRACK or CRACKERJACK: a star bicycle rider, equivalent to 'hot shot' today.

FLYING START: the racer is timed from the moment he crosses the starting line, having already ridden a lap to gain speed.

GEAR: expressed in inches, the gear number is multiplied by 3.14 to determine the distance on the road covered for each crank revolution – the higher the number, the greater the distance covered for each crank revolution, i.e. the higher the gear.

HANDICAP RACE: the opposite of what it appears to mean. Slower riders are given a time or distance advantage. In a handicap race, riders are given a rating according to ability, experience and current performance, from the fastest, *the scratchman*, to the slowest, the *limitman*. They are given a staggered start. The *scratchman* has to work his way through a field of riders to win, a feat demanding great strength and speed.

HEAT: the first rides in which contestants are eliminated until they reach the semifinals and finals. A race between two contestants, a *match race*, is usually decided on the basis of the best of three heats.

HIGH-WHEEL BICYCLE: the precursor of the modern or *safety bicycle* in the United States. In Britain, it was known as the 'ordinary' bicycle or 'penny farthing.' It had an enormous front wheel with cranks attached directly to it. The *safety bicycle* quickly rendered the high-wheel bicycle obsolete.

JOCKEYING: riders constantly changed their position on the track, watched each other carefully, as they tried to assert psychological and tactical superiority and find a good position on the track in the early stages of a race. Often involved some physical contact. Jockeying for a good position continued throughout the race, and could become intense and dangerous on the final lap.

JUMP: a sudden strong, powerful surge of speed with which one rider tries to get in front of another. A rider may jump from a low speed or from an already high speed.

LAP: one circuit of the track.

LEAD OUT: as the finish of a sprint race neared, one rider had to choose to lead out, which was always a risky tactic, even for a very strong rider, since others would follow him and sit *on his wheel.*

LIMIT or LIMITMAN: the rider who is rated the slowest or weakest in a *handicap race* and, therefore, is granted a time or distance advantage over the opponent.

LOAFING: generally used prejoratively. Occurs when competitors, while they are *jockeying* for position at the beginning of a race, ride extremely slowly, watching and waiting for the others to make a move. They might even come to a complete standstill. Loafing was part of the *tactics* of sprint racing, since it was better to be

in second or third position until the final yards of a race. Often a non-competing *pacemaker*, who competitors were obliged to follow, was put into a race to prevent loafing.

LONG-DISTANCE RACE: in excess of 25 miles on the track.

MATCH RACE: a race between only two riders, in which *combinations* were eliminated and a true test of speed and tactical ability was run off. Match racing was the highest level of sprinting on the track, star pitted against star.

MEET or MEETING: interchangeable terms meaning an event or an afternoon of bicycle racing, consisting of many different kinds of races.

MIDDLE-DISTANCE RACE: from 5 to 25 miles on the track.

ON THE WHEEL: a rider on the wheel of another rider follows closely behind him, enjoying the benefit of his slipstream.

OPEN RACE: a race open to all amateurs and professionals who wished to enter.

PACING or PACE MAKING: a rider paced by another rider, or by a pacing machine, gains a considerable advantage in that wind resistance, the biggest obstacle to his forward movement, is reduced. See *tactics.*

PACING MACHINE: similar to a motor cycle, driven either by steam, electricity or gasoline during Taylor's time, behind which a cyclist was able to go faster than when he was unpaced.

PLACE: a rider wins a place if he finishes with the first three or four.

POCKET: when a rider is in a pocket or pocketed, his freedom of movement on the track is restricted tactically by other riders. Usually considered unsportsmanlike, and sometimes punished by judges or referees. A *combination* worked together to put another rider in a pocket.

POLE: a white line painted on the surface of the track marking the inside limit of the legal riding area, rather like the white lines of a tennis court. To be on the pole is a highly sought after position since it is the shortest distance around the track. A rider on the pole can legally only be overtaken on his right side, not on his left.

PURSE: the total amount of prize money for which professional riders competed in a race.

PROFESSIONAL: any rider who was registered as a professional and competed for cash prizes. The top professionals were often sponsored by bicycle and tire manufacturers and might, in fact, enjoy the support of more than one company. In the 1890s, just as today, a gray area was occupied by those outstanding amateurs who nevertheless frequently accepted equipment and support from manufacturers.

PURSUIT RACE: a race in which two individuals or two teams of riders compete over a measured distance, or a certain number of laps, starting on opposite sides of the track. Each tries to overtake the other and establish the faster time.

QUADRUPLET: or QUAD: a four-man bicycle used for *pacing* single riders.

QUINTUPLET or QUINT: a five-man bicycle used for *pacing* single riders.

SAFETY BICYCLE: the bicycle as we know it today, with two wheels of equal size, driven by cranks connected to the rear wheel.

SCORCHER and SCORCHING: a cyclist who rides fast for his own pleasure on public roads, often used to indicate disapproval, but also used by other cyclists as a term of admiration. Scorchers were often criticized for terrorizing horses and slower cyclists.

SCRATCH or SCRATCHMAN: the rider who is rated the fastest and strongest in a *handicap* race.

SHORT-DISTANCE RACE: up to 5 miles on the track, but often one-third, one-half or 1 mile, the most common distances for sprint races.

SPRINT: short distance race or an intense burst of speed.

STANDING START: the racer is timed from being stationary.

TACTICS: sprint racing on the track is an extremely tactical sport, a good tactical head is at least as important as speed and strength. A cyclist who sits closely behind, or *on the wheel* of another rider, always gains a considerable advantage, often crucial in deciding the outcome of a race. The first rider bears the full impact of wind resistance and therefore works harder than the second rider, who sits in his slipstream and enjoys the benefit of some shelter.

Nearly all the tactics involved in short-distance sprinting on the track relate to this simple fact. The rider who is in the leading position coming around the last *banking* before the finishing line is considered to be in a disadvantageous position, since his opponents, sitting *on his wheel*, are conserving energy and may overtake him with a sudden surge on the line. In the preliminary stages of the race, therefore, there is frequently a lot of *loafing* and *jockeying*, because none of the riders want to be in first position. Today, tactics in sprint racing are still essentially the same.

TANDEM: a bicycle built for two, often used for pacing a single rider.

TRIPLET: a bicycle built for three, often used for pacing a single rider.

TRACK: bicycle racing tracks in the United States in the 1890s were (and still are) oval in shape, with straight sides and semicircular *bankings*. Tracks were built either of cement or wood; some of the more primitive ones were grass or cinder and unbanked and also served as horse-racing tracks. In the big centers, New York and Boston, tracks were erected indoors for events like the six-day races. The riders always rode counterclockwise. On one side of the track was the grandstand, and spectators usually chose a position anywhere around the perimeter of the track. The best position, of course, was at the finishing line.

WHEEL and WHEELMAN: the bicycle as a machine and the cyclist who rode it. Wheel is interchangeable with bicycle in the 1890s, wheelman is interchangeable with cyclist.

BIBLIOGRAPY

A. AUTOBIOGRAPHY AND TAYLOR SCRAPBOOKS

The two most important sources of information for the present biography were Taylor's autobiography, *The Fastest Bicycle Rider in the World*, Worcester: Wormley Publishing Company, 1928, and the scrapbooks which Taylor kept during his racing career, now in the possession of his daughter, Mrs. Sydney Taylor Brown.

The autobiography, the importance, merits and weaknesses of which are discussed in Chapter 13, throws light on many aspects of Taylor's career and personality, beginning at an early age, though it does not give any information about his life after his retirement from bicycle racing in 1910.

The scrapbooks contain newspaper and magazine clippings from the United States, France and Australia, as well as photographs, race programs and other material. Taylor conscientiously clipped and saved newspaper articles about his career between 1894 and 1909. They were crucial in allowing me to document and reconstruct the unfolding of Taylor's career. Without them I would have needed many additional months of painstaking searching in microfilmed newspapers. Often on the basis of information contained in the scrapbooks, I was able to deepen and expand my research.

B. BOOKS AND ARTICLES BY AND ABOUT MAJOR TAYLOR

Listed below are the most important books and articles by and about Taylor. Many of the hundreds of newspaper articles which describe and report his life and career will be found listed in the notes.

Coquelle, Robert. "Le Nègre volant Major Taylor." *La Vie au Grand Air*, Paris, March 10, 1901, 130—131.

Grivell, H. "Curly." Highlights from the Life of Major Taylor. *Sport Radio Press*, (Australia), date unknown.

Hamelle, Paul, and Robert Coquelle. *Major Taylor, Ses Débuts, Sa Carrière, Sa Vie, Ses Aventures*. Paris: 1904, reprinted 1907.

Keene, Judy. "Major Taylor, Bike Champ from Indianapolis." *Indianapolis Magazine*, May 1977, 41—54.

Lucas, Robert. "The World's Fastest Bicycle Rider." *Negro Digest*, May 1948, 10—13.

Marrel, Albert. *Les Champions du Cycle*. Rive-de-Gier: Bruyère, 1903.

Martin, Maurice. "Le Match Jacquelin—Major Taylor au Parc des Princes. *La Vie Illustrée*, Paris, May 24, 1901, 128—129.

Opitz, Edmund A. "The Fastest Bicycle Rider in the World." *Bicycling*, August 1971, 8—9.

Palmer, Arthur Judson. "The Fastest Man on Wheels." *Sports Illustrated*, March 14, 1960, 7—11.

Percival, Bob. "Remembering Father, the Bike Champ." *Indianapolis Star Magazine*, February 12, 1984, 24—25.

—. "He Raced the Best." *Pittsburgh Press*, April 29, 1984, 16—24.

Ritchie, Andrew. "Major Taylor, World Champion and Black Pioneer of America." *Competitive Cycling*, November 1976, 22.

—. "Major Taylor takes on Europe." *Competitive Cycling*, December 1976, 3.

—. "Major Taylor's Letters." *Competitive Cycling*, November 1978, 12—13 and December 1978, 7.

—. "Black Bicycling Champion was World's Fastest Racer." Boston: *Bay State Banner*, May 28, 1987, 7.

Sanders, William. "Major Taylor, Great Man and Cyclist." *Bike World*, July 1975, 40—43.

Taylor, Marshall W., 'Major.' *The Fastest Bicycle Rider in the World: The Story of a Colored Boy's Indomitable Courage and Success against Great Odds*. Worcester: Wormly Publishing Co., 1928.

—. *The Fastest Bicycle Rider in the World*. Abridged reprint. Brattleboro: The Stephen Greene Press, 1972.

—. "Ma Tournée en Europe." *La Vie au Grand Air*, Paris, May 4, 1901, 222—225.

—. "Ma Dernière Saison de Course." *La Vie au Grand Air*, Paris, August 24, 1907, 134—135.

Scioscia, Mary. *Bicycle Rider*. New York: Harper & Row, 1983. (children's book.)

Stahlin, Oskar. "Major Taylor, L'ascension pénible, la gloire et la fin tragique du champion noir." *Englebert-Vélo Magazine*, Paris, January 1950, 19—22.

Violette, Marcel. "La Rentrée de Major Taylor." *La Vie au Grand Air*, Paris, May 11, 1907, 323—324.

Weecxsteen, Pierre, "Major Taylor, un grand sprinter." *Le Cycle*, Paris, July—August, 1982, 35—38.

Williams, G. Grant. "Marshall Walter Taylor, The World Famous Bicycle Rider." *The Colored American Magazine*, Boston, September 1902, 336—345.

C. Books Containing a Substantial Reference to Major Taylor

Barton, Rebecca Chalmers. *Witnesses for Freedom: Negro- Americans in Autobiography.* New York: Harper & Brothers Publishers, 1948, 45—48.

Henderson, Edwin B. *The Negro in Sports.* Washington, D.C. Associated Publishers, 1939.

McCullagh, James C. *American Bicycle Racing.* Emmaus: Rodale Press, 1976, 20—23.

Kountze, Mabrey. *50 Sports Years Along Memory Lane.* Mystic Valley Press, 1978, 163—168.

Palmer, Arthur Judson. *Riding High, The Story of the Bicycle.* New York: E. P. Dutton, 1956, 174.

Smith, Robert A. *A Social History of the Bicycle.* New York: American Heritage Press, 1972, 162—169.

Wesley, Charles H. *International Library of Negro Life and History,* Vol. 9. New York: Publishers Company Inc., 1968, Essay by Edwin B. Henderson: 52—53.

D. Newspaper Sources

The story of Major Taylor's life was told, to a very large extent, in newspapers and magazines. From 1894, when he was only sixteen years old, until his death in 1932, Taylor's career and activities were recorded and reported in newspapers and magazines in the United States, Canada, France, Germany, Italy, Belgium and Australia. His is among the most extensively documented athletic careers and one of the most extensively documented black American lives of the period.

Many American newspapers, for instance the *Chicago Tribune*, the *New York Times*, the *Boston Globe*, the *Worcester Telegram*, and many others (see Note 2, Chapter 3), had a regular daily or weekly bicycling column in the 1890s, which discussed social aspects of the new bicycle fad and reported bicycle racing in great detail. Sometimes, especially in the smaller cities, and on the occasion of important race meetings, bicycle racing was reported on the front pages of American newspapers. Bicycle racing was so popular that almost every daily newspaper gave at least some coverage of it. *Scientific American* gave extensive coverage of social and technical aspects of cycling through the 1890s.

In France (see Note 3, Chapter 9), Major Taylor's European career was reported by two sports newspapers, *Le Vélo* (1894—1904) and later *L'Auto-Vélo* (1900—1903), which became *L'Auto* in 1903. These two papers gave priority to bicycle racing over other sports, though L'Auto became increasingly involved with motor-racing and aviation. The important illustrated weekly magazine *La Vie au Grand Air* also contains extensive written and photographic coverage of Taylor's racing career (see List of Illustrations).

E. SPECIALIZED CYCLING SOURCES

The huge growth of the bicycle industry and the sport of bicycle racing in the 1890s saw the rise of many publications devoted specifically to cycling. In the competitive marketplace, some were short-lived and the less successful were absorbed by the stronger and more economically healthy. They are hard to find now and the best collections of complete runs of turn-of-the-century cycling periodicals may be found at the Library of Congress and the Smithsonian Institution in Washington, D.C.

The most useful in documenting Major Taylor's career are listed below:

American Cyclist (Hartford, Conn.), 1890—1898; merged into *Bicycling World*.

The Bearings (Chicago), 1893—1897; incorporated in *Cycle Age*.

Bicycling World (New York), 1879—1915.

Cycle Age and Trade Review (Chicago), 1897—1901; incorporated into *Motor Age*.

Cycling Gazette (Cleveland, Ohio), 1895—?.

Cycling Life (Chicago), 1894—1897; incorporated into *Cycle Age*.

The Referee and *Cycle Trade Journal* (Chicago and New York), 1893—1897; incorporated into *Cycle Age*.

The Wheel and *Cycling Trades Review* (Chicago and New York), 1888—1900; incorporated into *Bicycling World*.

Wheelmen's Gazette (Indianapolis), 1886—1895.

F. OTHER PUBLICATIONS CYCLING AND SPORTS

Barth, Gunther. *City People, The Rise of Modern City Culture in Nineteenth Century America.* New York: Oxford University Press, 1980. (See Chapter 5, "Ball Park," for discussion of the significance of sports at the turn of the century. This chapter also has extensive and useful notes. See also Barth's "Sources,": 272—4, for many general sports history references.

Bastide, Roger. *Petit-Breton, La Belle Époque du Cyclisme.* Paris: Éditions Denoel, 1985.

Betts, John C. *Organized Sports in Industrial America.* New York: Columbia University, 1951. (Ph.D dissertation).

—. "Sporting Journalism in Nineteenth Century America." *American Quarterly,* V, Spring 1953, 39—56.

Dulles, Foster Rhea. *A History of Recreation: America Learns to Play.* New York: Appleton-Century-Crofts, 1965.

Duncan, H.O. *Vingt Ans de Cyclisme Pratique.* Paris: F. Juven, 1897.

Grivell, H. *"Curly." Australian Cycling in the Golden Days.* Unley (South Australia): Courier Press, date unknown.

Gronen, Wolfgang and Walter Lemke. *Geschichte des Radsports und des Fahrrades.* Eupen (Belgium): Edition Doepgen Verlag, 1978.

Hamelle, Paul and Robert Coquelle. *Thorwald Christansen Ellegaard.* Paris, 1912.

Henderson, Edwin B. *The Black Athlete, Emergence and Arrival.* New York: Publishers Co., 1968.

—. *The Negro in Sports.* Washington, D.C.: Associated Publishers, 1939.

Kobayashi, Keizo. *Pour une Bibliographie du Cyclisme.* Paris: Federation Française du Cyclotourisme, 1984.

Laget, Françoise and Serge Laget. *Le Cyclisme. Courlay: Éditions Jadault, 1978.*

Lucas, John A. and Ronald A. Smith. *Saga of American Sports.* Philadelphia: Lea & Febiger, 1978.

Mandell, Richard D. *Sport, A Cultural History.* New York: Columbia University Press, 1984.

McCullagh, James C. *American Bicycle Racing.* Emmaus: Rodale Press, 1976.

Mead, Chris. *Champion — Joe Louis, Black Hero in White America.* New York: Penguin Books, 1985. (Has extensive notes on sports history.)

Ritchie, Andrew. *King of the Road, An Illustrated History of Cycling.* London: Wildwood House; Berkeley: Ten Speed Press, 1975.

Roberts, Randy. *Papa Jack, Jack Johnson and the Era of White Hopes.* New York: The Free Press, 1983.

Smith, Robert A. *A Social History of the Bicycle.* New York: American Heritage Press, 1972.

Swann, Dick. *The Life and Times of Charlie Barden.* Leicester: Wunlap Publications, 1965.

Young, A. S. *Negro Firsts in Sports.* Chicago: Johnson Publishing Co., 1963.

Zimmerman, Arthur A. *Points on Training for Cyclists.* Leicester: F.W.S. Clarke, 1893.

BLACK HISTORY

Bennett, Lerone. *Before the Mayflower, A History of Black America.* New York: Johnson Publishing Company, 1962.

Bergman, Peter M. *The Chronological History of the Negro in America.* New York: Harper and Row, 1969.

Franklin, John Hope. *From Slavery to Freedom, A History of Negro Americans.* New York: Alfred Knopf, 1947.

Hughes, Langston and Milton Meltzer. *A Pictorial History of the Negro in America.* New York: Crown Publishers, 1956.

Lacy, Dan. *The White Use of Blacks in America.* New York: McGraw-Hill, 1972.

Meier, August. *Negro Thought in America, 1880—1915.* Ann Arbor: University of Michigan Press, 1963.

Woodward, C. Vann. *The Strange Career of Jim Crow.* New York: Oxford University Press, 1957.

INDEX

Library of Congress Cataloging-in-Publication Data

Ritchie, Andrew.
  Major Taylor : the extraordinary career of a champion bicycle racer / Andrew Ritchie. —
Johns Hopkins paperbacks ed.
      p.   cm.
  Originally published : San Francisco : Bicycle Books, 1988. With new front matter.
  Includes bibliographical references and index.
  ISBN 0-8018-5303-6 (pbk. : alk. paper)
  1. Taylor, Major, 1878-1932.   2. Cyclists — United States —
Biography. 3. Bicycle racing — History.   I. Title.
GV1051.T3R58   1996
796.6´092 — dc20
[B]   95-44486